Keeping watch

Keeping watch: Monitoring, technology and innovation in UN peace operations

A. Walter Dorn

**United Nations
University Press**

TOKYO · NEW YORK · PARIS

United Nations University Press
United Nations University, 53-70, Jingumae 5-chome,
Shibuya-ku, Tokyo 150-8925, Japan
Tel: +81-3-5467-1212   Fax: +81-3-3406-7345
E-mail: sales@unu.edu   general enquiries: press@unu.edu
http://www.unu.edu

United Nations University Office at the United Nations, New York
2 United Nations Plaza, Room DC2-2062, New York, NY 10017, USA
Tel: +1-212-963-6387   Fax: +1-212-371-9454
E-mail: unuony@unu.edu

United Nations University Press is the publishing division of the United Nations University.

Cover design by Helen Chilas

Cover photographs by (clockwise from top) UN Photo/Martine Perret; UN Photo/John Isaac; and MCpl Danielle Bernier, DGPA/J5PA Combat Camera, National Defence (reproduced with the permission of the Minister of Public Works and Government Services, Canada, 2010)

Printed in the United States of America

ISBN 978-92-808-1198-8

Library of Congress Cataloging-in-Publication Data

Dorn, A. Walter.
Keeping watch : monitoring, technology and innovation in UN peace operations / A. Walter Dorn.
    p. cm.
  Includes bibliographical references and index.
  ISBN 978-9280811988 (pbk.)
  1. United Nations—Peacekeeping forces. 2. Peace-building—Technological innovations. I. Title.
JZ4971. D67   2011
341.5'84—dc23   2011021070

To those who gave their lives in the service of peace while on mission for the United Nations. When we improve upon their efforts to secure the peace, we honour their sacrifice.

Endorsements

"In *Keeping Watch*, Walter Dorn makes a persuasive case for bringing the technology of UN peacekeeping into the 21st century – and not a decade too soon, because the time-honored approach of throwing ill-equipped troops at unstable places just is not working. With a unique mix of substantive and technical expertise, Dorn demonstrates how dozens of existing and emergent technologies – from thermal imaging to crowd-sourcing – could be vital force multipliers for peacekeepers, who can't keep the peace if they don't know the score. Anyone with an interest in peacekeeping should own this book and use it."
William Durch, *Director of the Future of Peace Operations Program, Stimson Center*

"As the senior editor of the international journal *Intelligence and National Security*, whenever I receive a manuscript on the subject of intelligence and international organizations, A. Walter Dorn is the first reviewer I turn to for help in evaluating the submission. In *Keeping Watch*, his deep knowledge is on display. This book is chock full of fascinating charts, tables, drawings, and photographs to accompany Dorn's signature careful analysis and flashes of original insight. He demonstrates in lucid prose how technology can be highly useful in monitoring, mitigating, and preventing international conflict. Here is a study that should be standard fare in every university course on international conflict and cooperation – indeed, one that citizens everywhere would benefit from reading."
Loch K. Johnson, *Regents Professor, University of Georgia*

"Walter Dorn is one of the most thoughtful and knowledgeable analysts of peacekeeping and security policy, and this book makes an important contribution to a field that needs far more public discussion."
Bob Rae, *Member of Parliament for Toronto Centre and Liberal Foreign Affairs Critic in Canada's House of Commons*

"Dr. Walter Dorn is the 'dean' of the peace intelligence scholars, having both founded and nurtured the field since his seminal work on UN intelligence successes in the Congo. This book covers the technical side of UN intelligence, and complements work on harnessing distributed human intelligence. From the Brahimi Report to the High Level Panels on Threats and on System-Wide Coherence, there has been a pattern of 'emerging intelligence'. This book is the newest contribution – an absolutely essential, practical, and inspiring contribution to help create a prosperous world at peace."
Robert David Steele, *CEO, Earth Intelligence Network*

"The engagement of the United Nations in peacekeeping has increased rapidly over the past decade. In the search for ways to enhance UN operations, the UN Special Committee on Peacekeeping Operations in 2006 requested a study on how technical monitoring and surveillance can be used to ensure the safety and security of United Nations peacekeeping personnel and improve the operational effectiveness of peacekeeping missions.

Dr. Walter Dorn, engaged by the UN's Department of Peacekeeping Operations as an independent expert, conducted research and came up with findings which successfully laid the grounds for further development of the idea of monitoring technology in UN peacekeeping. He continued to assist DPKO in establishing an action plan to systematize the knowledge, identify priorities, implement the proposed solutions and set the way forward, in close cooperation with member states.

Dr. Dorn's work was welcomed by the Special Committee. It helped the United Nations understand and appreciate the usefulness of modern technology in peacekeeping. What is also important is that it helped to overcome a psychological barrier which hindered efforts to bring these capabilities into the UN peacekeeping effort.

The book *Keeping Watch* expands on the author's *Tools of the Trade?* report to the Special Committee and his other papers on the subject. It provides a very interesting insight into UN peacekeeping operations from the perspective of the possible use of modern technology. It helps the reader understand, for example, the issues that need to be considered when using technology such as unmanned aerial vehicles. This book will be a beacon for the use of modern technology in peacekeeping operations at a time when the UN seeks to overcome the complex challenges it faces in the field."

Zbigniew Szlek, *Senior Military Adviser, Permanent Mission of Poland to the United Nations*

Contents

Figures

Tables

Abbreviations

Note: the abbreviations for UN peace operations are in Appendix 1.

AH	attack helicopter
ALR	artillery-locating radar
AMSTAR	Advanced Man-portable Surveillance and Target Acquisition Radar (also known as Australian Man-portable Surveillance and Target Acquisition Radar)
ASR	Air Surveillance Radar
AU	African Union
AWACS	Airborne Warning and Control System (aircraft)
C4ISR	Command, Control, Communications, Computers, Intelligence, Surveillance and Reconnaissance
CCTV	closed-circuit television
CIT	communications and information technology
CITS	Communications and Information Technology Service
CNDP	Congrès national pour la défense du peuple (National Congress for the Defence of the People)
COB	Contingency Operating Base
COE	Contingent-Owned Equipment
CSI	commercial satellite imagery
DCOS	Deputy Chief of Staff
DDR	disarmament, demobilization and reintegration
DFS	Department of Field Support
DMZ	demilitarized zone
DPA	Darfur Peace Agreement
DPKO	Department of Peacekeeping Operations (UN)
DRC	Democratic Republic of the Congo

DSS	Department of Safety and Security (UN)
DVN	digital video network
DVR	digital video recorder
ELINT	Electronic intelligence
EOD	Explosive Ordnance Detachment (of MFO)
EUFOR	European Union Force
FAC	Forward Air Controller
FARDC	Forces Armées de la République Démocratique du Congo
FLIR	forward-looking infrared
FWF	former warring factions (in Bosnia)
GIS	geographic information system
GoS	Government of Sudan
GPR	ground-penetrating radar
GPS	Global Positioning System
GSR	ground surveillance radar
HD	high-definition
HUMINT	human intelligence
IAEA	International Atomic Energy Agency
ICC	International Criminal Court
IDF	Israel Defense Forces
IDP	internally displaced person
IED	improvised explosive device
IFOR	Implementation Force (NATO force in Bosnia)
IP	Internet Protocol
IR	infrared
ISTAR	Intelligence, Surveillance, Target Acquisition and Reconnaissance
IT	information technology
JAM	Joint Assessment Mission
JMAC	Joint Mission Analysis Centre
JOC	Joint Operations Centre
LAN	local area network
LPR	license plate recognition
LSX	Ledra Street Crossing
MAC	Mixed Armistice Commission
MFO	Multinational Force and Observers
MOSS	Minimum Operating Security Standards
MOU	Memorandum of Understanding
NATO	North Atlantic Treaty Organization
NEO	network-enabled operation
NEW	National Election Watch
NGO	non-governmental organization
NVD	night-vision device
NVE	night-vision equipment
OMIK	Organization for Security and Co-operation in Europe Mission in Kosovo
OP	observation post
OPFOR	opposing force

P5	the five permanent members of the UN Security Council
PIR	passive infrared (sensors)
PKO	peacekeeping operation
PLO	Palestine Liberation Organization
POC	protection of civilians
PTZ	Pan Tilt Zoom (cameras)
REMBASS	Remotely Monitored Battlefield Sensor System
RFID	radio frequency identification
ROE	Rules of Engagement
SAR	synthetic aperture radar
SFM	Sinai Field Mission
SFOR	Stabilisation Force in Bosnia and Herzegovina
SIGINT	signals intelligence
SLA	South Lebanon Army
SMS	Short Message Service
SOFA	Status-of-Forces Agreement
SOP	standard operating procedure
TCC	troop-contributing country
TOE	Table of Organization and Equipment
TOW	tube-launched, optically-tracked, wire-guided (type of missile)
TRA	Threat and Risk Assessment
UAV	unmanned/uninhabited aerial vehicle
UGS	unattended ground sensor
UN	United Nations
UNMO	United Nations Military Observer
UNMOVIC	United Nations Monitoring, Verification and Inspection Commission
UNOSAT	United Nations Operational Satellite Applications Programme
UNPOL	United Nations Police
UNSAS	United Nations Standby Arrangements System
UNSCOM	United Nations Special Commission

Foreword

Lieutenant-General The Hon. Roméo A. Dallaire (Retired)

I am pleased to contribute the Foreword to Professor Walter Dorn's important book on improving UN peace operations. These operations are much needed in today's world and are in need of constant innovation. Violent extremism, whatever its origin and wherever it raises its ugly head, is everyone's business. Peace operations have become one of the most important tools the international community has to achieve conflict resolution. We can no more abandon peace operations than we can turn our back on dying children in catastrophes or give up our hopes for a more peaceful world.

The past failures of the international community in UN peacekeeping should catalyse new commitments to peace rather than a withdrawal from UN operations. Rather than discard peacekeeping altogether because of its chequered history, we need to learn from its failures as well as its successes. The lessons of the 1990s should be incorporated into the current generation of operations.

Peace operations have evolved considerably and more resources are now dedicated to them than ever before. The annual UN peacekeeping budget of US$8 billion is more than twice as large as when I commanded a peacekeeping force in Rwanda in 1993–1994. The number of uniformed peacekeepers deployed in UN missions has now surpassed 100,000. The mandates of the new missions are generally stronger – though still not strong enough. The Security Council explicitly requests its twenty-first-century missions to protect civilians, an enormous task that requires the use of robust force and detailed intelligence on all manner of threats.

The United Nations Assistance Mission for Rwanda (UNAMIR) in 1993–1994 showed the problems of a lack of intelligence and analysis in peacekeeping. We found ourselves working in an information vacuum, at times groping in the dark to identify and confront shadowy forces and unofficial networks that became apparent only after the genocide began.

Information needs to come not only from human sources but also from modern intelligence, surveillance and reconnaissance technology. From hand-held metal detectors that are used to detect underground weapons caches to satellite imagery that helps paint the big picture, the United Nations needs to make better use of modern technology. It needs to be aware of the enormous potential of advanced technology to save lives and alleviate human suffering. To this end, practical studies and in-depth research are extremely valuable.

Dr Walter Dorn is well qualified to write on this subject. He has been studying the United Nations for decades. Because of his training in physics and chemistry and his leadership in the Canadian Pugwash movement of scientists, he is well acquainted with applications of science and technology. He has a multidisciplinary background and a depth of knowledge that are rare, even in the present-day era of technological advancement. He also has practical experience in field operations and, as a professor at the Canadian Forces College, is in daily contact with military officers from around the world. Moreover, as is evident in this book, he is deeply dedicated to UN peace missions and to the cause they serve. It remains only for the international community to summon the political will to act on the sage advice offered in this book, and to implement Dr Dorn's timely recommendations.

Preface

Wars and conflicts exact a terrible toll on people well beyond those caught in the cross-fire. Massive human displacement, lost lives and livelihoods, deteriorating health and governmental services, the demise of justice and broken societies are all results of endemic violence. The cycle of insecurity empowers warlords and militarists, emboldens combatants and inflates military budgets in regions unable to afford such diversions. As well, it has repercussions around our interconnected world.

The world desperately needs *effective* peacekeeping. Helpless civilians caught in conflict need impartial forces to protect them. War-weary fighters need opportunities to stop their shooting and lay down their weapons. Moderates need outside assistance to sustain fragile cease-fires. Durable peace agreements backed by credible verification and enforcement by the international community are the best means for progress in local governance, for implementing the rule of law, for fostering greater prosperity and for a return to normalcy. But all too often the international forces deployed by the United Nations are unprepared and under-equipped, unable to meet the challenges in the field, unaware of emerging threats and unable to take proactive action to prevent escalations of conflict.

Since truth is the "first casualty" of war, I posit that winning back the truth is the first job of the United Nations peacekeeper. Piercing the "fog of war" is critical to any response. Conflicts are routinely fuelled by rumour, false reports, misinformation, disinformation and propaganda. The peacekeepers serve as the eyes and ears of the international community, and often its limbs as well, frequently placing themselves in harm's way to monitor threats, protect civilians and create some order from bloody chaos. But the challenges of monitoring conflicts are many. Over large areas, at night and in difficult terrain, the human eye is insufficient, especially for border surveillance, sanctions monitoring and detecting early signs of violence. Spoilers of fragile peace processes try to keep their plans and preparations for attack secret, often using the cover of darkness; the United Nations must make use of all possible tools to keep watch over shadowy forces and conditions in the field.

With this challenge in mind, I ask how modern science and technology can help peacekeepers maintain their watch and carry out robust peace operations. This book is one answer to the issue I have been pondering since I was an undergraduate student in the physical sciences. If the reader permits me to describe the relevant personal background, I start with the words that inspired me to try to link the fields of physical science and political science. The scientist-sage Albert Einstein (Lynd 1939) told his students at Princeton University (United States):

> Concern for man himself and his fate [humanity itself and its fate] should be the chief interest of all technical endeavours. Never forget this in the midst of your diagrams and equations.

As a physical sciences student at the University of Toronto in Canada in the 1980s, I asked myself how the subjects I was studying (chemistry and physics) could make a difference in a world weary of the Cold War. Technology to support arms control verification seemed like a fruitful area, so I directed my graduate work to help develop sensors for the detection of chemical and biological warfare agents. In parallel, I served as the UN Representative of the Canadian organization Science for Peace, making bimonthly trips to New York. This allowed me to become familiar with the world organization, carefully observing UN operations and practices, gathering information from experienced contacts inside and outside of the organization. I watched with sadness and alarm as important UN operations became stuck in Somalia, Rwanda and Bosnia. I wondered what could be done better. I visited several conflict areas and in 1999 served on the UN mission administering a referendum in Indonesia-occupied East Timor. Although the UN mission proved successful, it was accompanied by tragedy, including of a personal nature. Several friends, colleagues and a member of my team were killed in the Suai massacre of 6 September 1999. This experience reinforced my conviction that the United Nations needed a strong intelligence architecture and much better technical tools to gather information for preventive action.

I sought to convey this link between technology and peacekeeping by developing and teaching courses at the Pearson Peacekeeping Centre in

Nova Scotia, Canada, in particular a course titled "Live, Move and Work: Technology and Engineering in Modern Peacekeeping". I also conducted research at Yale and Cornell universities on improving the capacity of the United Nations. Building a research bridge from the physical to the social sciences brought me to a professorship at the Royal Military College of Canada, where I was able to broaden the research. During a sabbatical in 2006, Canada's Permanent Mission to the United Nations in New York offered the opportunity to carry out a study for the United Nations on surveillance technology for peacekeeping. I presented the preliminary results to the United Nations Special Committee on Peace-keeping Operations in 2007, which welcomed the report. A year later, when the United Nations' Department of Peacekeeping Operations needed help in implementing the general proposals, I was given a golden opportunity to study how specific technologies could be applied to parti-cular operations. With financial support from the Department of Foreign Affairs and International Trade (DFAIT) Canada, the United Nations sent me on research trips to UN missions in Haiti, Cyprus and the Demo-cratic Republic of the Congo.

This book is the culmination of the field experiences and trips, inter-views at UN headquarters and a quarter-century of studying UN peace-keeping. It incorporates and publicizes the findings of the two reports I have written for the United Nations and of work done at Sandia National Laboratories. Through the research I discovered just how far behind the United Nations is in employing modern technology. I joked with UN staff that I wanted to help bring the United Nations into "the 1990s"!

I observed a growing "monitoring technology gap" of several dimen-sions. This gap exists between the United Nations' mandates and its means, between the nations contributing to UN operations (especially between developed and developing nations), between the United Nations and some of its important partner organizations in the field (for example, the European Union and the North Atlantic Treaty Organization), and even between the United Nations and some parties it is supposed to be watching closely. Some warring governments, rebels and criminal gangs have better surveillance technologies than either the United Nations or the national police/military forces with which the United Nations works in war-torn lands.

Through this life work, I hope to help advance the technological ca-pacity of the United Nations, making practical and forward-looking re-commendations without appearing too critical of UN staff struggling to make do with what they have. I have sought to illustrate the centrality of the monitoring functions in United Nations' operations, and describe the capabilities and drawbacks of the range of technologies based in outer space, in airspace or on the ground. I hope to increase awareness not only of the United Nations' deficiencies but also of its future potential. The world organization can strengthen its "information power" using both human and technological sources, including social media based on the Internet, to better serve as an instrument of peace.

In this book I develop the main thesis about the tremendous utility of technologies for monitoring in peacekeeping (Chapter 1) before providing a background overview of the evolution of peacekeeping (Chapter 2), showing the expansion of monitoring requirements over time. I assess the United Nations' many needs for impartial information and intelligence (Chapter 3) and survey the broad range of technologies that can be applied to the problem (Chapter 4). Aerial surveillance (Chapter 5) turns out to be a key information-gathering method but one that is greatly underutilized in UN missions, like many other technologies. This was borne out in case studies of both traditional and modern multidimensional missions in the field, with some notable and encouraging exceptions (Chapters 6 and 7). What UN headquarters' policies and standards exist for the creative use of monitoring and surveillance technology? The subtitle of Chapter 8, "Starting from near zero", points to the answer. Why is the United Nations so far behind most modern militaries? Several answers are found by looking at the challenges and problems in deploying technology (Chapter 9). Given the United Nations' sputtering efforts at improving its technological proficiency, I make a series of recommendations (Chapter 10) on general capacity-building and on deploying specific technologies for specific missions. My conclusions (Chapter 11) are prefigured in this preface but I also suggest a few ways forward.

A physical scientist by training and a political scientist by current profession, I tried to marry the two fields while pursuing a convoluted career. Benefiting from a decade of teaching officers in the Canadian Forces and other militaries, I incorporated their experiences into the research. I was able to test some ideas on officers with experience using technology in the field. As an "operational professor", I also sought to go to the field to observe UN operations first-hand. Through this work, I have sought to determine how peacekeeping can make effective use of modern tools. This research experience has enhanced my conviction that, with better technological means and connectivity, the United Nations can save more lives, alleviate more suffering and foster more of the harmony that is so desperately needed in this world.

Acknowledgements

I have many people to thank for helping me in this intellectual adventure – exploring the theory and practice of peacekeeping and the applications of technology. Professor John Polanyi at the University of Toronto first propelled me in this direction with an inspiring speech and a personal interview in 1982 on a proposed International Satellite Monitoring Agency. George Ignatieff, as President of Science for Peace, encouraged me to look at how science and technology could assist arms control and the United Nations, where he had served as Canadian ambassador and earned the moniker "peacemonger", of which he was rightly proud.

When I was consulting for UN Studies at Yale, the distinguished Jim Sutterlin, formerly with the US State Department and the United Nations, provided invaluable encouragement and insights, especially on early warning proposals. At Sandia National Laboratories, David Barber of the Cooperative Monitoring Centre gave me support and wise advice when I spent three months there as a Visiting Scholar looking at possible peacekeeping technologies. At Cornell University, Professor Matthew Evangelista gave tremendous support as I began the long book-writing journey.

At the Royal Military College of Canada (RMC-C), I must thank Lieutenant-Colonel (ret'd) Dr David Last and Dr Joel Sokolsky (then Politics Department head, now Principal), who provided me with opportunities to teach and to conduct research at the College. This helped me link theory to practice, given that the RMC-C students were past or future peacekeepers.

At the United Nations itself, I received much kind support. In the United Nations' Military Planning Service, two Chiefs, (successively) Colonels Ian Sinclair and Bryan Norman, and a Deputy Chief, Shayne Gilbert, provided invaluable opportunities, including places to work and people to meet while on frequent visits to New York and to field missions. Lieutenant-Colonel Harald Lixenfeld, the United Nations' first Capability Development Officer, offered many insights into recent UN developments and kindly accompanied me on a visit to Haiti.

The Chief for Aviation Projects, Kevin Shelton-Smith, provided great insights into the United Nations' procurement process, especially when I served as a consultant on a project for unmanned aerial vehicles (UAVs). Despite Kevin's herculean efforts over three years, the initiative to equip the UN mission in the Congo with advanced UAVs sadly ended without success, though valuable lessons will be learned for the future.

Among the Military and Police Advisers community in New York, I am especially appreciative of Colonel Zbigniew Szlek of the Polish mission, who spearheaded the acceptance of my first study (*Tools of the Trade?*) in the Special Committee on Peacekeeping. Colonel Mike Hanrahan, the military adviser of the Canadian mission, is to be thanked for first suggesting to DPKO in 2006 that I serve as a consultant on monitoring technologies, resulting in that first study.

I am grateful to Canada's Foreign Affairs department (DFAIT) for its generous support from the Global Peace and Security Fund. Special thanks go to Tara Denham, Tony Anderson and Lieutenant-Colonel Brad Bergstrand for their advice and project administration. The DFAIT grant allowed me to obtain research help in the preparation of my second UN report and this book.

My research assistants provided invaluable help. I thank my reliable copyeditor, Jennifer Birtill, whom I met while at the International Criminal Court. Former police officer Mike Dubé helped explore potential police technologies. Robert Pauk, a former peacekeeper who remains ever committed to the cause, and Dr Peter Langille, an expert devoted to improving peacekeeping, prepared studies with me on Cyprus and Darfur, respectively. I gratefully include the results of both studies in this book. Similarly, Nick Martin skilfully helped draft parts of the smartphones analysis.

I am grateful to those who reviewed the drafts of the book, including Lieutenant-Colonel Richard Kelderman, Robert David Steele, Ryan Cross and Cameron Harrington. I much appreciate the organizations that supported its printing and publication: the Department of Foreign Affairs and International Trade Canada and United Nations University Press, especially Vesselin Popovski and Naomi Cowan. The copyeditor, Liz Paton, did a meticulous job and showed much-appreciated patience as the manuscript was finalized. My graphic artist, Helen Chilas, did a wonderful job of translating my suggestions into an appealing cover and two maps in the text. I warmly thank the peacekeeping hero Lieutenant-General Roméo Dallaire (Ret'd), now a Canadian Senator, for kindly contributing the Foreword to this work. Those who kindly provided endorsements of the book (Dr Bill Durch, Professor Loch Johnson, the Hon. Bob Rae, Colonel Zbigniew Szlek and Robert Steele) deserve gratitude for their generosity.

Finally I owe a lifetime of gratitude to my parents, Trudy and the late Paul Dorn, for their life-long support and encouragement.

1

Introduction: Technology for peace

Rapid technological advancement has impacted military affairs in extraordinary ways. New technologies have led to more explosive, powerful and precise weapons. They have steadily increased the ability to monitor an enemy or opponent. Technology changed the way wars are fought. Has it also changed the way peace is kept?

Unfortunately, the technological revolution has barely touched the peace operations of the United Nations. In particular, the surveillance equipment ("soldier's kit") of UN peacekeepers has changed little since the inception of peacekeeping. There remains a compelling need to modernize UN operations, especially given the ambitious new mandates assigned to the United Nations. These tasks go far beyond traditional UN operations. Peacekeepers today are not merely positioned between two opposing armies but are now often deployed across entire countries. Their tasks include protecting civilians from ethnic violence, providing security for entire populations, preventing civil wars and massacres, combating criminality and building nations from the ashes of war. To do these many tasks, UN peacekeepers must locate and intercept clandestine arms shipments, monitor potential spoilers of peace processes, uncover evidence of atrocities for courts and tribunals, and even govern large territories during transitional periods. The extensive list of UN mandates and peace operations, past and present, is provided in Appendix 1, showing the expansion over time.

The new and difficult tasks in modern multidimensional missions require substantial technological resources for monitoring and observing,

Keeping watch: Monitoring, technology and innovation in UN peace operations, Dorn, United Nations University Press, 2011, ISBN 978-92-808-1198-8

yet UN member states have been reluctant to invest the United Nations with modern observation means. Peacekeepers continue to rely on old-generation tools, mostly binoculars. For this and other reasons, UN peacekeepers have been overwhelmed in such places as Angola, Bosnia, Cambodia, Darfur, Somalia, Southern Sudan and Rwanda.

Meanwhile, the technological "revolution" in the world has given birth to tremendous scientific and commercial progress, having many potential applications for peacekeeping. Most easily discernible are the advances in information technology (IT) and communications. Global telecommunications, the Internet, personal computing, hand-held devices and wireless and digital networks, especially social media such as email, blogs, wikis and popular sharing interfaces (Facebook and Twitter), have changed the way people live, move and work in the "information age". The United Nations has not left itself out completely. The UN system for communications is the one area that has evolved alongside the commercial sector. Yet for monitoring and surveillance there has not been parallel progress in UN operations, despite a commercial revolution in sensor technology. Inexpensive products such as high-zoom digital cameras, web cameras (webcams) and camcorders have become common household items. Closed-circuit television (CCTV) and digital video networks are making shops and streets safer in cities around the world. But the concept of video monitoring of strategic locations in war-torn cities is a novelty in peacekeeping. Motion detectors are in widespread use in home alarm systems and in driveways, for instance in night illumination systems to alert householders to visitors and potential intruders, but they are not yet the tools of peacekeepers in the world's hottest conflict zones. High-resolution satellite imagery, which 20 years ago was the sole preserve of military and intelligence agencies, is now available free on personal desktops worldwide through services such as Google Earth, but the United Nations has yet to use near-real-time satellite imagery in its operations. Model airplane enthusiasts can fly small-scale airplanes equipped with miniature video cameras, but the United Nations has yet to purchase professional-level unmanned aerial vehicles (UAVs). Other organizations such as the North Atlantic Treaty Organization (NATO) and the European Union have readily adopted a wide range of advanced technologies in their peace support operations, but the United Nations has not seized the opportunity.[1] Given that monitoring is a central element of every UN peacekeeping mandate, it is strange that monitoring technologies are missing from the organization's standard toolkit. It is also tragic that they are not used by the United Nations in the world's conflict zones, where detection of dangerous movements of arms and fighters could help prevent truce violations, large-scale atrocities or clandestine smuggling of weapons or humans.

In the communications field, as mentioned, the United Nations has successfully harnessed some new technologies. The United Nations' Department of Field Support (DFS) maintains a communications system that is world-class, rapidly deployable anywhere on the globe and capable of voice, video and data transmission at the operational level. Purposely redundant and complementary systems such as UHF, HF, cell and satellite phone networks are deployed in most missions. New York also maintains high-quality video teleconference links with many peacekeeping operations. The Department of Peacekeeping Operations (DPKO) has an advanced information technology architecture, providing crypto-fax, email, Internet and, since 2006, intranet access to all field missions and most field personnel.[2] Many UN databases contain excellent, up-to-date information resources and are easily accessible from remote locations. For example, the Contingent-Owned Equipment (COE) database is available to personnel at headquarters and in the field.[3] Moreover, the United Nations' Official Document System database has been available free of charge to the general public since 2004.[4] Tens of thousands of UN documents are added annually.

The driving processes of globalization, digitization, miniaturization and the convergence of technologies (e.g. multifunctional phones) have greatly helped the communications/IT functions of the United Nations. Surprisingly, there has not been a direct impact on the United Nations' capacity for observation. Satellites are routinely used by the United Nations for intercontinental communications but they are not used for timely reconnaissance. Similarly, the use of aircraft for UN transportation is impressive. The United Nations' mission in the Democratic Republic of the Congo (DRC) – Mission de l'Organisation des Nations Unies en République démocratique du Congo (MONUC) – runs the largest carrier (transport) fleet in Africa,[5] but the potential for aerial reconnaissance in peacekeeping has only just begun to be explored in a systematic fashion. The United Nations' "Contingent-Owned Equipment Manual" sets the standards for equipment brought to the field by national contingents (United Nations 2008). It lists 34 types of communications technology but only 6 monitoring technologies, and even those 6 are not adequately defined or described (see Chapter 8).[6]

Fortunately, commercial off-the-shelf technology for monitoring is becoming cheaper, lighter and better in virtually all categories and is increasingly easier to procure and deploy. The microprocessor revolution, which experienced an unprecedented improvement of 10 orders of magnitude (a factor of 10 billion) in price-to-performance ratio over four decades,[7] has led to a proliferation of "intelligent" sensors and surveillance systems. Data can now be conveniently added to geographic information systems (GIS) that are readily available on the commercial marketplace at a fraction of the previous price or even free on some cell phones. However, the United Nations continues to distribute only cartography products and paper maps and has yet to make the jump to shared GIS databases, which would allow direct input anytime from users such as UN police and military observers in the field. Fortunately, this capability is likely to come soon, given the considerable progress that has been made in the DPKO's cartography units in the missions.

Modern militaries around the world have a keen awareness of technological evolution, especially the enormous impact on operations from increased intelligence, speed and precision. The terms "revolution in military affairs" and "network-enabled operations" or "network-centric warfare", based on GIS, are now common in military circles, especially in the Western world. Such systems convey the reality that new technologies combined with new strategies have substantially changed military operations, especially through advanced electronic networks. Many militaries have been quick to take advantage of the sensor revolution, deploying ruggedized night-vision equipment (now in the fourth generation) and ground-based radars for air/ground surveillance and making use of aerospace reconnaissance. The military concept of C4ISR (Command, Control, Communications, Computers, Intelligence, Surveillance and Reconnaissance),[8] with its strong emphasis on information collection and sharing, has long been viewed as an essential field of military study and operations.

Notwithstanding this rapid evolution of sensor technologies in modern militaries and across modern societies, the United Nations has been slow to apply sensors to the military and civilian domains of its peacekeeping operations. The world organization is subjecting its personnel to unnecessary risks by not utilizing modern technologies that can monitor the most dangerous areas from a safe distance and help gain a broader awareness of safety and security threats.

Technological deficiencies in monitoring and a lack of "situational awareness" have already led to tragedy. In Rwanda in 1994, Force Commander Roméo Dallaire complained of being "deaf and blind in the field". Not being able to corroborate reports of a planned genocide or to monitor radio conversations of genocidal militiamen or to track arms flows, he lacked the detailed intelligence to secure UN headquarters support for preventive action (Dorn and Matloff 2000). Moreover, after the genocide began, he also lacked the fighting forces needed for an effective response. This led to a loss of UN credibility in Rwanda and a UN failure in the eyes of the world, though the fault lay more with the nations in the Security Council that delayed and obfuscated instead of providing desperately needed support.

In the neighbouring DRC, an estimated 3–4 million people have perished since 1996 in widespread strife, including two civil wars, the second of which could be termed a "continental war" given the presence of opposing fighting forces from many African nations. At the beginning of the Congo/Zaire crisis, the United Nations proved unable even to provide accurate and consistent counts of moving refugees (Dorn 2005). Large shipments of illegal armaments are routinely imported into the DRC as vast quantities of minerals are illegally shipped out, without United Nations detection or interdiction (UN Security Council 2004). Rogue militias routinely carry out illegal "tax" collecting, looting, smuggling, kidnapping and killing in areas of the country with no real-time watch from the United Nations. Furthermore, on average one peacekeeper dies each month while serving in the Congo.[9] Although military leaders in MONUC clearly expressed the operational requirements for surveillance technologies (see the case study in Chapter 7), the UN planning and procurement process has proven too slow in response.

The harrowing consequences of the technological deficiencies in UN missions are illustrated by the November 2008 headline on the front page of the *New York Times*: "A Massacre in Congo, Despite Nearby Support." As hundreds were killed in Kiwanja and the village burned, over 100 UN peacekeepers were merely a kilometre away, "struggling to understand what was happening outside the gates of [their] base". The commanding officer had to "grope his way through a fog of rumour, speculation and misinformation". The officer complained: "During this whole time, there was an informational vacuum" (Polgreen 2008). The rebel militias of Laurent Nkunda held Kiwanja and Rutshuru and advanced towards Goma. Fortunately, the United Nations deployed some advanced technologies to counteract this advance, showing what a tremendous difference technology can make. As the rebel forces approached Goma, the United Nations deployed its Mi-35 attack helicopters equipped with state-of-the-art day- and night-viewing cameras. The high-zoom features enabled the helicopters to identify advancing targets, to confirm ground reports that there were no civilians or UN or government forces nearby, and to aim precise fire. With this help, UN forces prevented an attack on Goma, something the United Nations had failed to do in Bukavu four years earlier. The lack of intelligence in 2004 was similar to the famous inadequacies of previous missions, such as in Rwanda.

A *few* UN missions have used a *few* technologies to great advantage, as described in detail later in this book. The United Nations Interim Force in Lebanon has deployed several sophisticated radars for both air and ground surveillance. The United Nations Peacekeeping Force in Cyprus has become the first UN force to install CCTV cameras to monitor areas in a conflict zone. They are located in sensitive hotspots along the "Green Line" that winds its way through Nicosia separating two armies. The United Nations Stabilization Mission in Haiti has used heliborne cameras that transmit imagery in real time to mission headquarters. Moreover, the

United Nations in Haiti used sophisticated means to procure "intelligence" about the gang leaders who literally ruled Cité Soleil and its impoverished inhabitants. In 2007 the UN force was finally able to wrest control from the criminal elements, stop countless murders, incarcerate the wrongdoers and restore a semblance of the rule of law.

These cases, examined in detail later, indicate how technology has helped the United Nations to gain better general awareness and specific knowledge (intelligence) about hostile elements. It has also enabled the United Nations to protect its personnel and the local populace and better fulfil mission mandates. Sadly, cases where technology was used to its potential are the exception rather than the rule.

Fortunately, the United Nations has in recent years gained greater awareness of the need to harness technological tools and is slowly working on solutions. In 2008, DPKO launched a short-term project to enhance the deployment of low-and-medium-cost technologies in selected missions (Guéhenno 2008). The United Nations' "New Horizon" report, produced by DPKO and the DFS, outlined a "new field support strategy" that included "a better use of technology to support lighter, more agile deployment" (DPKO and DFS 2009: vi). The two departments recognized that robust peacekeeping "requires enhanced situational awareness" (2009: 21) and pledged "to enhance information-gathering, analysis and security-risk assessment capacity" (2009: 25). Their strategy "calls for the introduction of modern technology" (2009: 21) while identifying "critical shortages" in "observation/surveillance, including high resolution; night operations capability; data management and analysis" (2009: 27).

The UN Special Committee on Peacekeeping Operations (aka the C-34, which stands for the Committee of 34, reflecting the original number of members, but which today is composed of more than 120 nations which are contributing to UN operations) requested "the Secretariat to develop appropriate modalities for the use of advanced monitoring and surveillance technologies" (UN Special Committee on Peacekeeping 2008: para. 50). In 2009, it noted "progress made towards a wider and systemic use of technology in peacekeeping operations" (UN Special Committee on Peacekeeping 2009: para. 42). In 2010, however, the Special Committee requested "further effort in this direction" (UN Special Committee on Peacekeeping 2010: para. 43). A full list of Special Committee statements on this subject is provided in Appendix 2.

This book was written to help promote progress in peacekeeping. As outlined in the Preface, the work analyses the expanding UN monitoring functions in conflict zones. It seeks to identify the information requirements in missions and the extent to which they are met. It identifies lessons to be learned and mistakes not to be repeated. Cases of specific technology use in particular missions were researched and described.

All of this must be founded on a broad understanding of UN missions as they have evolved over time.

Notes

1. In several peacekeeping missions, other organizations or governments flew UAVs but not under the UN chain of command. In Bosnia, the United States flew Predator drones in areas where the United Nations Protection Force was stationed. Later, the NATO-led Implementation Force and Stabilization Force missions used drones. Various nations deployed drones in the NATO-led Kosovo Implementation Force. In the Democratic Republic of the Congo, the European Union flew Belgian B-Hunter UAVs, in part to support the UN Mission in the Congo (MONUC).
2. The United Nations has not yet brought data transmission to the tactical level (i.e. the individual soldier in the field), largely because communications within a contingent remain the responsibility of the contingent. Also, UN personnel often complain of blackout periods, when email cannot be used, and of delays in the transmission of messages across the UN networks in the field and to UN headquarters.
3. The COE database is not available to the general public, but information on the COE system can be found at <http://www.un.org/en/peacekeeping/sites/coe/about.shtml> (accessed 5 January 2011).
4. The United Nations' Official Document System is available at <http://documents.un.org/> (accessed 5 January 2011).
5. MONUC's many air assets consist of 24 fixed-wing aircraft and 62 helicopters. Military helicopters: Mi-17 (16); Mi-35 (4); Mi-25 (4); Lama/Alouette (4). Civilian air assets (Contractors): Mi-8 (30), Mi-26 (4), Hercules (6), An-24 (3); An-26 (2); An-72 (1); Il-76 (3), Beechcraft-200s (3), Boeing 727 (2), HS-125 (2), Dash turbo props (2), as of 10 January 2006, available at <http://www.monuc.org/news.aspx?newsID=9576> (accessed 2008). MONUC's fleet of over 86 aircraft is greater in number than South African Airways' 49 aircraft, though the latter are mostly considerably larger (see <http://www.flysaa.com/Utility_Navigation/About/index.html>, accessed 2008). Of MONUC's annual $1.1 billion budget, almost a quarter is spent on aircraft and fuel (US$ are used throughout this book).
6. The 34 types of "major" communications equipment are listed under 6 categories: VHF/UHF-FM transceivers (8 types); HF equipment (4); satellite equipment (10); telephone equipment (5); airfield communications (4); and miscellaneous (3, including underwater). The monitoring technologies fall under 2 categories ("observation" and "identification") and list only 6 types. The deficiencies of the COE Manual are described in Chapter 8. The Standard Cost Manual 2005 (DPKO 2005a) lists 4 types of observation technology and 175 types of communications equipment.
7. In the early 1960s, the "state-of-the-art computer" had 1 kilobyte (1,000 bytes) of "core storage" and cost over $10,000, whereas today a laptop with 1 terabyte (1,000 billion bytes) of hard disk space can be purchased for under $1,000. This is a 10-billion-fold improvement in the price-to-performance ratio over 50 years.
8. In the 1980s, the term C3ISR was used because computers had not yet made such a high level of impact as to warrant adding the extra "C".
9. The most dangerous current peacekeeping operations, based on fatalities per year (given in parentheses) over the length of the mission until 2009, are: United Nations Mission in Liberia (28.3), United Nations Mission in the Sudan (15), United Nations Mission in the DRC (14), United Nations Operation in Côte d'Ivoire (13), United Nations Operation in Burundi (11.5) and United Nations Stabilization Mission in Haiti (10).

2

The evolution of peace operations

The League of Nations ... should be the eye of the nations to keep watch upon the common interest, an eye that does not slumber, an eye that is everywhere watchful and attentive.

US President Woodrow Wilson, Paris Peace Conference, 25 January 1919[1]

The United Nations has done far more than its predecessor, the League of Nations, to keep watch over the peace and security of the world. In fact, no other organization in history has as much experience in monitoring peace agreements and treaties as the United Nations. Since World War II, it has verified fragile peace arrangements between numerous conflicting parties:

- colonial powers and independence-seeking groups;
- "communist" and "capitalist" forces, usually parties fighting proxy wars for the superpowers during the Cold War;
- rebel groups and governments in Central America and in the former Soviet Union after the Cold War;
- warring states in the Middle East;
- armed factions in Southeast Asia (Cambodia and East Timor) after periods of genocide;
- ethnic groups in Africa, Asia and Europe;
- superpowers seeking international confirmation of their troop withdrawals (e.g. US withdrawal from the Dominican Republic in 1965 and Soviet withdrawal from Afghanistan in 1988–1989).

Missions that the United Nations sends to the field "to prevent, manage, and/or resolve violent conflicts or reduce the risk of their

Keeping watch: Monitoring, technology and innovation in UN peace operations, Dorn, United Nations University Press, 2011, ISBN 978-92-808-1198-8

recurrence" are broadly called peace operations, though the United Nations retains the older term "peacekeeping operation".[2] The UN definition of peacekeeping (peace operation) has changed several times, but the following contains the basic elements:[3]

> Peacekeeping is the deployment of international (UN) military, police and civilian personnel to a conflict area with the consent of the parties to the conflict, acting impartially in order to:
> * stop or contain hostilities;
> * supervise the carrying out of a peace agreement;
> * assist with humanitarian relief, human rights compliance, and nation-building.

United Nations peacekeepers, sometimes called "Blue Helmets", "Blue Berets" and even "Blue Caps" (civilian peacekeepers) because of the colour of their headgear, have monitored areas and activities from disputed borders to entire countries, from cease-fires to disarmament and demobilization, and from human rights to national elections. These soldiers and civilians have served as "early warners" of war, investigators of complaints,

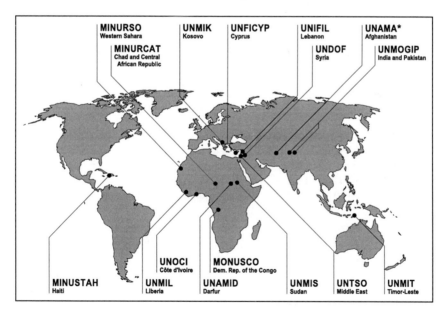

Figure 2.1 Missions administered by the UN Department of Peacekeeping Operations.
Source: Based on UN Map No. 4259 Rev. 11(E), January 2010 (DPKO 2010b), updates available at <http://www.un.org/en/peacekeeping/bnote.htm> (accessed 6 January 2011).
Note: The United Nations Assistance Mission in Afghanistan (UNAMA, marked with *) is technically a "political mission" though it is led by DPKO.

verifiers of compliance, evaluators of human rights, and witnesses to raging conflicts. They have also been called upon to intervene forcefully to prevent a build-up of tensions and the escalation of violence.

Experiencing both successes and failures, UN peacekeeping has evolved considerably over time, though the term peacekeeping is more identified with the older (traditional) types of mission. The mandates have become more complex and the monitoring tasks more elaborate. Over the decades, conflicting parties have generally given peacekeepers more access and more responsibilities and, on paper at least, pledged more cooperation. Particularly after the Cold War there was a dramatic increase in the mandates and number of UN peace operations in the field. In the 1990s, for instance, the number of new missions was double the number created in the previous 40 years. A map showing the current UN peace operations is shown in Figure 2.1, with abbreviations for the missions. A list of all UN operations (1948–2010) with their full titles is provided in Appendix 1, along with brief descriptions of the monitoring and other mandates.

A review of all UN peace operations shows that they can logically be divided into four broad functional categories corresponding roughly to four "generations" over its 60-odd year history.[4] Each new category or generation brought new tasks and additional monitoring requirements.

Four types of peace operation

Observer missions

UN OBSERVERS. Their beat – no man's land. Their job – to get the facts straight. A frontier incident, an outbreak of fighting ... Which nation is responsible, whose story is true? The UN must know. So its peace patrols keep vigil to prevent flare-ups, supervise truces, investigate and report. Already this vital work has helped to end bloodshed, bringing a promise of peace to millions of people.
UN poster, Department of Public Information, c. 1960[5]

The oldest type of peace operation is the "observer mission", characterized by the above quotation. The main purpose is to observe the deployments and activities of the armed forces of two or more conflicting states, usually in relation to a cease-fire agreement that is often negotiated between states with UN mediation. Sometimes the mission name, as well as the mandate, includes the ambitious term "supervision", but conditions rarely put these UN operations in such an elevated position over the parties. The unarmed observers on the ground, however, had many opportunities to help de-escalate and contain violence. In addition to the "observe and report" function, they attempt to influence parties to quell violence using advice, aid and mediation.[6] The first official UN peacekeeping operation, which is still operating in the Middle East, was the United Nations Truce Supervision Organization (UNTSO). A full list of observer missions is provided in Appendix 1, Table A1.1.

Interposed forces

The second type of operation was first formed in 1956 when a "UN force", not simply an observer group, was deployed to the Sinai to separate the Egyptian army from the invading forces of Israel, France and the United Kingdom. This proved to be the key to end the Suez crisis. In this and other "second-generation" operations, UN troops were interposed between conflicting armed forces. These forces typically number in the thousands, whereas observer missions usually number in the hundreds. Unlike soldiers in observer missions, the peacekeepers in these operations are armed. Also they are deployed in preformed units (e.g. battalions) not as individual observers on secondment. By separating combatants physically, these more robust forces reduce the number of military contacts and flare-ups and allow more effective monitoring of the tense zones (no man's land) between the parties. To prevent parties from violating cease-fires or gaining new ground, the UN peacekeepers must keep constant watch over the positions of the combatants and try to anticipate any forward movements of military forces from agreed positions, sometimes even placing themselves in the way of such advances.

In his pioneering report to the General Assembly on the proposed United Nations Emergency Force (UNEF), UN Secretary-General Dag Hammarskjöld set out the basic principles that have guided this type of operation (UN Secretary-General 1956). The Force was to be:

- under the command of the Secretary-General (as the earlier missions, including UNTSO, had by then become);
- recruited from member states other than the five permanent members of the Security Council (i.e. China, France, the Soviet Union, the United Kingdom and the United States were excluded from direct, on-the-ground participation owing to their Cold War strategic involvement in most disputes in the world);
- paid by the United Nations, except for the salaries of troops, which would continue to be covered by the contributing states, though the United Nations made a contribution per soldier;
- impartial, i.e. the forces would not favour one side over the other in the conflict; and
- non-offensive, using armed force only in self-defence.

Hammarskjöld negotiated with Egypt[7] an agreement that was to become a model for future Status-of-Forces Agreements (SOFAs), which the United Nations signs with host states. The SOFAs cover a wide range of issues, including the freedom of movement and legal immunity of the UN peacekeepers.

Almost all of the traditional operations (i.e. the first and second types) have required and received invitations from the host state. The observer missions and forces could hence be withdrawn upon request of the host state, as did indeed transpire when Egypt requested the withdrawal of UNEF prior to the 1967 war. Thus the operations are of limited value once the parties are determined to engage in serious fighting.[8]

Multidimensional operations

The third generation of UN operations (multidimensional) arose from the changed character of most conflicts following the Cold War, as described in a general fashion in Table 2.1. With internal conflicts increasing

Table 2.1 From Cold War to hot wars: Different types of conflict and peace operation

	Cold War	Post–Cold War
Predominant conflicts	*Inter*state, inter-alliance	*Intra*state, internal
Origins	Ideology; power bloc rivalry	Ethnic/tribal/religious animosities, secessionism
Main threats	Armed attack or invasion	Civil war, human rights violations (including genocide and torture), terrorism
Goals	National and international stability; conflict management	Human security; conflict resolution; comprehensive multidimensional peace agreements; conflict prevention
Means	Deterrence; negotiation of cease-fires and troop withdrawal agreements; traditional peacekeeping; Chapter VI of UN Charter	Cooperation, mediation, modern multidimensional peacekeeping (traditional peacekeeping PLUS humanitarian action, disarmament, elections, enforcement, sanctions, economic assistance, peacebuilding); Chapter VII of UN Charter
Locations	State boundaries	Throughout a nation or region
Peacekeepers	Soldiers (non-P5, i.e. not the permanent members of the Security Council)	Soldiers, police, civilian monitors and experts (elections, human rights); including the P5

in both number and intensity, the United Nations became much more in-volved *within* states. The United Nations sought to foster a sustainable peace between warring factions, not just a cease-fire, and to assist in the difficult task of nation-building. This required multidimensional peace-keeping encompassing a wide range of functions and methods, including the traditional observation of armed forces, the delivery of humanitarian aid, human rights promotion, and the supervision of elections. Whereas the previous two types of operation monitored mainly military activities, the new missions needed to monitor a wide diversity of activities, including political, humanitarian, police, judicial, electoral, economic and human rights activities. The United Nations had not only to disengage the fight-ing forces but also to reform the security sector as a whole, especially since unreformed agencies posed a threat to the fragile peace process. New training was required for border guards, prosecutors and judges, and even for officials in intelligence agencies. In some missions the tasks ex-panded to include the supervision of entire departments of government, including defence and foreign affairs. The United Nations found itself at the forefront of efforts to fight crime, control cross-border smuggling and enforce sanctions.

Though a forerunner operation (ONUC) was staged in the early 1960s in the Congo, over 30 multidimensional operations have been launched since 1989, when the pioneering operation in Namibia (UNTAG) was created. Major powers, including the permanent members of the Security Council (the P5), actively participated in such modern operations.

Transitional administrations

At the end of the 1990s a fourth type of operation was created for the purpose of "transitional administration". In such cases, the United Nations finds itself not merely supervising a peace accord but actually governing an entire territory during a transitional period. The main cases of transitional administrations are the missions in Kosovo (UNMIK) and East Timor (UNTAET). Although East Timor became self-governing in 2002, Kosovo officially remains under United Nations administration.

The number of UN peacekeepers increased dramatically with each new type of operation. In an observer mission, some 500–700 military person-nel were typically deployed. With UNEF (1956), the strength jumped to 5,000; similarly for other interposed forces. With the rise of multidimen-sional peacekeeping at the end of the Cold War the number of uniformed peacekeepers (military plus police) grew to over 10,000 per mission – with some 80,000 in the field at the 1990s peak. After the United Nations completed its missions in Cambodia (UNTAC, 1993), Somalia (UNOSOM

II, 1995) and Bosnia (UNPROFOR, 1995) – peacekeeping in Bosnia was taken up by the North Atlantic Treaty Organization (NATO) – the total number of peacekeepers fell back to the 10,000 mark. But in the twenty-first century, the demand for peacekeepers has grown dramatically in two "surges": the first to handle the two transitional administrations (UNMIK and UNTAET); the second for the missions in the Democratic Republic of the Congo (MONUC) and in Darfur (UNAMID). The number of uniformed UN peacekeepers exceeded 100,000 for the first time in March 2010. Today, the United Nations deploys more soldiers to the field than any other entity except the United States government. The developed and developing worlds contributed approximately equal numbers of peacekeepers to UN operations in the 1990s, but since 2000 the main contributing nations of military and police personnel have been from the developing world.[9]

The number of uniformed peacekeepers (military and police) after the Cold War is graphed in Figure 2.2, showing the two surges since 2000. The

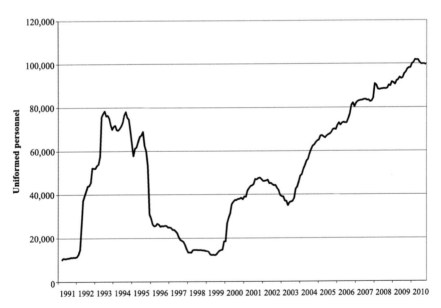

Figure 2.2 The number of uniformed personnel in UN peacekeeping since 1991. *Note*: I designed an earlier version of this chart while on sabbatical at the United Nations, using DPKO data mostly available at <http://www.un.org/en/peacekeeping/contributors/>. The chart was published (with permission) and is continuously updated by the United Nations on its website at <http://www.un.org/en/peacekeeping/documents/chart.pdf> (accessed 6 January 2011).

numbers in the field were at an all-time high by 2010. Adding the civilians (both international and local), the total number of personnel in peacekeeping was an unprecedented 125,000.

The purpose and methods of each of the four major categories of peace operation are summarized in Table 2.2. The 70-plus operations are listed within each category in Appendix 1, providing the "alphabet soup" of UN acronyms and indicating the monitoring activities of these missions. Since the first operation was created in 1948,[10] the vast majority (over two-thirds) were launched after the end of the Cold War.[11] Though the third type, multidimensional missions, is the most common, there are still missions of the other types in operation today, as shown in Appendix 1.

All UN peace operations must maintain a delicate balance between the conflicting parties in order to keep the peace. The United Nations cannot appear to be dominant or it will be accused of being an "occupying" force. Still, in many conflicts where parties respect military strength above all, some force may well be necessary to keep the peace. Various forms of dominance may be needed, especially in multidimensional operations and transitional administrations. This was exemplified in the non-UN mission run by NATO in Bosnia and Herzegovina – IFOR/ SFOR (Implementation Force / Stabilisation Force) – where "information dominance" quickly became a key component of mission success (see Chapter 7). In UN multidimensional operations of the twenty-first century, the United Nations finally began to make use of "information power", creating its own analytical centres within its field missions (Dorn 2010).

Armed force remains a valuable deterrent, but minimum force only should be applied, given the inevitable resentment that comes after death and destruction. So, for the United Nations at least, "information power" is a more important tool than "military force". And when the latter is required as a last resort, information also plays a central role in determining when and where to apply force. Multidimensional UN operations generally aim to be robust as well as flexible. Expanding the United Nations' information horizon allows it more options across the spectrum from soft to hard power.[12]

As UN operations evolved across the four types, the monitoring and information requirements grew. These needs must be reviewed before exploring the appropriate technologies to match the missions. Historically, the United Nations has used a host of methods, including observation posts, checkpoints, foot and vehicle patrols, and occasionally aerial reconnaissance, but few technological means. This is surprising given the importance of monitoring.

Table 2.2 Four types or "generations" of UN peace operation

Type of operation	Purpose	Means and methods	First missions
Observer missions	Determine if parties are respecting a cease-fire or other peace agreements, and assist in local settlements	Monitoring through foot and vehicle patrols, observation posts, checkpoints, etc. Mostly UN military observers	UNTSO (1948–) in the Middle East was the first official mission of this type; UNMOGIP (1949–) in Kashmir followed shortly thereafter
Interposed forces	Prevent or put an end to combat between opposing armies	Placing peacekeeping troops, mostly battalions, between combatants. Using patrols, checkpoints (fixed or mobile), searches, escort, show of UN presence/force	UNEF (1956–67), stationed between Israeli and Egyptian forces, was the first peacekeeping force
Multidimensional operations	Oversee or assist in the implementation of a complex peace agreement, which may involve disarmament, demobilization and reintegration of former combatants, humanitarian assistance, electoral assistance, human rights, civilian police, mine clearance, etc.	All of the above, plus protection of assembly areas and civilians, storage and destruction of surrendered weapons, escorts and protection of key personnel/facilities, oversight of police forces and other parts of the security sector, etc. Uses military, civilian police and civilian peacekeepers	ONUC (1960–4) was the first of this type; UNTAG (1989–90) in Namibia pioneered this type of mission in modern times; UNTAC (1992–3) in Cambodia saw a large increase in UN roles and responsibilities

16

	Protection of civilians (vulnerable populations)	Humanitarian aid convoys, road clearing, evacuation plans for vulnerable persons, securing sites such as refugee camps and designated territory. Uses military forces and civilian police, humanitarian workers, etc.	UNPROFOR (1992–5) in Bosnia had responsibility for "UN Protected Areas" but did not have the means; these missions work in close cooperation with humanitarian agencies (e.g. UNHCR); virtually all missions created in the twenty-first century included this mandate
Transitional administrations	Govern a territory during a transition to independence and self-governance	Comprehensive missions covering all aspects of society (from military and legal to education and sanitation). Uses soldiers, police and administrators of all types	UNMIK (1999–) in Kosovo and UNTAET (1999–2002) in East Timor are the main examples. Earlier, UNTEA (1962–3) in West New Guinea (Indonesia)

Notes: UNTSO – UN Truce Supervision Organization; UNMOGIP – UN Military Observer Group in India and Pakistan; UNEF – UN Emergency Force; ONUC – UN Operation in the Congo; UNTAG – UN Transition Assistance Group; UNTAC – UN Transitional Authority in Cambodia; UNPROFOR – UN Protection Force; UNHCR – United Nations High Commissioner for Refugees; UNMIK – UN Interim Administration Mission in Kosovo; UNTAET – UN Transitional Administration in East Timor; UNTEA – UN Temporary Executive Authority.

Notes

1. Quote in Wilson (1986: 265).
2. This definition of peace operation is drawn from *United Nations Peacekeeping Operations: Principles and Guidelines*, the "capstone" document of the Department of Peacekeeping Operations and the Department of Field Support (DPKO and DFS 2008). NATO uses the term "peace support operations", which include the following types of operation: peacemaking, peacebuilding, humanitarian assistance, peacekeeping, peace enforcement and prevention. The following are my brief explanations of the terms: peacemaking – negotiations for a sustainable peace; peacebuilding – creating the physical and social infrastructure for peace; humanitarian assistance – providing the means for human beings in distress to survive; peacekeeping – providing security, cease-fire verification and military assistance; peace enforcement – using force to press parties to abide by their agreements and international law; and prevention – to stop a conflict from starting or escalating. Official NATO definitions can be found in NATO (2010b).
3. This definition of peacekeeping is based on one taken from the UN website <http://www.un.org/Depts/dpko> in February 1999.
4. The peacekeeping literature usually considers only two categories or generations: traditional peacekeeping and second-generation (or modern) peacekeeping. This breakdown ignores the fact that "traditional" peacekeeping is itself divided into two categories: observer missions (first used in 1946–1948 in Greece, Indonesia, Korea and Palestine) and armed forces interposed between conflicting parties (first used in 1956 in Egypt). Similarly, modern (post–Cold War) missions are of two types. In the 1990s, the range of functions increased dramatically to include many non-military functions. This constituted multidimensional missions. At the turn of the century, another jump was made, with some new missions actually governing entire territories during a transitional period (transitional administration). Hence the concept of four types or generations of peacekeeping, introduced for the first time here, is more precise than the usual two.
5. The UN poster is visible in a photograph from the UN Department of Public Information (1960).
6. In all generations of peacekeeping operations, the United Nations tries to prevent or reduce fighting through negotiation, mediation and the exercise of its "good offices", but it can succeed only to the extent that the parties allow.
7. David Ben Gurion, the Prime Minister of Israel, stated in parliament that "on no account will Israel agree to the stationing of foreign forces, no matter how called, in her territory, or in any of the areas occupied by her" (United Nations 1996: 45). Although UNEF was not stationed on Israel, UNTSO continued to operate there (with its headquarters still in Jerusalem) and the UN Interim Force in Lebanon later worked in areas occupied by Israel in Lebanon.
8. The United Nations Iraq–Kuwait Observation Mission, which occupied territory on both nations, is an exception. The Security Council created the mission under Chapter VII and, under international law, it cannot be withdrawn without the authorization of the Council, even if the states (i.e. Iraq or Kuwait) demand its removal. Some other missions (e.g. UNOSOM in Somalia) have had similarly strong mandates.
9. In 1995, the developed world (as represented by the nations of the Organisation for Economic Co-operation and Development) accounted for 51 per cent of UN uniformed peacekeepers; 10 years later, the contribution had fallen to only 8 per cent (my computations). After 1995, NATO began to take on major peacekeeping responsibilities, starting in Bosnia and later in Kosovo. The European Union also deployed short-term forces in 2003 and 2006 to the Democratic Republic of the Congo in support of the ongoing UN-led peace process.

10. UNTSO, created in 1948, is considered by the United Nations to be its first peacekeeping operation, since it came under the control of the UN Secretary-General. Earlier missions of the United Nations, though not under the Secretary-General's control, could also be considered as peacekeeping operations, namely the Commissions sent to Greece (1946), Indonesia (1947) and Korea (1947). In those multinational missions, the personnel directly represented states and not the United Nations as a whole.

11. The end of the Cold War is taken to be 1988, even before the 1989 fall of the Berlin Wall. It became clear in 1988 that the Soviet Union, under Mikhail Gorbachev, was no longer going to participate in the superpower arms race. In December 1988, Gorbachev announced unprecedented and unilateral cuts to the Soviet armed forces. Earlier, in February 1988, the Soviet Union declared it would start repatriating troops from Afghanistan under UN observation. The Soviets had begun constructive engagement in the UN Security Council since 1986. On 17 September 1987, Gorbachev made his dramatic proposals for strengthening the United Nations, including wider use of peacekeeping forces and enhanced monitoring powers for the UN Secretary-General. See Mikhail S. Gorbachev, "Reality and the Guarantees of a Secure World", *Pravda* and *Izvestia* article available in UN Secretary-General (1987).

12. For a creative and broad overview, see Steele (2010a).

3

Monitoring: The constant need

Monitoring is a basic function of all UN peace operations, past and present, and in some cases it is the primary function. All mission mandates have included observation, monitoring (i.e. observation over time) or verification (i.e. monitoring to determine if parties are living up to agreements). Almost two dozen missions have had these tasks explicit in their mission names.[1] The peace operations created in the twenty-first century have been explicitly tasked by the Security Council to monitor many activities and areas, including:

- arms embargoes and military assistance to illegal armed groups;
- cease-fires and demilitarized zones;
- commercial activities such as illegal mineral exploitation that fuel conflicts;
- disarmament, demobilization and reintegration of ex-combatants;
- elections;
- human rights;
- international/internal borders;
- malicious acts and escalations of armed violence;
- minefields for marking and clearing;
- no-fly zones and flight bans;
- security sector reform (e.g. of armed forces, police, corrections, customs and even intelligence agencies);
- strategic areas (e.g. airports) and persons (threatened VIPs);
- trafficking in illicit materials and human beings;
- UN protected areas such as safe havens or refugee camps;
- vulnerable places (e.g. refugee camps) and groups (e.g. children).

Keeping watch: Monitoring, technology and innovation in UN peace operations, Dorn, United Nations University Press, 2011, ISBN 978-92-808-1198-8

There is plenty of evidence from the field and from academic studies that UN monitoring, however imperfect, helps to promote cooperation among former warring parties, to prevent conflict, to reduce unwarranted fears and worst-case assumptions, and to reduce cheating and rogue/spoiler problems (Lindley 2007).

In addition to mandated monitoring, for its own security every UN operation must maintain constant situational awareness around UN camps and facilities. Missions must also be vigilant about a myriad of threats, including possible risks on the main supply route, on roads travelled and in areas visited by UN personnel. In addition, operations need to learn details about the wider environment such as the intentions and locations of potential spoilers who might seek to disrupt the peace process, the mood of belligerent crowds or mobs, the hideouts and armaments possessed by renegade forces, and much additional information about actual or potential threats, both natural and human-made.

For all these mandated and implied tasks, peacekeeping operations (PKOs) need a wide set of monitoring tools and methods. Technical means can help the United Nations meet these enormous monitoring challenges. But before reviewing specific technologies, an analysis is provided to show the kinds of advanced capabilities required to handle the recurring problems facing PKOs. This chapter also looks at some of the mission structures that are needed to process, analyse and disseminate information, including the Joint Operations Centre and Joint Mission Analysis Centre. Case studies of specific missions are provided later (Chapters 6 and 7). In general, UN missions face at least six pressing needs: protecting UN personnel; protecting civilians; night-time awareness; detecting illegal trafficking; accurate and precise intelligence; analysis of the data.

Protecting UN personnel: An essential responsibility

The safety and security of UN personnel sent to the field should be foremost in the minds of UN leaders who assume a solemn responsibility for the civilians and military personnel they dispatch to the field. Protection requires accurate threat and risk assessments, early warning of emerging threats and a proactive approach based on wide-ranging information-gathering. Especially in highly volatile areas, where personnel might be exposed to direct or indirect fire, landmines and unexploded ordinance or even ambush, the United Nations needs far more than an occasional "presence" to observe possible threats. It needs a thorough day and night watch over large areas well beyond UN camps, something few missions provide. There are rarely enough personnel to do the job. Moreover, employing vulnerable human observers presents a serious dilemma for the United Nations.

The reliance on a human presence, particularly from unarmed United Nations Military Observers (UNMOs), gives rise to a "Catch 22" dilemma. When conditions become dangerous or the parties become hostile, current information in conflict areas is most needed and most valuable, requiring close observation. But at such critical times, the observers often have to be withdrawn for their own security, creating an information vacuum. As will be demonstrated, technologies can help resolve this dilemma.

Despite the United Nations' care and caution, over 2,500 personnel have lost their lives from various causes since the beginning of UN peacekeeping in 1948. Table 3.1 analyses the fatalities listed in the Department of Peacekeeping Operations (DPKO) Casualties Database according to the three types of personnel and the four types of incident causing death. By examining how (and to whom) the fatalities have occurred, it should be possible to explore ways and tools to help avoid them in the future.

The table shows that, over the history of peacekeeping, accidents have accounted for the greatest number of fatalities, followed by malicious acts and illness, with a small percentage of other causes (often undetermined). Military personnel have suffered by far the greatest number of

Table 3.1 Fatalities in UN peace operations

| | Incident type | | | | |
	Accident	Malicious act	Illness	Other	Total
Military	848	627	519	115	2,109 (87%)
Police	57	21	65	12	155 (6%)
International civilian	51	30	73	8	162 (7%)
Total	956 (39%)	678 (28%)	657 (27%)	135 (6%)	2,426 (100%)

Source: Raw data provided by the United Nations' Casualties Database (1948–2009).

Note: The Casualties Database is maintained by the DPKO Situation Centre, which provided these data to me by email from Q. Wilson on 21 June 2010. The Situation Centre notes that "prior to 2006, the requirement and procedures for recording civilian fatalities were lacking, and, therefore there is a risk that for years prior to 2006 not all civilian fatalities, particularly local fatalities, were recorded" (email to me, 30 January 2006). Because of this, fatalities of local UN staff are not included in the table. For the record, the data on fatalities of local staff (1948–2009) are: 52 by accident, 47 by malicious act, 124 by illness and 18 other, for a total of 241 deaths, which is 9 per cent of the total. Including locals, the total number of fatalities in peacekeeping up to 31 December 2009 was 2,682.

fatalities (87 per cent), though only 3 per cent of these fatalities were military observers. Since the number of military personnel serving in peacekeeping is many times that of civilian personnel,[2] a better indicator of risk is the number of fatalities per 1,000 personnel serving. For 2005, they are: 1.51 for uniformed personnel (i.e. military and police) and 2.92 for international civilians. This indicates, surprisingly, that an international civilian is almost twice as likely to die in a UN mission as a uniformed person, probably because the latter are generally younger and better trained and protected in danger zones.[3] In addition, the data show that a much higher percentage of the civilians die of illness, probably because they are older and less fit than the soldiers.

The United Nations can take many measures to mitigate fatalities in each category. In particular, monitoring technologies can be deployed for prevention, protection and rescue. A sample list of applicable technologies would include:

• *for accidents*: vehicle management and tracking systems (a proven example is "Carlog", described later); night-vision equipment for driving on unlit roads; better weather-forecasting using radars and satellite imagery;

• *for malicious acts*: better threat assessments using surveillance systems for detection, including: the presence of mines, recent military/militia activity, arms smuggling, the possibility of ambushes and many other indicators of potential violence; artillery-tracking radar for incoming fire; access control/identification technologies for UN buildings and camps; convoy trackers and positioning devices (based on Global Positioning Systems, or GPS) and, in the case of robust engagements, "identify friend from foe" technology;

• *for illness*: many medical monitoring technologies for diagnosis and prognosis (not covered in this study).[4]

By extending the range of observation and awareness, technologies can allow observers to avoid hazards while still keeping tabs on the conflict. Remote sensors can serve as the eyes and ears of the United Nations in danger zones. Devices on the ground and in the air can capture details of the conflict for remote viewing by distant observers.

Protecting civilians: Vigilance required

After some terrible experiences during the 1990s, when massacres occurred in plain view of helpless peacekeepers, the Security Council included the protection of civilians in the mandates of new PKOs in the twenty-first century.[5] In addition to such explicit responsibility, many peacekeepers feel it is their moral as well as their legal duty to protect the vulnerable within their areas of operation. Some countries also include this in their national Rules of Engagement (ROE) prior to deployments. Furthermore, the "Responsibility to Protect" doctrine has been adopted at the UN summit level, although it is only slowly being operationalized.[6]

To achieve civilian protection in conflict zones, accurate early warning of attack is essential. Before sending rapid response forces to prevent or mitigate tragedy, timely information/intelligence is needed. As the United Nations readily admits, too often it has found itself in the dark about spoiler intrigue, arms and militia movements and a host of other dangerous activities. Then it can only react to tragedies after they have occurred rather than work to prevent them in the first place (UN Secretary-General 1999). UN investigations are usually conducted after violations have been committed, when the results of atrocities are plain to see. Even then, it may be difficult to locate hidden graves, determine the sequence of events and identify the individual perpetrators.

Technologies not only are useful for post-violence forensic analysis but can increase awareness for conflict prevention, for instance by monitoring both distant and proximal threats to protected areas and people. Aerial reconnaissance can help detect movements of armed bands towards vulnerable civilian population centres, such as refugee camps or urban communities. Closed-circuit television and motion sensors can alert security forces to intruders in the offices/residences of protected persons (e.g. VIPs) and provide a record of the events if violence does occur. Although no panacea, this technology can be useful for preventive deployments and rapid response.

A bolder proposal is to place video cameras in the hands of the local population to help identify and deter perpetrators. This, however, raises a moral dilemma. Although the ability to record violent activities may serve as a deterrent, camera-holders may also be seen as a threat to belligerents, exposing them to risks of retaliation. The merits of observation equipment in local hands must be assessed in each case. For protection, cameras can be equipped with telephoto lenses for distant viewing, ruggedized for robust handling and miniaturized for discreet photography, as the situation may warrant. Distant or hidden cameras would be out of reach of the perpetrators. Pictures, even taken with cell phones, could constitute important evidence in national or international courts.

Not least, "crowdsourcing" (discussed below) can be an indispensable means to assist the protection of civilians. Through the use of phone and computer messaging, the affected population can provide a timely picture of what is going on, though the reports will need to be corroborated by UN staff with information gained near the scene of the fighting.

Night-time awareness: Coming out of the dark

The Athenians now fell into great disorder and perplexity ... in a night engagement (and this was the only one that occurred between great armies during the
war) how could any one know anything for certain?

Thucydides, *History of the Peloponnesian War*, 431 BCE (1972 edn)

Throughout history, violent and nefarious activities have been carried out
under the cover of darkness rather than in the revealing light of day.[7]
Thus the United Nations must try to detect and deter such nocturnal actions and preparations. If fighters operate at night, then so must peacekeepers. But traditionally peacekeeping has been a "daytime job". With
the exception of night guards, scheduled peacekeeping activities are done
almost entirely during daylight. Even now, UNMOs typically finish their
work at the end of the day, usually 1700 or 1800 hrs, returning to their
base or dwelling as the sun sets. This is not only because of the dangers
that might lurk in the dark and attack patrols but also because there is
little that can be seen at night with the unaided eye. This leaves the
United Nations blinded for about 10 out of 24 hours, giving the forces of
violence free rein for many hours each day.

To surmount the "darkness barrier" and claim the night back from the
forces of violence, the United Nations must make night operations routine. This is possible thanks to the advancement of night-vision equipment, allowing troops to follow terrain on foot or drive vehicles at night
while being on the lookout for threats.

In 2006, the Eastern Division of MONUC – United Nations Mission in
the Democratic Republic of the Congo (DRC) – instigated the pioneering practice of establishing mobile operating bases in faraway locations
for four to seven days a week. The soldiers were equipped with some
night-vision goggles to allow them to patrol the jungle at night. These
"night flash" operations cooperated with local "village vigilance committees" that reportedly banged pots and pans in order to sound the alarm.
The UN forces, with 50–70 soldiers in a group, used their night-vision
equipment to help locate and confront intruders and attackers. For large-
scale combat operations, in November 2006 MONUC authorized the
night-time deployment of Mi-25/35 attack helicopters, which are equipped
with advanced thermal imagers as well as image intensifiers to allow
pilots to engage their targets at night. A detailed description is provided
in the case study in Chapter 7.

Other technologies to extend monitoring at night include ground
surveillance radars and acoustic/seismic sensors. These can alert peacekeepers to potential threats such as intruders into UN demilitarized or

protected areas. Once peacekeepers became accustomed to operating with night-vision equipment, they ask not to patrol at night without them. Night vision can also help overcome the limitations on night flying by providing pilots with extra vision for manoeuvring, landing on unfamiliar terrain and detecting nearby threats on the ground or in the air, especially weapon-carrying forces.

Monitoring arms embargoes: Detecting illegal trafficking

Widespread weaponry in conflict areas is the bane of peacekeepers. Conflicting parties seek to gain advantage with more and better armaments. Arms races, even on a rudimentary level, can result in massive stockpiles and great tragedies. Small arms (weapons carried and used by individuals), in particular, have caused widespread death and destruction. They have made modern conflicts more combustible and crime more extensive, feeding cultures of retribution and downward spirals of violence.

For these reasons it is imperative to somehow deal with the weapons that fuel the fires of violence. However, reducing or prohibiting weapons imports is enormously difficult in war-torn areas because borders are typically porous and there is high demand, including for personal protection. The Security Council often mandates arms embargoes in conflict areas, and frequently asks PKOs to monitor and implement the embargoes. Furthermore, it tasks PKOs with disarmament programmes to reduce weaponry in the overall population.

Disarming unwilling parties is one of the most difficult challenges in peacekeeping operations. Some missions have even refused to do this job for fear of retaliation. This reluctance is understandable. Before confronting smugglers and militia forces, it is important to know what kind of weaponry they possess and to pinpoint the arms routes. In this deadly "cat and mouse" game, the United Nations is at a great disadvantage if it possesses observation technology that is inferior to that of the smugglers who seek to evade detection. In fact, many arms smugglers are better equipped (e.g. with night-vision equipment) than the peacekeepers, allowing them to outmanoeuvre the United Nations at almost every turn. A UN Group of Experts investigating the weapons embargo on militias in the Eastern Congo assessed MONUC's capacity. It concluded that, in order to achieve its mandate, the mission "needs to be provided with the appropriate lake patrol and air-surveillance capabilities, including appropriate nocturnal, satellite, radar and photographic assets" (UN Security Council 2004).[8] This case is described in Chapter 7.

Peacekeepers must often search for weapons moving across national borders or within nations, a very difficult challenge since the weapons are usually hidden, stowed or stored until needed. The discovery of armaments is facilitated by metal detectors and ground-penetrating radar to find buried arms caches. X-ray machines can detect weapons smuggled through luggage. At vehicle checkpoints, mirrors and video cameras can be used to look for explosives under cars. Although X-ray machines exist to scan entire vehicles, including tractor-trailers and sea containers, this equipment would be too expensive and require too much infrastructure for most UN missions. However, walkthrough X-ray machines are already used in some UN missions, as are metal detectors of the walkthrough and wand variety.

To detect smugglers transiting over bodies of water such as the Great Lakes on the eastern border of the DRC, it is not sufficient to observe simply with the human eye. In order to maintain a wide-area watch, maritime radars are required while sending fast patrol boats to inspect or board suspicious boats. To catch weapons imported by aircraft, the United Nations must maintain surveillance over the airspace and determine where illegal flights are landing before initiating interdictions. Surveillance *of* the air and *from* the air are both needed.

Robust operations: Accurate and precise intelligence required

As the United Nations has learned from its well-publicized failures, PKOs need the capacity to apply force, as a last resort, to maintain the peace. This means being able to move up the force spectrum against recalcitrant groups that have spurned previous offers of settlement, rehabilitation and reintegration, etc. Often such "Chapter VII" action entails combat under the force's ROE and in conformity with the Security Council mandate. Armed engagements should be as precise as possible, targeting only the spoilers without collateral (civilian) damage.

Before engaging in direct confrontation and combat, peacekeepers need a solid command of the information sphere in the area of operations. Such situational awareness necessitates precise information about locations, unit structures and weaponry ("order of battle" in traditional military doctrine), plus more complex factors such as the level of support among the local population for the United Nations and for the "hostiles", the parties' intent and ability to use human shields, and the intelligence capacities of the hard-line elements. Unfortunately, overstretched PKOs often lack such intelligence.

When spoilers see that the United Nations is aware of their actions and has the means to uncover their preparations before they strike, they will think twice about challenging the peace process. These notions of robust observation and action are being put to the test in places such as the DRC (see Chapter 7).

When operating in a war zone and engaging in combat, the technologies needed include: imagers to distinguish between civilians and armed combatants (who might use human shields); night-vision devices for camp protection and night operations; weapons detectors; and devices to "identify friend from foe" to avoid shooting friendly forces. In the attack helicopters used in the DRC, UN pilots have the possibility of "seeing" their targets before "engaging" (firing on) them, including at night. But only a few of the United Nations' military aircraft are permitted to fly at night.

Analysis: Thinking through the data

Ensure that sufficient information about the situation at hand is obtained and that it is analysed adequately so that it provides policymakers with an incisive and valid diagnosis of the problem.

Alexander George (1980: 10)

Thanks to advances in the field of information technology, the amount of information currently at the fingertips of UN analysts and decision-makers is orders of magnitude greater than before the dawn of the information age. However, the basic intelligence process has remained the same. "Raw" information from the field needs to be gathered, collated, synthesized, analysed and disseminated from a variety of human and technical sources. Unfortunately, in today's peace operations, experts on intelligence and technical monitoring are few and far between, including operators of the devices and interpreters/compilers of the data.

With the encouragement of the United Nations Special Committee on Peacekeeping, DPKO took a major step in 2005–2006 by developing structures for information-gathering and analysis. Joint Operations Centres (JOC) and Joint Mission Analysis Centres (JMAC) are now required components of all PKOs (DPKO 2006a). The JOC/JMAC structures present an opportunity to include experts in the analysis of outputs from monitoring technologies.

Under the current Concept of Operations, the JOC deals with current- and near-term information whereas the JMAC looks to the medium and long term. (It might be useful to shift the focus for the JOC to current operations, and for the JMAC to deal with analysis, as the names indicate, regardless of the time horizon.) In any case, technical information is useful for both. Since the JOC is designed to operate 24/7 for mission-wide situational awareness and for support of current operations, it especially needs (near) real-time information from in-field observation assets. It also needs to know how to rapidly redeploy these assets to meet any immediate information gaps. JMAC also needs this information but not on such a short time-scale.

In developing and implementing JOC and JMAC procedures in various missions, it is important for the United Nations to identify the technologies that could help meet the various Mission Information Requirements, Priority Information Requirements and urgent Requests for Information. It would also be useful to identify optimal "checkpoints and choke points". These are places where technical monitoring would have the most significant impact, for example in increasing security and/or suppressing illegal/violent activities. It should be possible for intelligence officers to direct information-gathering operations and foster intelligence-led peacekeeping.

JOC and JMAC units require specialized skill sets, including those relating to technology:

- geographic information systems and GPS reference systems;
- digital video processing, editing and networking;
- basic interpretation of feeds from various sensors;
- relational databases and cross-referencing;
- quantitative and statistical analysis, graphing and charting using standard and advanced software;
- specialized search engines beyond those already widely used for Internet searches;
- encryption tools (e.g. private and public key) and data authentication (e.g. watermarked images).

The professional members of the JOC and JMAC need to understand the strengths and weaknesses of the various monitoring technologies and sensor systems. Missions also need personnel with specialized expertise in order to:

- identify the specifications for equipment purchases;
- optimize technical monitoring devices;
- deal with telecommunications and bandwidth challenges;
- use artificial intelligence for digital analysis, pattern recognition, change detection and automation software related to the monitoring technology;
- identify artefacts in imagery and other technological products;
- conduct image analyses (formerly called photo-analysis), for example to "read" output from radar products and infrared imagers and to recognize the signatures of various armaments and vehicles;
- other specialized skills (e.g. forensic investigations, crater analysis).

JOC and JMAC personnel need to create "information synergy" from different sources and methods, especially technical information that can confirm or deny human sources. In addition, day and night observations can complement each other. Useful JOC/JMAC analytical products would help mission planning, execution and security risk assessment. The two organizations are mandated to support *informed* decision-making at all stages. Because various monitoring assets are deployed, an "information hub" is needed to put "the right information into the right hands". One benefit of technology is the ability to share the "data feed" or data segments from sensors with multiple UN sections. For example, feeding real-time video imagery to a range of computers allows multiple inputs into the analysis.

An important "information product" is the "Threat and Risk Assessment" (TRA). Its preparation involves, among other tasks, the compilation of risk factors and early warning indicators, and developments to be monitored by technical and non-technical means. Optionally, the TRA can include potential UN responses ("courses of action") and suggestions for prevention and mitigation strategies, including operational plans. From TRAs, analysts in JOC/JMAC, together with personnel from the UN Department of Safety and Security, can determine the security levels (e.g. using the current alert levels I–V) and recommend the appropriate security postures to protect UN staff and property.

Both information-gatherers and analysts need to be aware of moral and legal limits on technical information-gathering. Issues of privacy and political sensitivities, along with practical difficulties associated with technical monitoring, will be discussed in Chapter 9.[9] During a crisis, such as one involving hostages or combat, it may be acceptable to increase the means of detection to include new devices such as signal (cell phone) interception, though ordinarily this should be used with caution and sensitivity to the parties concerned. At all times, a proper balance must be achieved between privacy and military necessity.

The dissemination of information/intelligence products in order to influence decision-making is a traditional challenge for analysts. To draw attention to their assessments, they have used prioritized reports (e.g. flash reports) to complement routine ones. Information technology has, of course, made sending the results to decision-makers and other users/ clients much easier, but there is a frequent problem of "information overload and under-use". With so much information arriving electronically, it can be difficult to separate valuable, timely information from the trivial, a difficulty also known as the "signal to noise problem". Search engines, file-finding tools and databasing help ease this difficulty by making it easier to locate, flag, highlight and prioritize desired information. But the challenge remains for analysts to provide the right level of detail in timely analysis for busy decision-makers.

Notes

1. For example, the United Nations Disengagement Observer Force (UNDOF), the United Nations Observer Mission in Georgia (UNOMIG), and the United Nations Angola Verification Mission (UNAVEM I, II and III).
2. In recent years, the number of civilians (local, international and UN volunteers) serving in peacekeeping has risen to about 20 per cent of the number of uniformed personnel (military and police).
3. A much more detailed statistical analysis (with charts) of UN peacekeeping fatalities is available upon request.
4. For basic information on medical technologies, see DPKO (1999).
5. The Security Council's first resolution on the protection of civilians in armed conflict (Resolution 1265 of 17 September 1999) stressed the importance of including "special protection" provisions in the mandates of PKOs.
6. The Responsibility to Protect (or R2P for short) was expounded in the document *The Responsibility to Protect: Report of the International Commission on Intervention and State Sovereignty* (ICISS 2001). The principle was endorsed in the *2005 World Summit Outcome* Document (United Nations 2005). The United Nations has incorporated protection of civilians (POC) language into many of its mission ROE, including on the use of deadly force. Further, an "operational concept on POC" and an outline of POC strategies was drafted in 2010.
7. Some 41 per cent of UN PKO fatalities have occurred at night, even though there are far fewer UN activities carried out at night than during the day. I derived this statistic from fatality data collected by the DPKO Situation Centre. The night-time statistic includes only those fatalities for which the time of the incident has been recorded.
8. The report was summarized for the press in a press release of 27 July 2004, available at <http://www.un.org/News/Press/docs/2004/sc8156.doc.htm> (accessed 6 January 2011).
9. Two relevant publications of mine are Dorn (1999) and Dorn (2005).

4

Survey of monitoring technologies

Technology supplements rather than substitutes for the human presence in the field. Face-to-face interactions with armed factions and local civilians will always be the basis for peacekeepers to build trust and understanding. However, peacekeepers need all the information they can get to be safe and secure in complex and dangerous environments, and to carry out their monitoring mandates effectively. Human vision and communication are limited in distance, in duration and at night. There is much that technology can do to:

- increase the range, area coverage and accuracy of observation;
- permit continuous (e.g. 24-hour) monitoring;
- increase effectiveness, including cost-effectiveness in some cases;
- decrease intrusiveness;
- record events for transmission and future viewing.

Technical information complements human observation by creating a larger and more detailed picture of the area of operation. The United Nations can easily move beyond the "mark one eyeball", sometimes aided by binoculars, and deploy a variety of appropriate technologies as a standard part of the peacekeeper's toolkit.

The human eye sees only a small slice of the electromagnetic spectrum: visible light of wavelength 400 to 700 nanometres. Instruments are capable of measuring a range that is at least 15 orders of magnitude larger, from X-rays (less than 3 nanometres in wavelength) to radio waves (centimetres to thousands of kilometres). Furthermore, the unaided human eye has limited optical resolution[1] and no capacity for zooming. Electro-

Keeping watch: Monitoring, technology and innovation in UN peace operations, Dorn, United Nations University Press, 2011, ISBN 978-92-808-1198-8

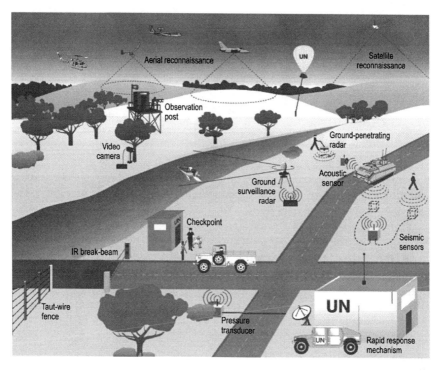

Figure 4.1 Composite diagram showing potential sensors and platforms for peacekeeping.

optical sensors can extend the human capacity many-fold, enhancing observation, interpretation and assessment. Sensors can also record images for wider dissemination.

Besides electromagnetic waves, other forms of energy can also be measured (e.g. acoustic/seismic signals, quasi-static electric/magnetic fields), as can materials (nuclear particles, chemical/biological agents). This chapter focuses on the detectors and technologies that can be most useful, illustrated in Figure 4.1.

The composite diagram in Figure 4.1 depicts a wide range of useful technologies for peace operations. A "top to bottom" explanation reveals the four possible regions to place sensors: outer space, airspace, ground level and underground. From outer space (top right), modern reconnaissance satellites can legally observe all areas of the Earth, with enough resolution to count cars and even people. In the air, helicopters manned and manned aircraft (including radar-equipped reconnaissance aircraft), and balloons (tethered, guided permit even higher-resolution surveillance of large areas.

Ground observation posts (middle left in Figure 4.1) can be equipped with imaging equipment, such as video cameras attached to high-power binoculars or night-vision devices. For open areas, as often found in buffer zones and waterways, ground surveillance radar can detect intruders or movements of persons, vehicles or boats. For smaller passageways, acoustic or seismic arrays can be used to detect movements, possibly to alert peacekeepers to oncoming vehicles or to initiate mobile UN checkpoints or to trigger a rapid reaction force. Similarly, pressure transducers or infrared (IR) break-beams could alert the United Nations to vehicle movements, especially at night, on roads that have no UN checkpoints. Ground-penetrating radar can help locate buried weapons, mass graves, landmines or underground bunkers or tunnels. Areas that are UN protected or sensitive can be blocked off with taut-wire fences, which not only serve as barriers but also send signals when touched or climbed or cut, indicating the location of intruders to UN guards or forces.

A UN station (bottom right in Figure 4.1) could dispatch mobile patrols or interception forces to respond to incoming information. It could also send the imagery and information gained by the sensors to other nearby stations and to mission headquarters for real-time (or near-real-time) viewing. The United Nations could even use loudspeakers located at sensitive sites to issue voice commands to trespassers, even though the observers and other UN personnel might be far away at the station.

The United Nations has, in isolated instances, used some of these technologies. Some advanced contingents have brought them to the mission as part of their National Support Element. These technologies are covered in detail below, with examples from UN operations, if deployed at all. A summary of potential technologies and their applications is also provided in Appendices 3 to 6. This chapter gives a thorough examination of the technological resources the United Nations has used in the past or could use in the future.

Satellite and aerial reconnaissance

High-resolution satellite imagery was for decades the sole preserve of the superpowers. From the very dawn of the space age, however, UN supporters have envisioned the possibility of UN satellite reconnaissance for peacekeeping and humanitarian purposes (Dorn 1987). In 1981, a UN study even recommended the creation of an International Satellite Monitoring Agency. Though UN ownership of satellites proved far too expensive, commercial companies began selling increasingly higher-resolution and superior satellite imagery at affordable prices with discounts for humanitarian agencies. Since 1999, images of 1 metre resolution or better – a capability once highly classified – have been readily available on the open market.[2]

To capitalize on the host of new satellite imaging applications, European nations in 2000 led the development of an International Charter on Space and Major Disasters (International Charter 2010) designed to provide a "unified system of space data acquisition and delivery to those affected by natural or man-made disasters". This joint endeavour of international organizations, the private sector and the scientific community allows authorized users "to request the mobilization of the space and associated ground resources ... of the member agencies to obtain data".

One result of this initiative was the creation of the United Nations Operational Satellite Applications Programme (UNOSAT) to harness the possibility of inexpensive data for peacekeeping and humanitarian purposes.[3] Under the motto of "satellite imagery for all", UNOSAT operates a 24/7 Rapid Mapping Service for UN agencies and their implementation partners. An impressive example of its mapping capability was shown during the Lebanon–Israel crisis of July–August 2006. Damage assessments were provided a few weeks after the fighting stopped to assist with rebuilding.[4]

Most commercial satellite imagery does not arrive until two weeks or more after it is ordered by the United Nations. This turn-around time is too long for operational use. So the vast majority of UN-ordered satellite imagery is used to make maps. The United Nations has not moved to near-real-time imagery, which is considerably more expensive. However, such imagery would be extremely useful in countries such as the Democratic Republic of the Congo (DRC) and Sudan, especially in determining the recent locations and movements of militia. Some governments have this capability, but share near-real-time imagery with the United Nations only on a "need-to-know" basis as determined by their own national security criteria. Shorter turn-around from commercial sources is possible, and in the future, as the technology advances, images of current operations should be available and affordable.

Unlike satellites, aircraft can provide imagery in hours since they can be leased and controlled directly by the United Nations. The world organization has carried out aerial reconnaissance in several of its missions. In 2006, the UN Mission in the DRC (MONUC) established an "Observation Aviation Unit" as an Eastern Division asset, with four Lama (Alouette) light helicopters, each providing a "glass bubble" around pilot and passenger. When street protests and mobs were a threat in Kinshasa, two of these helicopters were brought to the capital for urban monitoring. In another instance, the United Nations had its first experience tasking uninhabited or unmanned aerial vehicles (UAVs), which were brought by the European Union Force (EUFOR) to help MONUC during the election period from June to November 2006. These UAVs helped spot and track illegal arms imports near the city by the two main conflicting parties. EUFOR also deployed mirage jets with photo-reconnaissance capabilities.

Finally, balloons (aerostats) could serve as another useful observation platform, although such possibilities have not yet been employed by the United Nations. When tethered to the ground they could also serve as a landmark, for example to identify borders. Because aerial reconnaissance is such an effective means of monitoring and because there are so many varieties of aircraft, Chapter 5 is devoted specifically to the subject. In addition, the many uses of geographic information systems, as an integral part of mapping, charting and geodesy, are explored later in this chapter.

Mobile cameras (still and video)

A photograph describes circumstances, actions and justification much better than written or verbal explanations. All worth-mentioning incidents, events, locations, personalities, equipment and [anything] else must be photographed/filmed for conveying writte[n] message to all concerned.
> Guidelines from the Eastern Division Commander of MONUC,
> Maj. Gen. Patrick Cammaert (2005a)

Cameras have been used since the beginning of traditional peacekeeping, though often in a strictly limited fashion owing to the sensitivities of parties, especially opposing armies, that the United Nations has stood between.[5] Belligerents worried that photographs could show changes in their forward positions, which could be used by the other side. They also wanted to hide and deny evidence of their own violations. In modern operations where traditional lines between the parties are more fluid and spread over large areas – or even are nonexistent – cameras are an important tool to provide evidence of violations, which might be presented to the parties or even to a national or international court.

Personal hand-held cameras are now providing evidence of breaches of international law, just as they are of domestic law.[6] As commercial technology becomes increasingly better, higher resolution and less costly, UN field operations will undoubtedly benefit, particularly if ingenuity is used to find new and creative methods and places for their use.

An early innovative approach using simple technology was demonstrated in Cambodia in 1992–1993. Under the 1991 Paris Peace Agreement, the United Nations Transitional Authority in Cambodia (UNTAC) had the right of unrestricted access to information in the offices of government agencies and political parties. UN mission leaders were aware that assassinations of opposing political leaders were probably being planned in the field offices of political parties. To confirm this, UNTAC sent personnel to inspect regional offices. Using photocopy machines placed in the back of trucks, the teams made copies of files and correspondence for later translation from Khmer. The United Nations identified and exposed plots, which helped prevent assassinations and planned violations of the peace agreement, including undermining the elections of July 1993. The UN surveillance practice probably struck fear in the minds of potential perpetrators and limited their ability to communicate their plots with each other. This kind of monitoring operation would be technologically easier today because of the widespread availability of portable scanners, digital cameras and electronic translators. Even cell phones with cameras can be used to photograph and transmit page images.

Cameras and other image-capturing devices are also used in the rapidly unfolding field of biometrics. Biometric technologies permit the unique identification of humans based upon intrinsic traits that can be physical – such as fingerprints, facial features, hand/palm geometry and retina/iris patterns – or behavioural – such as gait or manner of speaking.[7] The United Nations' aviation agency already sets the world standards for biometric machine-readable passports (UN News Centre 2005). For UN peacekeeping endeavours, important applications would be to confirm identities for voting, payroll or access purposes. For instance, the European Union conducted iris scans on Congolese soldiers as a requirement to receive their pay. This ensured soldiers were paid only once per period – to prevent fraud. It also safeguarded against commanders inflating their personnel numbers to receive extra funds themselves. Another application could be to identify known criminals or insurgents who might be applying for positions in local police or military forces or for local UN employment. Such an application requires the development of a large database of fingerprints or other biometrics, which might raise privacy concerns. However, in post-conflict situations it might well be justified. During the siege of Goma in 2008, for instance, many of the rebel fighters who had previously participated in a disarmament, demobilization and reintegration programme renounced their integration into the Congolese army and returned to fight in the bush. They were rumoured to have secretly entered Goma in large numbers intending to seize it, but such infiltration was unverified; biometrics at checkpoints on roads leading to the town during the critical period would have been a small measure to help identify such individuals and make their entry harder.

Another example of a mature monitoring video technology is the license plate recognition (LPR) system, which can be fixed or mobile.

These systems have proved very useful for policing in the developed world. Mobile units are often placed in police cars/vehicles to scan, detect and identify licence plates on cars. Fixed LPR systems capture and automatically report on vehicles travelling through designated zones. The systems store the vehicle information in a database for quick and easy reference. This is particularly useful to find stolen vehicles and persons wanted for felonies. The Washington State Patrol installed a fixed system to check all the plates of vehicles boarding ferries (Port Orchard Independent 2008). They check them for AMBER alerts, reported stolen vehicles, wanted persons and suspected terrorists. One officer of the Arizona Department of Public Safety used an LPR-equipped patrol vehicle to recover more than 400 stolen vehicles over five years (Stockton 2009).

In a UN Police (UNPOL) context, this type of system can perform valuable security and detection functions for intersections and choke points (e.g. bridges), toll or vehicle portals, customs checkpoints and more. For example, vehicles approaching checkpoints or known hotspots would have their licence plate recorded and queried to reveal any enforcement action pending against the owner of the vehicle or simply to identify vehicles frequenting particular trouble areas for intelligence-gathering purposes.

These systems would be especially useful at border points. They could be used to spot vehicles likely to carry contraband and to track down known criminals. At key sites, the cameras can be permanently placed to keep a continuous watch.

Fixed video and motion sensors

Both portable and fixed video cameras have improved vastly in capacity and decreased drastically in size and cost. Additionally, an exponential increase in computer processing power, network speed and storage capacity[8] has created a "revolution" in digital closed-circuit television (CCTV) or, using recent terminology, digital video network (DVN).[9]

Commercially, CCTV/DVN technology has evolved from analogue cameras and recorders to hybrid analogue/digital systems and to fully digitized systems. Digital video recorders (DVRs) allow imagery to be more easily transmitted, stored and analysed. Analytic software within the recorders can detect motion and send automatic email/text alerts upon detection. A further evolution, from which the United Nations should benefit, is the Internet Protocol (IP) camera, which can even be connected to the World Wide Web.

Such IP systems allow imagery to be transmitted and viewed in real time throughout a local area network (LAN). Access can be password protected and signals encrypted before being transmitted. In Iraq it was discovered that insurgent groups were downloading unencrypted video feeds from US UAVs – (Shane and Drew 2009). The United Nations would also have to prevent signal interception through encryption in some of its operations so that imagery is used not to assist aggression but to discover it.

High-definition (HD) IP cameras with smooth imagery – "real-time" rates of 30 frames per second (fps) or more and frames with 1080 pixels – are now becoming inexpensive. IP cameras can connect anywhere on the network, including through a wireless connection or the nearest hard-wired "node". For cameras with the Pan Tilt Zoom (PTZ) feature, the movement commands are transmitted through the same transmission line as the video signal. Two-way audio is also possible with speakers built into the video camera system, allowing warnings to be made to would-be violators and communications with those seeking assistance. The power needed for the camera can be transmitted over the wire ("Power over Ethernet") so an additional power supply is not needed. Alternatively, if the device is wireless and removed from power sources, it can be solar powered, though perhaps for only several hours a day.

IP-type systems contain purposeful redundancy. A single error in the system cannot cause a system-wide disruption. Like the Internet more generally, the system is designed to find alternative routes to convey information. A comparison of analogue, IP and HD-IP cameras is provided in Table 4.1, showing the evolutionary progress in such systems.

Most IP cameras contain internal motion sensing through software that will start a recording only when detecting motion in the field of view. Some video software (e.g. Video IQ iCVR) allows customers to search for a person or vehicle of interest simply by clicking on their image. Video IQ automatically searches across terabytes of video from any of the Video IQ cameras and encoders on the network, though the result is highly dependent on the quality of the imagery.

To protect privacy within certain areas of the camera view, "masks" can be assigned internally so sections of the camera image are deliberately degraded. This allows the camera operator to hide certain areas from the viewer (for example, an entrance to a washroom) or from other parties.

At the high end, video cameras have high optical zoom capability (in the range of 120 times magnification) and can operate in very low or no-light conditions, with humans still identified at distances up to 3,000 metres.[10] High-quality HD cameras are now available at a low cost, as low as $100–200.[11] They come in small (pocket) sizes and are easy to operate and connect to computers to upload imagery.

Video systems became more common on UN premises after the tragic 19 August 2003 bombing in Baghdad. As a safety and security measure,

Table 4.1 The evolution of commercial video cameras

	Analogue	Analogue + DVR	IP video	High-definition IP video
Video quality	Good	Poor, generally	Very good (640 × 480)	Excellent (1920 × 1080) HD 1080i
Frame rate (images per second)	High (30 fps analogue)	Low (5–10 fps)	High (30 fps)	Very high (30–60 fps)
Storage capacity	Limited; tape-based	Fair; limited by proprietary nature of system	Very good; utilizes MPEG-4 compression	Excellent; utilizes new H.264 standard
Archival capability	Poor; magnetic tapes eventually degrade	Fair; manufacturer must have designed archival feature	Very good; video files are in standard format, easily archived	Very good; video files are in standard format, easily archived
Number of simultaneous users	Limited; can add only up to the point of signal degradation	Limited; only 5–10 viewing users at any given time	Limited only by system/network capacity, 30+ users	Limited only by system/ network capacity, 30+ users
Number of cameras per system	Limited by the number of wall monitors installed	15–30 cameras per server, typically	Virtually unlimited	Virtually unlimited
Analytic capabilities	None; "mark one eyeball"	Limited; motion-based recording	Advanced; depends on software package	Advanced; depends on software package
Degree of "openness"	Somewhat open	Not open; usually a proprietary or "black box" solution	Generally open; video streaming is based on open standards	Generally open; video streaming is based on open standards
Degree of difficulty for remote viewing	Very difficult	Difficult; requires specialized software	Easy; requires only a web browser	Easy; requires only a web browser
Security	No security	Limited security (username/ password)	Very secure (encrypted/ authenticated)	Very secure (encrypted/ authenticated)

Note: I am indebted to my knowledgeable research assistant, Gordon Hawkins, who provided the initiative and a lot of help in putting together this table.

UN field missions were given the go-ahead from UN headquarters to purchase video camera systems (CCTV/DVN). Such systems are now widely used to monitor the perimeters and some internal spaces in the headquarters and camps of many UN field missions.[12] However, the world organization has little experience of installing cameras outside UN premises.

Installing fixed cameras to view conflict areas has tremendous potential but has been little explored in peacekeeping. By contrast, other types of operations and organizations have taken such initiatives. The United Nations Monitoring, Verification and Inspection Commission (UNMOVIC) installed remotely controlled cameras inside and outside Iraqi factories to verify the non-production of weapons of mass destruction in Iraq.[13] The Organization for Security and Co-operation in Europe Mission in Kosovo (OMIK), which is a distinct component of the United Nations Interim Administration Mission in Kosovo (UNMIK), installed a network of some 130 cameras in or near its buildings, all electronically linked to its mission-wide LAN. More importantly, in the divided city of Mitrovica, two of its PTZ cameras keep a 24-hour watch on a bridge that is the site of frequent contention between ethnic communities. Any gathering of crowds can be observed remotely from the OMIK Operations Room or from any computer on the network, including at OMIK headquarters.[14] Imagery of swelling and violent crowds can trigger intervention by peacekeepers.

The United Nations Peacekeeping Force in Cyprus (UNFICYP), which monitors the "Green Line" that separates the two main ethnic communities on the Mediterranean island, is one of the few UN missions to use CCTV to monitor hotspots. Under a new concept of operation titled "concentration [of forces] with mobility", military leaders argued in 2004 that UNFICYP would be more effective with a mobile response force using monitoring technology (UN Secretary-General 2004; see also the case study in Chapter 6). They advocated a shift from static observation posts to mobile patrols and CCTV/heliborne surveillance, arguing that this approach would require fewer peacekeepers, enhance both operational efficiency and force protection, and create savings in personnel, logistics and administration. It took four years but, in 2008, the United Nations had six cameras observing sections of the Green Line in Nicosia, the divided capital of Cyprus. UNFICYP also had 100 CCTV cameras to guard various UN bases and facilities.[15]

The quality, range, resolution and built-in features of commercial CCTV cameras are rapidly improving, while the costs are decreasing, leading to an increase in their utility and appeal. For instance, many CCTV systems can now automatically detect movement or another stimulus within the field of view. This can alert and dispatch peacekeepers to known hotspots.

Motion detectors can be used not only to raise an alert but also to turn on illuminators at night. They can be used to detect and deter prowlers or other intruders into UN camps or protected/monitored areas. Detectors can be fine-tuned to go off only when people approach. Older motion detectors often had the challenge of differentiating humans from dogs, cats or even tree branches blowing in the wind. Today's passive infrared sensors are keyed to the temperature of the heat coming from the human body: infrared radiation of wavelength 9–10 micrometres. Typically a household motion detector costs only $20–30 and can activate a video camera. Such detectors are also available in solar-powered and rugged-ized form ($50–200), which means they can be left alone for long periods of time.

Cameras can also be installed inside vehicles. For instance, some are installed in taxis in various cities around the world to deter violence against drivers, with snapshots or video of passengers stored in an inaccessible part of the vehicle or transmitted in real time to a central location. The imagery can be shared with police should the need arise. This has been a powerful deterrent to violence and vandalism. But in some cases such cameras have become a target of attacks themselves, though they can be hardened and made vandal-proof or disguised to evade notice. Another innovation is the "Talking CCTV" camera, which has a speaker that allows police to interact and warn would-be violators. After detecting illegal or suspicious activities in remote locations the police can verbally issue "orders" to wrong-doers. They can also provide directions to lost persons and helpful instructions to UN personnel. If the camera is night-capable, this can be done at all hours.

Night vision

Hostile elements often use the cover of night to conduct illegal activities. As mentioned in the previous chapter, these include: attacking civilians, digging mass graves to hide atrocities; pushing cease-fire positions forward to gain advantage; raids across lines of control; laying landmines and improvised explosive devices (IEDs); preparing ambushes; and breaking sanctions though arms and people smuggling.

For all such cases, night-vision equipment (NVE) is an invaluable tool for the peacekeeper. The most effective type is a thermal imager that detects infrared (IR) radiation, particularly in the 8–14 micrometre (far-IR) wavelength band, from warm bodies at distances up to 5,000 metres and from vehicles up to 10,000 metres. Such devices can also peer through smoke and dust, though not as easily through fog and clouds. Thermal imagers can enable peacekeepers to spot warm bodies hiding in jungle growth or rubble (though not behind glass windows). Some thermal devices are heavy, but others can be worn as goggles, facilitating foot patrolling and night driving (for example, in aid convoys), spotting targets, as well as keeping track of other peacekeepers. Unfortunately, the United Nations has very few of these IR devices because of their high unit cost (over $5,000), although some are brought to the operations by participating militaries. Rather, the United Nations depends on a simpler form of night vision: image intensification.

Image intensifiers detect visible light and sometimes near-IR but not far-IR (heat) radiation. The devices "amplify" the ambient visible light before it reaches the eye. Standard off-the-shelf intensifier tubes have a light magnification factor of 25,000 or more. To be effective, there must be sufficient ambient light from either the night sky or artificial sources. Illuminators operating in the near-IR part of the spectrum are sometimes added to the devices so that nearby objects can be viewed more clearly in reflected light. Although the human eye cannot see when the illuminator is on, persons using this technology can see objects much more brightly because of the light they reflect. For distant objects, image intensifiers add extra hours of vision around dawn and dusk. Under ideal conditions (for example, a cloudless night with a full moon), a sentry using a third-generation image intensifier can spot humans moving 1,500 metres away. The UN-owned equipment standard requires "an effective range of 250 metres", considerably less than the standard of 1,000 metres specified in the United Nations' Contingent-Owned Equipment (COE) Manual. The cost of these image intensifiers varies from $300 to $3,000 per monocular or set of goggles, depending on the generation and quality.

The UN Department of Peacekeeping Operations (DPKO) owns several hundred night-vision devices, mostly binoculars, almost all of which are currently deployed in missions.[16] Most peacekeeping operations (PKOs) possess about 20 or so UN-owned devices, with four – the United Nations Operation in Burundi (ONUB), the United Nations Mission in Liberia (UNMIL), MONUC and the United Nations Mission in Sudan (UNMIS) – having over 50 devices each, still a small number compared with the thousands of personnel in a mission, many of whom should be doing night patrols and operations, as well as acting as night sentries. The UN devices are all second generation,[17] except for a single third-generation device, which the Property Management Unit database lists as in "fair condition".[18] Generation 2+ typically cost the United Nations just under $2,000 for binoculars. Though DPKO has tried to procure third-generation devices, it has so far been denied the required US export licenses.

Contingents are usually requested to bring their own NVE in accordance with the vague standards of the COE Manual. The NVE usually come in the form of headgear (goggles) but they can also be found as monoculars, binoculars or weapon sights. They are mostly image-intensification systems with some near-IR capability. Thermal systems are also brought to some missions by individual nations (mostly developed nations).

The United Nations does not have its own means for recording imagery from NVE. The Mi-35 attack helicopters flown in the Eastern DRC are equipped with fourth-generation forward-looking infrared cameras, but these are national (Indian) assets, and the digital video recordings from the cameras are not generally shared with the United Nations. Similarly, when EUFOR deployed to the DRC, its special forces brought fourth-generation devices, though these were not shared with the United Nations. EUFOR also brought night-vision sights from tube-launched, optically-tracked and wire-guided (TOW) anti-tank missile launchers.[19] These had an impressive range of over 4 km to view a person. In an earlier UN mission in Bosnia, peacekeepers took the night-vision sights off TOW launchers, brought for protection, in order to use the sights for observation, given the lack of proper night-vision equipment. Another important technology for both day and night detection – radar – was not deployed by the United Nations in Bosnia.

Radars

Though seldom used by the United Nations, radars have tremendous potential for keeping peace, just as they have for fighting wars. Whether deployed on the ground or on boats, aircraft or satellites, they can greatly increase situational awareness through imaging or tracking the movement of objects either on the ground, in the air or underground.

Ground surveillance radars (GSR), for instance, can detect a moving person or vehicle at up to 10 km, as long as there is an unobstructed line of sight to the target. Suspicious movement detected by the radar could then trigger investigations by patrols. As an example, the United Nations Interim Force in Lebanon (UNIFIL) set up US-supplied ground radar devices in the 1980s to detect infiltration along critical sections such as the Litani River and the Israeli border, and in Israeli controlled-areas. In spite of a large number of false alarms, mostly caused by animals, the system proved valuable. European states also deployed radars to Lebanon in 2006 to observe movements: land-based radar (Cobra systems), air-based radars on jets and helicopters and sea-based radars on frigates and patrol boats. These radars greatly extended the range and night capacity of UNIFIL.

GSR was also deployed by the Irish Quick Reaction Force during its deployment (2003–2006) with UNMIL. Two Advanced Man-portable

Surveillance and Target Acquisition Radar (AMSTAR) units were brought from Ireland. Various naval radars were also used by the UN Iraq–Kuwait Observation Mission (UNIKOM, 1991–2003) along the tense maritime border, particularly to observe freighter traffic in the seaways near Basra.[20] Unfortunately, there are no UN reports on the use or functioning of this or other UN-owned or UN-controlled radar systems. When the contingents left, they took both their equipment and their knowledge with them.

Other ground-based radars are available to identify and track mortar and artillery fire. For a short period, the United Nations Protection Force (UNPROFOR) in Bosnia obtained such units to locate the origins of mortar fire. In some cases they revealed disturbing evidence of atrocities inflicted by one group on its own members, presumably in order to garner international sympathy.

Air surveillance radars have proved essential for accurate detection of airspace violations, which are common in war-torn areas. Already in the 1960s, the United Nations Operation in the Congo employed two such radar sets, but the current mission in the Congo (MONUC/ MONUSCO[21]) has not yet used them, despite calls from mission leaders. Only in 2006 did UNIFIL gain the capacity for airspace surveillance radars, despite a long history of unauthorized aerial intrusions by aircraft from Israel. In the past, airspace monitoring was done by the naked eye. "Violation reports" were issued when two UN military observers of different nationalities identified a plane in the sky using nothing more sophisticated than binoculars.

During the 1990s, the North Atlantic Treaty Organization (NATO) carried out very sophisticated and effective monitoring of UN-mandated no-fly zones in the former Yugoslavia using its AWACS (Airborne Warning and Control System) aircraft. Every second week, the UN Secretary-General circulated documents with long lists of airspace violations, totalling many thousands of violations a year. When NATO took over operations in Bosnia, the sophisticated JSTARS (Joint Surveillance and Target Attack Radar System) aircraft complemented AWACS by detecting ground movements and providing radar imagery.

Synthetic aperture radar (SAR) is of special interest in military operations because of its ability to image day and night in all weather conditions and from high altitudes, even above clouds. A SAR consists of a modestly sized but high-power radar transmitter/receiver on an airplane or satellite. The radar achieves a high spatial resolution of a few metres by exploiting the motion of its platform and coherently processing the return signals from the ground. The system achieves a resolution many times more useful than the actual physical aperture of the radar antenna. The resolution is limited fundamentally only by the radar wavelength. SAR imagery from commercial satellites, such as RADARSAT, has helped the United Nations to confirm large refugee movements in places such as the Eastern DRC.

Ground-penetrating radar (GPR) would be particularly useful to detect weapons buried underground and to locate hidden tunnels or hiding places. Metal detectors can reach only a certain depth, whereas GPR can go deeper. Such radar technology is also useful in detecting hidden graves, which is important for human rights work and is already in wide use for geology, archaeology and civil engineering.

The United Nations has used hand-held radar guns, normally for vehicle-speed measurement and enforcement, in a few of its missions. These devices cost less than $100 each and can be useful at checkpoints, in demonstrations during local police training and to monitor the speed of the United Nations' own vehicles.

Through-wall vision/radar systems have not yet been used in UN operations, although the "radar scope" is an emerging and proven technology for high-risk police and military operations. A current, commercially available unit is about the size of a laptop computer and can detect people behind common wall materials, even enabling a count to be made of people in a room. It can image (two-dimensional) static objects and detect movement at a range of up to 20 metres. It can also give information about room dimensions. Video from the devices can be broadcast wirelessly to a remote display. It is described by one manufacturer as ready to go at the push of a button with no warm-up time or complicated boot-up procedures. Only minimal training is required to operate the device.[22] Domestic police examples include a broad range of tactical entry operations including: rescuing hostages; apprehending suspects barricaded inside an apartment; executing a high-risk warrant of arrest; and unobtrusive surveillance.

In peacekeeping, this technology could be used to view rooms into which UNPOL or UN military forces are about to enter, with force if necessary. In Haiti, the United Nations has liberated kidnapped people from their captors and has conducted cordon and search operations to arrest gang leaders in their hideouts. For such cases, the through-wall vision system would be useful to anticipate threats and reduce collateral damage.

Communications monitoring

To supplement the extended "eyes" of the United Nations using visual, infrared and radar remote sensing, peacekeepers have on rare occasions had electronic "ears" (radios with frequency scanners) to listen to radio and electronic communications. This controversial practice is not routinely employed in peace operations for privacy and other reasons. In some circumstances, however, it is entirely warranted – for example, when peacekeepers are being attacked or held hostage. Such monitoring has selectively but effectively been employed in several of the United Nations' large PKOs and much more extensively in NATO operations. The first documented use was in the UN Operation in the Congo (1960–1964), where the practice developed casually. In Northern Katanga, a battalion commander established an improvised radio interception system using a commercial receiver and local tribesmen as translators. Later in that mission, a more sophisticated interception system with a code-breaking capability was established to stop miscreant activities by mercenaries supporting secession in Katanga (Dorn and Bell 1995: 11). For the vast majority of operations, however, electronic interception has not been used. In the NATO-led Implementation/Stabilisation Force in Bosnia and Herzegovina and Kosovo Implementation Force, by contrast, advanced electronic intelligence platforms were routinely used to capture messages sent by radio, even those transmitted by frequency-hopping techniques. Of course, national laws should be respected during such undertakings, as discussed in Chapter 9.

The United Nations needs to be aware that its own communications are liable to be intercepted. Whereas NATO or EU operations deploy secure communications systems as a matter of course – secure satellite phones, radios, fax, etc. – as EUFOR did in the Congo in 2006, the United Nations does not. In fact, the commercial cell phones used by MONUC personnel were generally known to be monitored. The United Nations did conduct sweeps to detect bugs in some mission headquarters offices, but in general its counter-intelligence capability is very limited.

Acoustic and seismic sensors

Acoustic sensor systems enable sound (in the audible range and beyond) to be detected. Some systems can be simple and improvised. For example, in UNPROFOR, one-way radios were used as acoustic sensors inside weapons storage sites that were under UN lock and key. The understaffed UNPROFOR could not guard them 24/7. When parties broke into the sites, which happened frequently, the sensors captured the sounds of the heavy vehicles (for example, the starting of a tank engine). The signals, sent by radio, then alerted staff in the United Nations' local headquarters. In some instances, the weapons were recovered.

Seismic systems monitor low-frequency waves propagating through the Earth caused by either underground stimuli such as explosions or surface activity such as vehicles or even footsteps. Because the ground tends to attenuate seismic waves, the detection ranges of geophones are typically small (tens to hundreds of metres) for most kinds of surface disturbance. For underground explosions, the ranges can be much larger, depending on the detailed characteristics of the soil and the frequencies being sensed. Unattended ground acoustic sensors were successfully used in the United States' Sinai Field Mission (SFM) in 1976–1980. The sensors complemented remotely operated video cameras (both visible and IR) to notify watch stations of intruders moving through the strategic Giddi and Mitla passes. In areas near the passes where geological conditions were less favourable for seismic/acoustic detection, strain sensitive cables were laid across the terrain. Strain gauges then measured the deformation of the cable and the nearby ground by an intruder. The SFM was created and manned by the US government but closely coordinated with the United Nations Emergency Force II. By technical means, some 90 minor violations over nearly four years of observation were detected and resolved (Kontos 1980; Vannoni 1998). The United Nations, even 30 years later, still has not employed ground sensors, at least not to the level used by the SFM in the 1970s.

Ultrasound probing involves sending high-frequency sound waves through an object. The attenuated or reflected signals can then be used to characterize the contents of the object. Such probing was used by inspectors in Iraq to deduce whether munitions were empty or were filled with bulk, powder or liquid, something essential to know before starting to drill for testing and destruction. No examples of uses in peacekeeping have been uncovered.

Chemical, biological and nuclear sensors

Chemical agent monitors or "sniffers" are widely used in airports to detect explosives in luggage and hand baggage. Most systems are based on gas chromatography/mass spectrometry. These devices are becoming more compact, transportable and sensitive thanks to commercial instrument development. The large chemical/biological analytical toolbox is rapidly expanding. Sensor kits for biological agents have been developed commercially for testing air, water and soils. A number of research programmes are developing advanced chemical sensing for landmine detection, though the technology has yet to move from the prototype to the field in the form of inexpensive and widely available devices.

The three UN inspection bodies in Iraq – the United Nations Special Commission (UNSCOM), UNMOVIC and the International Atomic Energy Agency (IAEA) – have had substantial experience with chemical, biological and nuclear detectors. In UNSCOM, nuclear radiation detec-

tors were essential not only to uncover the Iraqi nuclear weapons programme but also for the personal safety of the inspectors, especially
during visits to destroyed nuclear sites. Geiger counters and gamma detectors are the main sensing devices, although for arms control many
other sensors are also used. Several UN PKOs have used hand-held narcotics and explosives detectors, mostly in UN-assisted airports and the
entrances of UN buildings.[23]

Positioning systems and "blue tracking"

In military parlance, "blue tracking" means following the movements of
the mission's own or friendly forces. In UN peace operations, the term is
appropriate not only because of the United Nations' identification with
the colour blue, but because the tracking capability is much needed for
UN safety and effectiveness. To best protect and make use of UN personnel, it is essential to know where they are. Of course, tracking other forces
is also important, for example red (hostile), green (friendly) or white
(other).

In one of the most successful applications of technology in modern
peacekeeping, the United Nations has deployed a vehicle fleet management system using Carlog devices to monitor the movements of UN
vehicles in most UN missions.[24] The Carlog device, which is permanently
fastened to the vehicle dashboard, automatically identifies the driver
(who must swipe his licence card through the Carlog reader and enter a
pass code to start the engine), the location and the route (thanks to an
offline Global Positioning System, or GPS), distances travelled, driving
behaviour (such as speeding, harsh braking or over-revving) and the time
of day (by the second). When speeding occurs, the Carlog's built-in alarm
system beeps and displays a flashing notice, often frustrating speeding
drivers. After accidents, the Carlog records can be reviewed to produce a
vehicle event history and to see if drivers might be fully or partly responsible. Persistent speeders may be reprimanded or even have their licence
revoked. The Carlog display also reminds drivers of the next scheduled
maintenance period. Used in conjunction with the FuelLog system, it
keeps track of fuel and calculates gas mileage.

According to DPKO transportation officials,[25] the proven benefits of
the Carlog system are extensive. These include: reduced accidents and
injuries, reduced repair costs, improved driving performance, better fuel
efficiencies, more regular vehicle maintenance (improving vehicle reliability), reduced paperwork (no manual trip-tickets), a reduced number
of unauthorized trips, improved vehicle security (by use of the ID pass
codes and swipe cards) and better vehicle allocation management. On

top of all that, Carlog allows for route planning and analysis to determine the most efficient routes and has provided the United Nations with the assurance of knowing where its vehicles have been.

The Carlog system does not continuously transmit the vehicle's location to a central data station in the mission. The radio frequency transmitters in the vehicles are too weak for that. The stored data are transmitted in a burst when the vehicle is within 150 metres of a receiving antenna, usually located at main UN facilities. With an upgrade to FleetLog3 it would be possible to conduct real-time vehicle tracking, which is widely used by trucking companies in the developed world. The FleetLog2 system used in MONUC costs about $500 per device.[26]

Besides Carlog, the standard HF communications system in UN vehicles also has a tracking option using GPS.[27] The current location of the vehicle could be displayed automatically on a screen in the car and/or on a computer map in an operations centre. The system can also produce an audible warning when vehicles approach a user-defined exclusion zone (for example, national borders), but this feature has not yet been activated in UN missions.

Real-time vehicle tracking by a central facility, although not available in peacekeeping, could be particularly useful for trips out of radio contact and for retrieving stolen vehicles. In UNPROFOR, an advanced system with uplinks to the INMARSAT satellite communications system was set up by one of the contingents to track aid and supply convoys in the mountainous region of the former Yugoslavia. Tracking and transmitting devices in cars could be helpful for rescue or other forms of assistance.

Radio frequency identification (RFID) tags can permit the tracking of the movement of almost any type of object, from pencils to vehicles, within well-defined spaces. Microwave RFID tags are already being used in the personal automobile market for long-range access control for high-end vehicles. RFID has many potential UN applications for tracking packages, equipment and even personnel (under certain conditions), and for verifying disarmed weapons in storage, among other possibilities. The rapid rise of GPS devices, wireless technologies, GPS-equipped phones and online connectivity will make such innovations increasingly easier and cheaper over time.

Cell phones and smartphones

Commercial telecommunications have made tremendous strides in recent decades worldwide in both military and civilian applications.[28] Between 2002 and 2009, cell phone subscriptions jumped globally from 1.0 to 4.1 billion, with over 60 per cent of the world's population having access (Jordans 2009). Figure 4.2 shows the growth in both the developed and

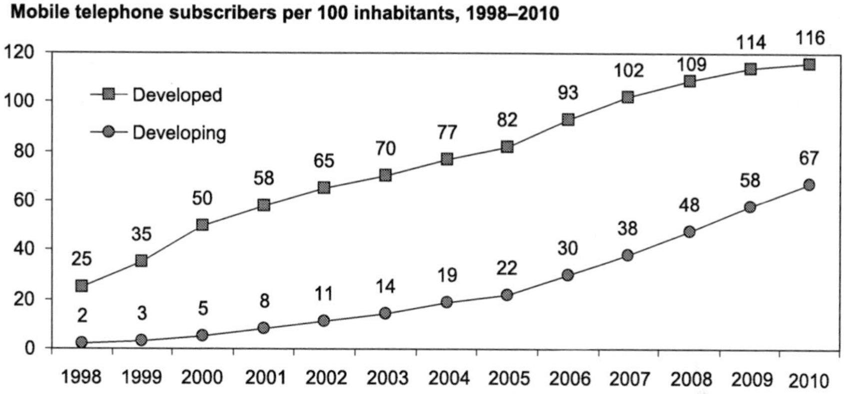

Mobile telephone subscribers per 100 inhabitants, 1998–2010

Figure 4.2 The dramatic increase in cell phone usage over one decade in both the developed and the developing world.
Data source: International Telecommunication Union, "Key Global Telecom Indicators for the World Telecommunication Service Sector", <http://www.itu.int/ITU-D/ict/statistics/at_glance/KeyTelecom.html> (accessed 7 January 2011).

the developing world. The devices have revolutionized the way societies communicate. They are now being used to grow businesses, transfer funds, increase personal mobility and provide better security to women and men all over the globe, where help in an emergency might be just a phone call away. They have enabled democratic movements to face authoritarian regimes, bringing about revolutionary changes in various parts of the world, especially in the Middle East and North Africa.

Cell phone systems are even available in some of the remote areas where UN peacekeepers are sent. Cell phone subscriptions have grown faster in Africa than in any other region of the world – from 54 million in 2003 to almost 350 million in 2008 (Poropudas 2009). In Haiti, the cell phone coverage rate rose from 6 per cent to 30 per cent between 2006 and 2010, despite a low 52 per cent literacy rate and widespread poverty. Fierce competition has lowered prices, increased services and widened area coverage in the developing world. Cell phones cheaply convey text messages (SMS, short for Short Message Service) around the world, although long-distance phone calls remain relatively expensive. (Where Internet connections are available, free voice and video conferencing is widely used, e.g. via Skype.)

The range of potential applications to peacekeeping and conflict monitoring is unlimited, but some examples demonstrate what has already been achieved. Cell phones are now widely used to alert conflict management professionals (local police, UN centres) and the wider population to perceived threats to safety and security. In Haiti, the United Nations has a hotline to receive reports of violence and kidnapping. In Jos,

Nigeria, a messaging system (FrontlineSMS) transferred text message security alerts to subscribers, including civilians, police and crisis management teams. One message read "Jos is tense, please avoid downtown today", creating a timely warning system based on the most ubiquitous communication tool in the region (Blyth 2009).

Election monitoring is a standard practice in UN operations for areas emerging from conflict, where elections are often hotly and sometimes violently contested. Election monitors and officials at polling stations have frequently used cell phones to call in or text their reports of election irregularities to field offices. The phones can provide video results of fraud, as in the 2009 Afghanistan elections, where UN officials had to void over 1.1 million ballots. In Sierra Leone's 2007 elections, the first after the bloody 10-year civil war, volunteer election monitors sent real-time reports to information hubs supported by the United Nations and non-governmental organizations (NGOs), both local and international. The National Election Watch (NEW) had thousands of volunteers across the country collect data on procedural irregularities, violence and ballot counting. The NEW headquarters in Freetown aggregated, processed and visualized the data. This allowed the organization to announce with confidence, and in a timely manner, that the Sierra Leonean elections, conducted after a tense and often violent campaign, had been largely free and fair.[29] International monitors, including the United Nations' peace-building office in country, echoed that conclusion.

The technique of "crowdsourcing" uses a larger segment of the population (a "crowd") to report on events, such as elections and violence. Ushahidi, which means "testimony" in Swahili, is a prominent platform, first created to track violence after the 2007 Kenyan elections. It has developed crisis maps to show locations and details of violence in the DRC, Haiti, Lebanon, Afghanistan and the Gaza Strip. Ordinary citizens can provide SMS and voice information on human rights abuses, outbreaks of violence and damage to infrastructure. Information is placed on geographical maps such as Google Maps, as shown in Figure 4.3 for earthquake-stricken Haiti.

Such systems have allowed UN and NGO workers, security staff and others to make decisions with greater clarity, since they allow users to get an idea of the trajectories of conflict in near real time (Loudon 2010). For example, if crowdsourced maps indicate a rise in violence at a particular village or on a particular street, UN protection forces can more rapidly determine where best to deploy scarce resources. However, there is a natural resistance within the United Nations to work with crowdsourced data since they do not usually come from identified or verified sources. Advocates of crowdsourcing systems respond that it is hard to falsify an event given the large number of sources, especially if pictures or videos

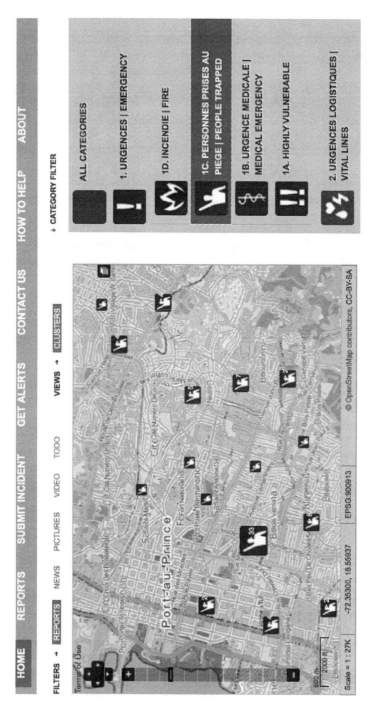

Figure 4.3 Map of crowdsourced incident reports of trapped persons in Port-au-Prince, Haiti, after the January 2010 earthquake.
Source: Ushahidi website, <http://www.ushahidi.com/> (accessed 1 December 2010).

are also presented. Such data can, in any case, become triggers for follow-up actions to verify and confirm reports or obtain leads.

More powerful cell phones called "smartphones" vastly increase the communication of information, including by email, Internet, camera, video/voice recorder, GPS and a growing number of online applications for social networking and interconnectivity (for example, Twitter and Facebook). Smartphones can also be attached through wires or wirelessly to a range of sensor systems and transmit sensor data. For instance, sensors that detect deadly chemicals can send their data through smartphones to rapid responders (Erdik 2006).

According to *The Economist* magazine (Economist 2009), by 2015 almost all handsets sold will be "smart".[30] As smartphones proliferate, the level and types of information transferred will increase dramatically, as will the potential for misuse. However, this problem can be intelligently controlled, though not extinguished. Transcription software and voice recognition allow smartphones to provide fairly accurate digitized records for forensic investigation.

Using cell phones or the Internet, peacekeepers in the field could obtain translation from a central translation service instead of relying entirely on a translator travelling with them. Alternatively, they could check the quality of the translations provided by persons who accompany them, especially to detect any translator bias, which is sometimes a grave problem in peace operations in divided societies. Telephonic interpretation services are also available commercially, and automatic voice translation software is making large strides.[31]

Customized smartphone software applications (apps) such as "The Guardian" can help peacekeepers and human rights observers upload still images and video, encrypt both SMS and voice messages, and speak in groups in a walkie-talkie fashion. In the event that an observer or a phone has gone missing, the NGO or UN field station can send an SMS to that phone and receive an automated response with the item's GPS coordinates. With the Guardian system, the phones can also be configured with a one-button erase feature or be accessed remotely by a colleague to delete any evidence if the phone falls into the hands of the perpetrators or their supporters. In addition, there are a growing number of relevant security and encryption software systems for human rights missions.[32]

Smartphones can instantaneously transmit images, sound recordings or video voicemail to secure servers and can have this information "stamped" with the time, the date and GPS coordinates. This can be used to show the location of human rights violations and allow the information to be placed in a geo-referenced database. Although images can be grainy, the resolution of smartphone cameras is rapidly increasing. Smartphones with Internet access can also allow peacekeepers access to virtually unlimited amounts of relevant data on the physical or social environment. Much valuable data can also be gained from information systems custom-built for UN field officials. The United Nations is just starting to do this.

Geographic information systems

Geographic information systems (GIS) are databases that link many types of data (for example names, images, reports and even RFID information) to geographical coordinates, that is, points on a map. Since mapping has long been a vital part of peacekeeping, GIS is already extensively used by DPKO to prepare maps of conflict areas, especially when up-to-date and high-resolution commercial maps are unavailable. GIS offers the potential for dynamic interactive maps,[33] change detection, overlays of selected data, analytical tools and other features.

The development of GIS is a technology-intensive area where the United Nations has made substantial progress over the past decade. The commercial availability of increasingly inexpensive and more accurate commercial satellite imagery and GPS devices, better Internet accessibility and user-friendly software (such as ArcGIS) has facilitated this progress. As a result of a Brahimi Report recommendation,[34] the first GIS units in the field were established in 2001 as pilot projects in MONUC, the United Nations Mission in Ethiopia and Eritrea and the United Nations Mission in Sierra Leone. GIS units are currently found in a dozen field missions, with 10 to 30 personnel in each unit, including military and civilian personnel.[35]

The United Nations is gradually evolving from ad hoc GIS arrangements to standardized structures and procedures.[36] The DPKO Cartographic Section at UN headquarters has developed GIS start-up packages for new missions as well as portable kits for GIS personnel deployed away from mission headquarters. The kits include: laptops and hand-held GIS PCs (personal computers that include GPS receivers), datasets, software, laser range-finders, digital cameras, portable printers and plotters.

The GIS units in the missions are providing much-used mapping services. For example, MONUC's GIS unit in Kinshasa has collected the GPS coordinates for Congolese villages and towns from UN military observers across the country. From these coordinates, it has created maps using geographical names common to the whole of MONUC, previously unavailable in that developing country. In addition to basic maps of administrative territories, tribal regions and UN deployments,[37]

MONUC's GIS unit has produced more specialized maps of many types, including:

- dangerous areas – for example, flood or flood-prone areas, areas mined or containing unexploded ordinance, and sectors cleared or uncleared of mines;
- security concerns – for example, incidents of accident/sickness/hostile fire, potential conflict zones, evacuation routes, mustering and regrouping points, checkpoints, security areas of responsibility, liaison offices, security warden zones;
- military locations – for example, Congolese army units, local militias, foreign armed groups, arms trafficking routes;
- disarmament, demobilization and reintegration locations – for example, Regrouping Centres, Integration Centres, Orientation Centres, special child soldier camps.[38]

The costs for a professional GIS service can be substantial. For a large mission, the GIS start-up package (including personnel) is of the order of $500,000. During operations, satellite imagery costs per scene are typically: $300 (low resolution); $1,000 (100 km^2, medium resolution, e.g. from SPOT) and $2,500 (100 km^2, high resolution, e.g. from RADARSAT or Quickbird) (UN Cartography Unit 2006). Prices are decreasing with time.

The very user-friendly GIS program "Google Earth" is available free in the basic version.[39] It is already used extensively for mapping by mission planners both at UN headquarters and in the field. Some databasing using Google Earth is also being done by field observers, although not with real-time adjustments.

Google Earth already includes human rights information on its Darfur map, showing villages that have been destroyed.[40] The information was supplied by the United States Holocaust Memorial Museum. This partnership, named "Crisis in Darfur", used high-resolution satellite imagery released by the Humanitarian Information Unit of the US Department of State in 2007 and July 2009. The data showed more than 3,300 villages damaged or destroyed, primarily between 2003 and 2005. The display compares "before and after" satellite images of attacked villages. The Museum claims to provide "the most detailed picture to date of the scope and nature of the destruction that occurred during the genocide in Darfur and after" (USHMM 2009). It also shows that the level of destruction decreased dramatically after 2006.

Although Google Earth images are usually over a year old and locations are not precisely geo-referenced (typically off by 100 metres), improvements are constantly being made and commercial upgrades and enhancements can be purchased. Eventually, high-quality and high-resolution real-time coverage can be expected at reasonable rates for areas of UN deployment.

Despite the progress in GIS, the current capability at the United Nations is quite limited compared with the great potential. The over-reliance on old paper maps means that much of the information in the hands of users is out of date, inaccuracies are not easily corrected and new data are not routinely entered. The creation of a widely accessible UN GIS database to supplement the distribution of paper maps would allow for quicker updating and error correction, user inputs and improvements, and relational linking to other databases. For instance, UN Military Observers could post their daily situation reports, including photos, on a common geo-referenced database so that records could be easily accessed, shared and compared for near-real-time analysis and archival purposes. In addition, these reports could contain electronic links to other documents in the database for quick referencing. Databasing also permits more detailed queries and statistical analysis to see how the reported pieces of information relate in time and space. Furthermore, a GIS database could display inputs in real time from a set of cameras and automated ground sensors to offer continuous monitoring.

Network-enabled operations

Once a GIS system becomes interactive in real time, allowing users from many different locations and functional responsibilities to feed into a common system, it becomes an organic network. If the system also allows observations, orders and instructions to be conveyed along with the technical information, it can provide a capability that the military calls C4ISR: Command, Control, Communications and Computers (C4) and Intelligence, Surveillance and Reconnaissance (ISR).

Many advanced militaries are adopting the practice of "network-enabled operations" (NEO) using computer/sensor networks.[41] Termed "net-centric warfare" in the United States, NEO provides military forces across great distances with a "common operating picture". The network can integrate information from any number of persons and sensors. NEO has been shown to speed up response times to threats and challenges. It also can be used to delegate authority lower in the chain of command, so those most able to respond locally (so-called "strategic corporals") are armed with the big picture to take decisive action in support of the mission. It also allows higher-ups to get a sense of the "tactical" situation. The advantages gained from NEO include greater synchronization and improved unity of command (Lito 2010).

The early promoters of the concept, including US Vice Admiral Arthur Cebrowski, argued that this modus operandi constitutes a "revolution in military affairs" (Cebrowski and Garstka 1998: 1):

> Network-Centric Warfare derives its power from the strong networking of a well-informed but geographically dispersed force. The enabling elements are a high-performance information grid, access to all appropriate information sources, weapons reach and maneuver with precision and speed of response, value-adding command-and-control (C2) processes – to include high-speed automated assignment of resources to need – and integrated sensor grids closely coupled in time to shooters and C2 processes. Network-centric warfare is applicable to all levels of warfare and contributes to the coalescence of strategy, operations, and tactics. It is transparent to mission, force size and composition, and geography. (Cebrowski and Garstka 1998: 9)

Sceptics have pointed out potential drawbacks, including the dangers of information overload and of the networks going down or being destroyed, compromised or misused. These challenges, common to all information-gathering systems, are addressed later in this book. Though manageable, they do need to be addressed when creating powerful networks, especially ones that determine the lethality of a response.

The development of network-enabled operations by the United Nations would more rightly be called an "evolution" in peacekeeping affairs rather than a "revolution", given the slow pace of the United Nations' technological change. But such a new operating method would allow a common picture to be offered to a wide range of participants. Observers at great distances, in the air and on the ground, could share their imagery and insights. This would allow the challenges of distance to be reduced. In particular, network-enabled peacekeeping could help make much better use of the third dimension of space – the air overhead.

Notes

1. The resolution capacity of the human eye is typically described as "0.5 arc minutes" for a "line pair". That is, when two lines are separated by less than $1/120$ of a degree from the observer, they can no longer be distinguished as separate. Given that the visible field of view is 120×120 degrees (maximum horizontal and vertical), one can estimate the number of bits of information the human eye is capable of seeing: $120\times120\times60\times60/(0.5\times0.5)$, which is about 300 megapixels. Commercial digital cameras are typically 3–10 megapixels, but advanced photo-reconnaissance cameras can record several orders of magnitude more information.
2. Ikonos, launched on 24 September 1999, was the first commercial satellite with a 1 metre resolution. Since then, several other satellites have been launched with a higher resolution, e.g. QuickBird 2 at 0.62 metres.

3. UNOSAT (<http://www.unitar.org/unosat/>) works on a not-for-profit basis and must be self-supporting. Therefore, images ordered by UN agencies carry a cost based on special prices negotiated with satellite image providers.

4. The UNOSAT Lebanon images are available at <http://www.unitar.org/unosat/maps> (accessed 7 January 2011). Another valuable website for imagery is Google Earth (<http://www.google.co.uk/intl/en_uk/earth/index.html>), though the free public imagery can be three years old. The United Nations is an "Enterprise Client" subscriber, so it can acquire a much larger range of imagery, including recent imagery. The turn-around time is still at least two weeks, though rush orders are possible at extra cost.

5. The issue caused some controversy in Lebanon in 2000 when the United Nations had video of armed groups kidnapping an Israeli soldier. At first, UN headquarters did not know the videotape was in existence and Israel demanded that the tape be given to it for its own investigations. This led the United Nations to consider its policies on cameras in the field. See United Nations (2001).

6. For example, see Crossette (1996).

7. An extensive manual is National Biometric Security Project (2005).

8. Terabyte (1,000 billion bytes) hard drives are now commercially available for under US$100.

9. Originally, the term "closed-circuit television" was used to make a distinction from televisions receiving public broadcasts. Closed-circuit meant that the image feed from the TV went back to a central location and was not openly transmitted. CCTV is now a generic term for a variety of video surveillance technologies, including images viewed on computer monitors.

10. The specifications for the Vumii Discoverii 3000 are given here (see Vumii Inc. 2010). The camera uses lasers to generate illumination.

11. US$ are used throughout this book.

12. The United Nations' CCTV security systems typically cost $10,000–20,000, including four or five cameras and a viewing/recording suite. Extra video cameras can cost from $1,000 to $3,500 each.

13. During the United Nations' verification operations (UNSCOM/UNMOVIC and IAEA) in Iraq prior to 2003, in the presence or absence of inspectors, sensors transmitted imagery and data by radio and telephone landline to the Monitoring and Verification Center in Baghdad, where remote viewing was carried out. For instance, IAEA cameras were able to observe the withdrawal of equipment from one Iraqi nuclear site in January 1999 the day before US bombs destroyed the facility (and the camera as well).

14. OMIK's two PTZ cameras, with a 100× zoom and waterproof casings, cost a total of about $3,000. Many additional features and accessories are advertised for the BioDVN suite, including a face recognition and identification module. See <http://www.security-labs.com> (accessed 10 December 2010).

15. The video surveillance cameras cost $225,500 for 93 cameras (approximately $2,500 each). With the associated equipment (computer, cabling, power supplies, etc.), the total equipment cost was about $400,000. For the maintenance of this CCTV system, DPKO budgeted $40,000 for 2006/7 (UNFICYP 2007).

16. The United Nations is also supplying the African Union Mission in Sudan with 360 night-vision goggles, according to a United Nations–African Union Agreement. See UN Secretary-General (2006).

17. Most are NVS 7-2 (generation 2+) devices from Newcon Optik (<http://www.newcon-optik.com>, accessed 7 January 2011).

18. Property Management Unit database query, Logistics Support Division, DPKO, New York, 27 September 2006.

19. TOW describes a missile technology invented in the 1960s that considerably improved over the decades and is still in wide use, though wireless guidance is now the norm for modern missiles.

20. DPKO's Item Master Catalogue lists a "Racal UNIKOM Radar Set Ground Surveillance System S-Band" from UNIKOM as being in the possession of the United Nations but in the inactive category. The UNIKOM radar was located at Umm Qasr, Iraq. It was used at night in conjunction with a searchlight to spot passing ships, especially oil tankers and freighters.

21. MONUC was replaced by the United Nations Organization Stabilization Mission in the Democratic Republic of the Congo (MONUSCO) on 1 July 2010.

22. For example, see Camero Inc. (n.d.).

23. MONUC has purchased eight hand-held narcotics and explosive detectors, at a total cost of about $200,000. Other missions having explosives detectors include (number of devices in brackets): United Nations Assistance Mission for Iraq (6), UNFICYP (2), UNMIK (1), UNMIL (11), and UNMIS (2). The UNFICYP detector is a Scintrex E3500 model, which claims nanogram limits of detection (specifications available at <http://www.scintrextrace.com/brochures/current/E3500.pdf>, accessed 7 January 2011).

24. The missions currently deploying Carlog (specifically Fleetlog2) with GPS are: UNMIK, United Nations Truce Supervision Organization, United Nations Disengagement Observer Force, UNIFIL, ONUB, UNMIL, MONUC, United Nations Stabilization Mission in Haiti, UN Mission for the Referendum in Western Sahara. The commercial vendor is found at <http://www.e-drivetech.com> (accessed 7 January 2011).

25. Email from Ebrima Ceesay, Officer-in-Charge, Surface Transport Section, DPKO, 21 December 2006.

26. MONUC purchased its Carlog system with 336 units for $173,100, or $514 per unit (MONUC 2007).

27. See Barrett Communications, available at <http://www.barrettcommunications.com.au> (accessed 7 January 2011). Among the models the United Nations currently uses is the Model 950 (125 watt) mobile transceiver.

28. This section draws heavily from an article by Martin et al. (2011).

29. See the MIT Press journal *Innovations*, which seeks "entrepreneurial solutions to global challenges", and articles by Schuler (2008) and Gabriel et al. (2008).

30. Commercial examples of smartphones include the Apple iPhone, RIM Blackberry, Google Nexus One, Palm Pre and the Treo.

31. An example of a company providing on-demand telephonic translation is Telelanguage. It claims to have interpreters trained in over 150 languages, enabling customers to connect to an interpreter within seconds around the clock (<http://www.telelanguage.com>, accessed 7 January 2011).

32. Some examples include TigerText (<http://www.tigertext.com/>, accessed 7 January 2011), Tivi (<http://www.tivi.com/, accessed 7 January 2011>) and Mobile Defense (<https://www.mobiledefense.com/>, accessed 7 January 2011). Information on "The Guardian" is available at Huffington Post (<http://www.huffingtonpost.com/rebecca-novick/technology-of-liberation_b_385294.html>, accessed 7 January 2011) and Netsquared (<http://www.netsquared.org/projects/guardian-secure-private-anonymous-telephone-built-google-android>, accessed 7 January 2011).

33. For an example of overlays, see <http://maps.google.com/> or Google Earth (<http://earth.google.com>).

34. The *Report of the Panel on United Nations Peace Operations* (widely referred to as the Brahimi Report, after its chairman, Lakhdar Brahimi) made the following recommendation: "Peace operations could benefit greatly from more extensive use of geographic information systems (GIS) technology, which quickly integrates operational information with electronic maps of the mission area" (UN Security Council 2000: para. 20(c)).

35. GIS has become so much a part of modern engineering that the engineering branches in several missions have their own GIS sections. The Cartographic Section at UN headquarters also provides services to the Security Council as well as GIS support for DPKO and missions in the field.
36. The United Nations has a GIS Operation Manual, templates for resource planning and budget guidelines and missions have Standard Operating Procedures for GIS units.
37. This would include, for example, the locations of civilian police, military observers, national battalions and UN Volunteers.
38. This list is a summary of the Map Index of the MONUC GIS unit. The Index was supplied to me in November 2006 by email. A full list of types would add the following map types: communications (radio and cell phone network coverage, radio checkpoints); electoral divisions (registration centres and polling stations, election risk analysis, logistics, cast votes for presidential and legislative assembly positions, spoiled ballots, alliance map, collection plan, voter turnout); humanitarian information (internally displaced persons, child protection/orientation, medical facilities); natural resources (eco-regions, hydrography, national parks, riverine maps, mineral and mining operations); public information (radio station coverage, including MONUC's Radio Okapi); transportation (transportation network, aircraft landing sites, helicopter ranges, roads status, arms trafficking and trade roads) and other purposes (locations of quick-impact projects).
39. The "Google Earth" program can be downloaded free from <http://www.google.com/intl/en_uk/earth/index.html> (accessed 7 January 2011).
40. The Darfur map can be found under the heading "United States Holocaust Memorial Museum: Crisis in Darfur" at <http://earth.google.com/intl/en_uk/outreach/cs_darfur.html> (accessed 7 January 2011). For other information, see <http://earth.google.com/outreach/cs_darfur.html> (accessed 7 January 2011).
41. Whereas the US military uses the term "network-centric warfare", the UK and Canadian forces use the term "network-enabled operations". For more on this, see Mitchell (2009).

5

Aerial surveillance: Eyes in the sky

Patrols by foot, jeep and armoured personnel carriers are the norm in peacekeeping; occasionally patrols have been carried out on bicycle as well. Fixed observation posts and road checkpoints also contribute to the mission picture. Such ground-level surveillance is obviously indispensable, but there are distinct advantages to using observation from above. Aerial and ground surveillance are complementary.

The United Nations has conducted aerial reconnaissance in some of its operations. However, the use of observation aircraft has been ad hoc and unsystematized in both UN doctrine and practice. Dedicated observation aircraft were employed in ONUC (the United Nations Operation in the Congo) in 1961 after it was discovered that pilots conducting transport flights observed important activities on the ground during their voyages. This prompted ONUC to begin mandatory debriefings of these pilots and later to deploy specialized reconnaissance aircraft, including jets.[1] In Yemen (1963–1964),[2] Central America (1989–1992) and several other locations, the helicopter was a key tool for observation as well as transportation. MONUC, the United Nations mission in the Democratic Republic of the Congo (DRC), is believed to have the largest and best heliborne reconnaissance capacity in UN history.[3] However, current commanders complain that their capacity is still far from adequate for the mandated task.

There is, unfortunately, no systematic record of UN aerial observation experience or any listing of the aerial imaging equipment used in UN missions.[4] Furthermore, there are no studies or even comparisons of the

Keeping watch: Monitoring, technology and innovation in UN peace operations, Dorn, United Nations University Press, 2011, ISBN 978-92-808-1198-8

benefits of aerial versus ground reconnaissance in peace operations. This chapter looks at the relative merits of these two important modes of observation, drawing upon selected UN operations and experiences. It also compares manned versus unmanned reconnaissance flights. The latter are increasingly used in both military and civilian applications in the developed world. The details of all such comparisons (air versus ground, manned versus unmanned) are, of course, case specific, that is, dependent in part on objectives, terrain, weather, and so on. But the broad factors outlined here point to the relative merits and the optimum configurations for effective monitoring in a wide range of environments, while also highlighting the problems of the various approaches.

Advantages of aerial reconnaissance

From the earliest days of peacekeeping, the United Nations has taken advantage of observation from altitude. Observations posts were placed on hilltops in the Middle East (Palestine, Lebanon and the Golan Heights) and Kashmir. But they provided useful views of specific fixed areas only – hilltops, unlike aircraft, are not moveable!

The "bird's eye view" is possible from aircraft, providing quicker coverage, a longer "line of sight" and a wider area of observation than on the ground. Aircraft can travel with great speed and there are generally fewer obstacles to block the view from the air. Once at the site, they can adopt the optimum observation altitude and angle for safe viewing.

Since aircraft can move faster than ground vehicles and go directly ("as the crow flies") to their destination, airborne observers can arrive at distant areas much more quickly. In addition, more territory can be covered during the observation period. Ground vehicles (for example, four-wheel-drive utility vehicles) can travel at a maximum of about 120 km/hour.[5] Under the poor road conditions typical of many conflict areas, jeeps must move slowly, perhaps 10 km/hour if at all, since many mountainous, riverine and jungle areas are impassable. By contrast, aircraft can easily overcome such terrestrial restrictions. Jets fly at typical cruise speeds of 500 km/hour, helicopters or two-seater planes at 200 km/hour, small tactical unmanned aerial vehicles (UAVs) at 100 km/hour and mini-UAVs at 50 km/hour. During an observation period, aircraft can slow down to dwell on an area, that is, circle by plane or hover by helicopter. Some gyro-stabilized cameras can "lock on" to their targets, keeping them in the centre of the picture even as the plane is moving.

During one aerial patrol (typically three to five hours duration), observers could, for instance, fly along an entire border of 500 km. Alternatively, such aircraft could cover an area of 500 km^2 or more. This could be done twice a day (or at night) for broad situational awareness and early warning. To follow the movements of the relevant actors (for example, armed bands, roving militia horsemen or smugglers along roads), the observation width ("swath") by eye or camera needs to be less than 10 km on the ground. At speeds of less than 150 km/hour and at low altitude, this would allow for detailed observation. Since low-flying aircraft (like ground vehicles) might be at risk of rifle or other fire, the optimum altitude must be determined. Fire from an AK-47 rifle, the most prevalent weapon in current conflict areas, cannot reach altitudes above 1,000 metres. And even at much higher and safer altitudes, for instance at 3,000 metres, advanced aerial observation equipment (geo-stabilized) can provide a resolution of 1 metre or better, allowing the tracking of individuals and vehicles.

The ability to vary the altitude of an aircraft allows the pilot to control the visibility of the plane. Aircraft can also fly above clouds for cover or find an altitude where they are nearly impossible to spot or hear. This makes it possible to monitor some illegal and clandestine activities that would otherwise be hidden as soon as the aircraft was detected. In addition, if criminal/violent elements are aware that the United Nations can operate silently, a powerful deterrent is created. Violators would fear detection, even if no aircraft were present.

If, on the other hand, a deliberate show of UN presence is desired, aircraft can fly at low altitudes. A highly visible "eye on the scene" could deter illegal activities or make them more difficult. Aircraft could even "buzz" an area at low altitudes to create a distinct impression.[6] During Operation Artemis, which aided MONUC in Ituri in the summer of 2003, a French Mirage jet on reconnaissance would deliberately break the sound barrier in the region to create a sonic boom that was clearly noticeable by all, including presumed wrongdoers. Aircraft can be painted in UN white or even with "glow colours" for greater visibility.

Flights at high altitudes offer less intrusiveness than a ground presence. At times, the United Nations must reduce its visibility either to accommodate local sensitivities or because national authorities have placed limitations on the freedom of movement of UN ground vehicles. While still observing national and international laws, UN aircraft can observe without being observed and move without attracting attention (satellites even more so). Of course, take-off and landing sites are needed, but they do not need to be near the observation area and can potentially be based in neighbouring countries. Permission to enter the airspace of a country would, of course, be required unless mandated by the Security Council.

Especially at night, aerial surveillance can provide a tremendous magnifying effect. When travel by ground is difficult and vision is limited (the range of most night-vision goggles is 500 metres or less), airborne forward-looking infrared (FLIR) and synthetic aperture radar (SAR) can alert the United Nations to illegal activities and movements of rebel fighters. Night flights for any purpose, however, are generally prohibited under UN rules because the United Nations does not possess night-time search and rescue capabilities and its aircraft are often not equipped with weather radars. In a few missions, however, contributors come well enough equipped to carry out such operations: for example, Norway and others in the former Yugoslavia, Australia in East Timor, a chartered company in Kosovo, and Russia in Sierra Leone.[7] In November 2006, MONUC was able to "break the night barrier" in the DRC after gaining permission from UN headquarters. Its Mi-35 helicopters used advanced infrared sensors to detect the movements of a renegade force advancing to attack the town of Goma. With this aerial intelligence, a combined UN–DRC force was able to halt the advance using night-flying attack helicopters.

In the future, UAVs could be used for night surveillance because the search and rescue requirement would not apply. Indeed, the European Union Force (EUFOR) did fly UAVs at night in the DRC from July to November 2006 with some remarkable successes, especially in uncovering illegal shipments of arms. For instance, the FLIR cameras were able to detect imported tanks moving by rail and small arms being transferred in small boats across the Congo River. UAV video imagery could be viewed at EUFOR headquarters in real time, so that commanders and analysts at headquarters could share a "common operating picture" and consider responses. Although there was no image feed to MONUC headquarters, recordings were shown to UN officials, for example to demonstrate illegal import activities clearly, thus allowing UN leaders to confront the violators.[8]

Reconnaissance by air is less constrained than on the ground. Host nations often insist that UN ground movements be escorted by the nation's troops or liaison officers, whose purpose is, more often than not, to keep an eye on UN personnel ("observe the observers") and prevent un-authorized detours. Air observation typically involves a lesser set of restrictions and limitations, although these may still be imposed by the host nation.

Advantages of integrated systems

Combining aerial and ground presences makes for a much more effective monitoring and response system. By air, large swaths of land can be reconnoitred separately or at the same time as by ground patrols. Advance surveillance flights can alert peacekeepers to dangers, locate them precisely through the Global Positioning System (GPS) and, in the future, automatically update GIS databases with the latest imagery for immediate viewing. Aerial images can help peacekeepers familiarize themselves with the terrain, their objectives and the dangers. They can assist training, planning and the operations themselves, as well as post-mission evaluation. Many hours will be saved if ground patrols can receive advance notification of roads that are impassable or bridges that are washed out, knocked out, closed or subject to militia checkpoints (or even to ambush!). Lives can be saved if potential threats are identified using aerial reconnaissance. For instance, during a MONUC battle with renegade militia leader "Cobra Matata" in the stronghold of Tchey in May 2006, heliborne spotters warned ground troops of militia fighters approaching stealthily. This allowed the UN forces to avoid a surprise attack and to respond appropriately.[9]

For UN operations to be robust they must be situationally aware and enhanced by aerial reconnaissance. Quick Reaction Forces, for instance, need to insert themselves with great accuracy at precise locations, which requires excellent geospatial awareness. This level of information, particularly about the hideouts of rogue militias or spoilers, involves advance (and advanced) surveillance, briefings for soldiers using detailed imagery and cueing from aerial assets to respond to the movements and actions of adversarial forces. Operating ahead of important convoys, aircraft can alert the convoys to potential threats in order to avoid them, for example through re-routing. Wide-area surveillance from aircraft can make the ground action quicker, more precise and safer.

During robust peace operations, reconnaissance from above is especially valuable in the pre-dawn period because militia often move into position at night and wait for dawn to attack. For instance, in the early morning of 28 May 2006, a joint Congolese–UN force walked into an ambush near Fataki soon after they began their march to search for rebel leader Peter Karim. An attack helicopter was called to suppress militia fire during their withdrawal, but it came too late for one Nepalese soldier who lost his life in the shooting.[10]

Similarly, Guatemalan special forces carrying out reconnaissance in Garamba National Park on the Congolese border with Sudan were ambushed early in the morning of 23 January 2006. The UN peacekeepers were searching for rebel Lord's Resistance Army troops who had infiltrated from Uganda. Eight Guatemalans were killed in the fire-fight, which started shortly after 0600 hrs and lasted four hours. This was the second-deadliest attack on MONUC.[11] Aerial reconnaissance using infrared night vision could possibly have identified the fighters in waiting, and would have better prepared the joint force of MONUC and the Forces Armées de la République Démocratique du Congo (FARDC).

Adding air power to ground force allows the United Nations to better prepare its night defences and offences. In Sake, 25 km from Goma, on 26 November 2006, MONUC established a security cordon to halt the advance of renegade Congolese brigades (the 81st and 83rd). When these brigades attacked MONUC/FARDC positions at 0525 hrs, MONUC was ready. Mi-35 helicopters flew the first helicopter night flight in MONUC's experience. The UN helicopters, equipped with advanced night-vision devices, spotted the attackers in the pre-dawn, distinguished them from friendly forces and then played a major role in the ensuing fight. The militia could not use tree cover or other terrain masking to obscure themselves from the foliage-penetrating Mi-35 FLIR cameras. Furthermore, the helicopter's rocket launchers and machine guns were aimed using (or "slaved to") the pilot's helmet-mounted night-vision goggles. Shortly after, UN and Congolese government forces regained control of the town of Sake with no MONUC/FARDC casualties. The 15,000 to 20,000 inhabitants of the town began to return and the city of Goma was saved.

In the Eastern DRC, airborne reconnaissance has located many militiamen, deserting soldiers and stragglers, prior to their being apprehended and arrested or becoming part of the peace process through *brassage* (that is, merging into the national army). More about the surveillance capabilities and work of the Mi-35 attack helicopters is found in the Congo 2008 case study in Chapter 7.

In summary, ground and aerial surveillance have different but complementary effects. The air provides a grand view of the terrain, whereas ground forces have the ability to interact more closely with people. A combination of air and ground surveillance permits a more persistent and targeted presence over larger areas. Aerial reconnaissance is a force multiplier. Locations that are too distant, numerous or dangerous for UN bases are better observed by aircraft. Various types of aircraft can be considered to optimize aerial effectiveness, including cost-effectiveness.

Enter the UAV

Unmanned or uninhabited aerial vehicles have in recent years found wide-ranging commercial applications in agriculture (crop-spraying and surveys), mineral exploration (especially in desolate and hard-to-reach regions), forestry management (fighting fires), telecommunications (as mobile relay platforms, including for emergency telecommunications in disaster zones), border or coastal watch and many other areas.[12] They are particularly popular in military circles for fighting wars and recently for keeping the peace as well.

Reconnaissance UAVs come in many different sizes, weights, capabilities and configurations. The payload can include many different types of sensor. Table 5.1 categorizes and characterizes the main types of UAV that could be used in UN peacekeeping.[13]

The smaller UAVs (especially mini-UAVs) are unstable in strong winds, making it hard to get steady video imagery, but sharp still images are possible using a fast shutter speed. Further, as high-resolution devices become lighter, smaller UAVs are becoming more capable. Similarly, small UAVs with less payload capacity are able to store images for download only once they have reached the ground, but the expansion of smartphone networks makes near-real-time transmission possible.

Mini-UAVs tend to run on batteries whereas the larger ones use gasoline or jet fuel. The petroleum-powered UAVs can attain a fuel efficiency of well over 200 km/litre.[14] Larger UAVs can support heavier payloads. Still, SAR payloads are of the order of 50–100 kg, so they are available only for tactical UAVs.

Ever smaller and smarter UAVs are under development. The near future might offer ultra-light or micro-UAVs (eventually possibly nano-UAVs) that are less than half a metre in wing-span and less than 2 kg in weight.[15] Autonomous take-off and landing UAVs are already available, as well as self-navigating UAVs using GPS waypoints. Generally these should be used only in a well-defined territory or air corridors where other aircraft are not present, though collision-avoidance systems are available.

The smaller UAVs have the benefit of being easier to transport (for example, by an individual), to launch (by hand or sling-shot) and to operate (for example, with joy-stick controls). They are cheaper to operate and to purchase (starting from $20,000 or less per UAV), and they usually cause less damage if they crash. On the negative side, they have limited range, endurance and payload capacity.

The deployment of "mixed packages" involving different categories of UAV allows the different advantages of each to be exploited, including cost and capacity benefits. For instance, travelling ground reconnaissance units could control mini-UAVs flying a short distance ahead, while a tactical UAV is used for more distant reconnaissance.

Manned versus unmanned aircraft

Advantages of UAVs

Unmanned flying machines are generally smaller, lighter and more fuel efficient than manned (or inhabited) aircraft. Also called remotely

Table 5.1 UAV types and characteristics

	Weight (kg)	Range (km)	Speed (km/h)[a]	Time aloft	Payload (kg)	Costs (US$)[b]	Example of functions	Sample models[c]
Mini-UAV	2–5	4–10	30–95	45 mins – 2 hrs	0.5–1.3	25,000[d]	Perimeter surveillance of UN sites and refugee camps	Desert Hawk, Dragon Eye, Raven
Sub-tactical UAV	10–20	Up to 1,000[e]	52–120	5–20 hrs	2–5.5	50,000+	Tracking humanitarian convoys; patrolling border segments	Aerosonde, Luna, Scan Eagle, Silver Fox
Tactical UAV	120–500	120–2,000[f]	90–200	3–20 hrs	3–200	1–10 million	Long border patrolling, large area surveillance, monitoring from high altitude	B Hunter, Crecerelle, CL-289, Phoenix, Shadow 200, Sperwer
Rotary-wing mini-UAV[g]	7–95	5–10	0–80	<2 hrs	4.5–30	Under 100,000	Observation in urban environments, e.g. of crowds from different angles	FFOS, STD-5 Steadicopter, SR200 VTOL, TAG M80, RMAX

Source: survey of models on the commercial market.

Notes: Micro-UAVs are also arriving on the market.

[a] Gives the range of possible speeds. Larger UAVs cannot fly as slowly as smaller ones since the "stall speed" generally increases with weight. Slow speeds can be advantageous for some observation roles, e.g. for a longer loiter time.

[b] Typical cost per UAV. For a system (including ground station with console, launcher) the cost ranges are: $60,000–300,000 (mini-UAV), $650,000–2,000,000 (sub-tactical), $2–20 million (tactical).

[c] This list emphasizes UAV models that have actually been deployed in military, forestry or other applications.

[d] For example, this is the cost for one Dragon Eye UAV; see <http://www.defense-update.com/products/d/dragoneyes.htm> (accessed 10 January 2011).

[e] For example, the producers of the Aerosonde UAV claim a range of 1,500 km with a regular payload; see <http://www.aerosonde.com/> (accessed 10 January 2011).

[f] For example, the producers of the Sperwer UAV claim a range of 200 km through direct link (line of sight), and further using relays; <http://www.sagem-ds.com/spip.php?rubrique127&lang=en> (accessed 10 January 2011).

[g] Larger (tactical) rotary-wing UAVs are also available; they are mostly converted manned helicopter models.

piloted vehicles, the greatest benefit of UAVs in peace operations is that there is no danger to pilot or other crew as none are on-board! This makes it possible to fly safely over raging conflicts.

To control UAVs, remote pilots remain at distances of up to 100 km or even further using repeater stations (which may be on the ground or in other UAVs in the air). With satellite communications, the remote operators can be on the other side of the Earth. The controllers can vary the altitude, direction and speed of the aircraft as well as the angles and zoom of the onboard camera(s). The imaging suite can include devices to capture visible light, infrared and radar signals. Autonomous (pre-programmed) UAVs exist, but this feature is not likely to be used in peacekeeping in the near future, except possibly for take-off and landing.

For night flying, UAVs offer tremendous advantages. The United Nations generally does not allow its planes to fly at night for fear of crashes. UN aircraft are typically not equipped with weather radars, which help spot approaching rains, stormy winds or other hazards at night. Nor does the United Nations have night-time search and rescue or combat search and rescue capabilities to react properly and quickly to crashes at night-time or in heavy conflict areas. With downed UAVs, recovery is not as time sensitive so they do not have the same stringent night-flying rules. Given the current lacuna for night surveillance in peacekeeping operations, UAVs offer a powerful tool to enhance effectiveness and security after dark.

UAVs are generally harder to detect and shoot down than manned aircraft, given their smaller size and decreased noise. Battery-powered UAVs make hardly any noise at all, certainly nothing detectable above the din of battle. At higher altitudes (for example, 500 metres above ground level), some smaller UAVs can be neither seen nor heard. It should be noted, however, that a Belgian UAV was shot down by a hunter in the Congo in 2006, but this was considered a highly improbable hit.

If a UAV crash does occur, day or night, the costs are much less than for a plane, most importantly in terms of human life. Also UAVs are much less expensive to purchase or replace. A mini-UAV with its control system typically costs less than $50,000; sub-tactical UAVs are available for $500,000 or less. And costs are decreasing while capability is increasing. Requirements for licensing, clearance and flight planning are also decreasing as the technology proliferates.

Though UAVs still need remote pilots and a crew for launch, control and maintenance, the number of such support personnel is less than for manned aircraft. Typically, 5–10 soldiers are needed to form a "flight" of two or three tactical UAVs – less for mini-UAVs. UAVs also require less training. Some mini-UAVs can be flown and operated successfully with only weeks of training (like model aircraft).

UAVs can be launched from many locations. Short runways are suffi-cient for most UAVs and some can take off vertically. Some mini-UAVs can be hand-launched. UAVs are also easier to transport: most mini-UAVs are human-portable; that is, they can be carried in a case by a single individual. Some fit in a backpack. Sub-tactical UAVs can be trans-ported in a minivan or on top of a utility vehicle (jeep), whereas tactical UAVs usually come with their own transport vehicle. UAVs are also easier to store, maintain and repair. All these features mean that UAVs have a "smaller operational footprint" in the field but the area coverage they provide can be as large as for manned aircraft.

UAVs also offer benefits to observers and analysts. In manned aircraft, onboard observers can easily become fatigued. Having more space and a greater ability to rotate personnel, ground-based observers at convenient locations can study monitors on large screens for longer periods of time. The endurance for human observers on a plane is typically four to six hours, and most planes need refuelling in even less time. UAVs can fly for longer periods because they are lighter and can be controlled by ground personnel on rotating shifts at a safe base to support longer flights. Any number of personnel can observe the video feed from the UAV.

Most UAVs are capable of longer loiter periods than planes, not only because they have more endurance but because they can achieve lower stall speeds, even as low as 30 km/hour (16 knots) for mini-UAVs, com-pared with 80 km/hour (43 knots) for small manned aircraft. Of course, rotary-wing aircraft have no stall speed. This "loiter on station" capacity is particularly useful to observe a localized activity closely for extended periods of time.

Rotary-wing (helicopter) UAVs can also range from small (mini) to large (tactical) UAVs. The latter are mostly converted manned-helicopter models with controls in place of the pilot's seat. Since few tactical rotary-wing UAVs are in existence, the numbers in Table 5.2 are only representative.

Advantages of manned aircraft

Unlike UAVs, the use of manned observation aircraft has historical pre-cedence in peacekeeping. The United Nations has considerable experience in practice, but little of it is recorded, described or analysed. The United Nations' first aerial cameras were used in the Congo as part of ONUC in the early 1960s. The subsequent mission in the Congo (MONUC) has, re-markably, less capacity though the need is as great. MONUC has four Alouette helicopters with a "glass bubble" for visual observation and no recording equipment except still and video cameras that might be carried aboard.[16] The Mi-35 helicopters have considerably more capacity: vari-able field-of-view low-light television and FLIR recording systems, as

Table 5.2 Rotary-wing UAV characteristics

	Mini-UAVs	Tactical UAVs
Weight	1–100 kg	500 kg or so
Range	1–10 km	<400 km
Endurance	<2 hrs	<10 hrs
Payload	1–25 kg	<150 kg
Speed	0–80 km/hr	<200 km/hr
Cost	Under $100,000 per UAV	Above $100,000 per UAV
Examples	SR200 VTOL, STD-5 Steadicopter, TAG M80	Vigilante 502, Vigilante 496, Eagle Eye

well as a helmet-mounted sighting and display system. But, being a prized Indian national asset whose exact resolution is kept classified, the fourth-generation FLIR video imagery is as a rule not shared with the rest of the mission. Only freeze-and-crop frames are provided to highlight certain observations, although a live feed would be technically possible for remote viewing. The Mi-35 FLIR cameras proved most useful during combat in spotting militia and allowing the helicopter gunship to engage them with weapons systems slaved to the reconnaissance devices. More on these systems is provided in Chapter 7.

The greatest benefit of manned aircraft is their multi-purpose capability for transportation and combat as well as observation. Soldiers can become familiar with the terrain from the air and be dropped close to their target, particularly with helicopters. Commanders can direct ground movements from helicopters, as they have done in the Congo. This dual use of manned aircraft allows cost efficiencies such as carrying out reconnaissance during or after the transportation of personnel or materiel.

Manned aircraft generally have a longer range (because of larger fuel tanks) and can fly at higher altitudes than most commercial UAVs. A typical operational range of 1,000 km is greater than most UAVs can sustain, except American UAVs such as Global Hawk, which are well beyond the means of the United Nations. Some aircraft, such as the Cold War U-2 spy plane, are designed to fly and photograph at very high altitudes of over 20,000 metres.

Aircraft also travel at greater speeds and offer a more "commanding presence". As mentioned, UAVs can provide a modest "show of presence" but a jet aircraft can streak rapidly and impressively above conflict areas, some even breaking the sound barrier.

Pilots in manned aircraft have a better "feel" for the aircraft than for a UAV, since they benefit from direct flight sensations (such as vibrations), unlike ground-based pilots. That is one of the reasons manned aircraft have a much lower crash rate than UAVs, where the pilot's life is not at stake.

Finally, direct observation from inside aircraft has advantages over remote viewing through computer screens of UAV imagery. Onboard personnel have three-dimensional and wide-angle (panoramic) views that cannot be achieved on computer screens. In addition, onboard cameras and screens can greatly increase the capacity of the unaided human eye for closer observation and for recording.

Like ground and aerial reconnaissance, integrating the use of UAVs and manned aircraft can offer the advantages of both types. Still other aerospace platforms are available for possible integration.

Aerospace platforms for reconnaissance

Overhead imaging can also be done from balloons and satellites.[17] These offer some comparative advantages. For instance, satellites can travel freely in outer space, permitting them to observe virtually any area of the Earth legally without requiring national consent. The relative merits of each platform are presented in Table 5.3. Each platform is evaluated on eight basic characteristics: six beneficial ones, then two undesirable ones.

The table shows the comparative strengths and the drawbacks: the high costs of manned aircraft, the limited payloads of unmanned aircraft and the very limited manoeuvrability of balloons and satellites. An advantage of satellites is that they cannot be shot down, at least not by the types of weaponry found in peacekeeping areas.

For some UN purposes, aerial manoeuvrability is not always needed. For instance, tethered balloons can be useful for observing important areas, corridors or choke points on a near-permanent basis. Cables keep the observation platforms in place and allow for the conveyance of electrical power and data signals. These large balloons can also serve as visible markers of borders or cease-fire lines, as navigation aids, as communications relays and as radio-station transmitters. Of course, these static objects might also be favourite targets for frustrated combatants. Some balloons consist of several sealed sections to reduce their vulnerability. If shot down, however, they can be repaired or replaced quickly and cheaply. Some aerostats are rapidly deployable, or redeployed, in as little as 10 minutes from the back of a ground vehicle.

Radar-equipped aerostat (balloon) systems are currently employed on several international borders (for example, US–Mexico) as part of national interdiction programmes for drugs and human trafficking. Held at a typical altitude of 500 metres, the view can extend for several kilometres. In Afghanistan, the 14-metre long RAID (Rapid Aerostat Initial

Table 5.3 Comparing different types of aerospace surveillance platform

	Range	Endurance[a]	Speed[b]	Altitude	Manoeuvrability	Payload capacity	Cost (financial)	Vulnerabilities
Fixed-wing aircraft (manned)	HIGH (<10,000 km)	Medium (max. 15 hrs)	HIGH	HIGH (<20,000 m)	HIGH (but cannot fly as slowly)	HIGH (<250,000 kg)	HIGH (for purchase, maintenance, fuel and personnel)	Possible fatalities; needs airfields for take-off and landing
Rotary aircraft (manned helicopter)	Medium (300 km)	Low (typically 3 hrs)	Medium (<350 km/hr)	Medium to HIGH (<10,000 m)	VERY HIGH (easy turns and stationary capacity)	Medium (<10,000 kg)	HIGH (for purchase, maintenance, fuel and personnel, inc. onboard pilots)	Possible fatalities
Unmanned aerial vehicles (UAV)[c]	Low to HIGH (1–1,000 km)	Low to HIGH (15 mins to 20 hrs)	Medium (40–300 km/hr)	Low to Medium (50–5,000 m)	HIGH	Low (1–150 kg)	MEDIUM (lower than manned aircraft, though dependent on type of UAV)	Can be shot down; weather dependent (esp. wind conditions)
Balloons (free or tethered)	Low (<100 km a day)	HIGH (10+ days)	Stationary or very low	Medium (<5,000 m)	Very low (wind dependent)	Low to medium (<500kg)	Low	Easily targeted and shot down
Satellites	VERY HIGH (but has fixed trajectory)	VERY HIGH (years, but revisit time can be days)	VERY HIGH (25,000 km/hr)	VERY HIGH (100–1,000 km)	Low (only certain types)	Medium (<5,000 kg)	HIGH (expensive to build and launch; imagery can be purchased cheaply[d])	Limited availability at specific time and place

Notes:
[a] Without refuelling.
[b] Ability to travel at slow speeds can be an advantage.
[c] Sub-tactical UAVs are considered.
[d] A high-resolution satellite can cost over $1 billion to build and $50 million to launch. Satellites of much lower cost, such as micro-satellites, are now coming on the market.

Deployment) aerostats are tasked with area surveillance and force protection against small arms, mortar and rocket attacks. They can stay aloft for over five days (Parsch 2005).

In addition to working with ground systems, aerial systems can be multilayered and hybrid to complement each other. Although aerospace reconnaissance provides unique advantages over ground reconnaissance, the best option is an integrated system to better detect threats and explore opportunities for peace and stability. Multiple information sources are needed to corroborate and probe sensitive and uncertain information in the dangerous environments found in many peacekeeping operations, past and present.

Notes

1. In ONUC, the United Nations' first air "recce" programme was begun one-and-a-half years after the operation was established in July 1960. Two Indian Canberra aircraft were designated for aerial reconnaissance. However, these planes proved to be inadequate, since they could take only vertical photographs because the window was designed for photographing bombing results. Later, Sweden provided two Saab 29C aircraft and a photo-interpretation detachment, which resulted in a substantial increase in intelligence on Katangese ammunition stockpiling and disproved many false reports of Katangese anti-aircraft batteries and underground aircraft shelters. See Dorn and Bell (1995: 11).
2. The United Nations Yemen Observation Mission (UNYOM) was mandated to observe an agreed disengagement between forces of Saudi Arabia, Egypt and Yemen. Air patrols, carried out by a Canadian unit with a dozen or so planes and helicopters, were essential in the mountainous border region, where foot patrols could cover only very limited ground. But, as in Lebanon in 1958, the United Nations came up against two limitations on UN patrols: traffic monitoring could be done only during daylight, and the ground inspection of various cargoes in moving caravans was difficult.
3. MONUC has 4 Lama (Alouette) observation helicopters and 4 Mi-25 and 4 Mi-35 attack helicopters equipped with advanced observation equipment. Along with the 28 transport helicopters (Mi-8T, Mi-8MTV, Mi-17, Mi-26), there are a total of 43 rotary-wing aircraft (data as of 24 March 2005).
4. Air flight is one of the most regulated forms of human activity worldwide, with detailed standards and specifications for safety and flight-worthiness. The United Nations generally abides by the standards set by the International Civil Aviation Organization. UN missions also have Standard Operating Procedures (SOPs) for flights and an Air Operations Manual. By contrast, the sub-activity of aerial reconnaissance is not well documented and only briefly mentioned in the SOPs.
5. Most missions have speed limits for vehicle travel. For MONUC, the limit was 60 km/ hour, lower for certain roads. In some missions, the time to reach the destination takes up the majority of the patrol time. For instance, in the United Nations Mission for the Referendum in Western Sahara, the "base to station time" required to reach the "berm" (the UN-monitored sand wall of separation) is two hours or more for some bases.

6. Even the sound of approaching aircraft can be intimidating, stimulating or warning (depending on the context). In the Eastern DRC, the mere sound of an approaching Mi-25/35 helicopter gunship caused militia forces to break up and flee.

7. Information provided by the Air Transport Section of the Department of Peacekeeping Operations, 28 February 2007.

8. EUFOR offered to provide images extracted from its UAV video feeds to MONUC within about 1–2 hours (i.e. in near real-time).

9. Personal interview with Brigadier General Duma Dumisani Mdutyana (Deputy General Officer Commanding of MONUC's Eastern Division), Kisangani, DRC, 30 November 2006. The militia leader signed a peace agreement later that year.

10. The helicopter provided armed protection for a group of seven Nepalese soldiers who became separated from the rest of the UN force (MONUC) but, when the helicopter went back to refuel, the soldiers found themselves surrounded by more than 300 militia and were taken hostage. After 42 days of negotiations, they were finally released unharmed.

11. Nine Bangladeshi peacekeepers died in a rebel ambush in the nearby Ituri district in February 2005. The DRC was the scene of the deadliest attack in UN history when, on 22 May 1961, 38 Ghanaians from ONUC were killed.

12. Two other commercial applications are: news gathering (for events that reporters cannot reach in time) and ground traffic reporting (to monitor traffic and accidents over major highways). See University of Florida's LIST Lab, "Brief History of UAVs", <http://www.list.ufl.edu/uav/UAVHstry.htm> (accessed 10 January 2011).

13. Larger UAV systems exist, e.g. US-manufactured Global Hawk UAVs, but they are not appropriate for the United Nations. They are not generally commercially available, their payloads are highly classified and the cost is extremely high. For example, the price of a Global Hawk aircraft, which can fly at extremely high altitudes over 20,000 metres, is $18–20 million.

14. The first UAV to fly autonomously across the Atlantic Ocean, Aerosonde *Laima* (13 kg), did so on a single tank of fuel with the benefit of supportive air currents (McGeer 1999).

15. For an example of light-weight sensors for UAVs, see Optical Alchemy's website at <http://www.opticalchemy.com> (accessed 10 January 2011).

16. Given the lack of permanent observation equipment onboard, when the Lama helicopters were deployed in Kinshasa in 2006 to observe crowd movements, the television cameras from MONUC's public TV unit and from Radio Okapi were used to produce some higher-resolution imagery. Personal interview with François Grignon (former chief of Joint Mission Analysis Centre, MONUC), Toronto, Canada, 4 February.

17. Also called aerostats, dirigibles, airships or blimps.

6

Traditional peacekeeping: Cases

Modern UN peacekeeping has evolved from traditional missions, as described in Chapter 2. The basic monitoring tasks found in the earlier traditional operations remain in the newer multidimensional missions, though many new requirements were added. Because traditional operations illustrate some of the fundamental challenges facing all operations, they are examined here. Historical cases also provide an overview of past UN experience and show how the United Nations arrived where it is today. In addition, seven traditional missions are still in operation today, four of them keeping watch in the Middle East.[1] (A full list of peace-keeping operations is provided in Appendix 1.)

The Middle East was the "cradle" of UN peacekeeping – the place where peacekeepers were first trained and where common problems were first encountered and partly resolved. In these Middle East missions, the main mandate was (and remains) monitoring and verification. What did the peacekeepers observe in traditional peacekeeping? What methods did the peacekeepers employ? What technologies were used, if any? How was information shared with parties? Did the parties cooperate or obstruct the United Nations in its monitoring? The real-life operations described in this chapter illustrate both the benefits and the problems of monitoring and technologies, past and present.

The Middle East has been the site of 10 UN peacekeeping missions – more than any other region of the world except Africa. Six operations were established to help foster peace between Israel and the neighbouring Arab countries. Two were created to monitor cease-fires between Iraq

Keeping watch: Monitoring, technology and innovation in UN peace operations, Dorn, United Nations University Press, 2011, ISBN 978-92-808-1198-8

and two of its neighbours: Iran at the end of the 1980–1988 Iran–Iraq War; and Kuwait after the 1991 Gulf War. Another two were created to verify the non-intervention of neighbouring states during the civil wars in Lebanon in 1958 and in Yemen in 1963–1964.

The following overview of missions is drawn mostly from the documents and publications of the United Nations.[2] In addition, a seminal early study, *International Peace Observation*, by David Wainhouse was consulted.[3]

Israel and its Arab neighbours

The first and longest-running peacekeeping operation in UN history, the United Nations Truce Supervision Organization (UNTSO), was actually established during, not after, the first Arab–Israeli war. Created by the UN Security Council on 29 May 1948 by Resolution 50 (1948) to supervise the truce (cease-fire) that the Council demanded of the warring parties, it soon assumed the task of verifying the four armistice agreements of 1949 negotiated between Israel and its four Arab neighbours, specifically Egypt, Jordan, Syria and Lebanon. The negotiations for these agreements were mediated by Dr Ralph Bunche, an American Under-Secretary-General from the UN Secretariat, who received the 1950 Nobel Peace Prize for his work.

The agreements established a cease-fire line called the Armistice Demarcation Line and various demilitarized zones (DMZs) between the Israeli and Arab nations' forces. The Armistice Demarcation Line of 1949 determined the borders of the Gaza Strip and the West Bank.

In UNTSO, the United Nations gained early experience with military observation and verification. The mission originated the concept of the United Nations Military Observer (UNMO) and determined that UNMOs should be unarmed, a tradition that continues today. The observers investigated armistice violations that came to their attention through complaints from the parties, from local civilians or from their own observation. After conducting on-the-scene investigations, often in conjunction with an attempt (sometimes successful) to mediate a local settlement, UNMOs would send reports to the UNTSO Chief of Staff, who was the top military officer and head of mission.[4] He might then protest to the offending party at a high level (sometimes at the head of state level) or raise the issue in meetings, joint or single, with the parties. In more serious instances, he would inform the UN Secretary-General.

Each of the four 1949 armistice agreements created a Mixed Armistice Commission (MAC) to allow liaison between the parties, specifically Israel and each neighbour. The MACs included an equal number of representatives, usually two or three, from Israel and the respective Arab state, with the UNTSO Chief of Staff or a designated senior UN officer serving as chairperson. As far as possible, issues were settled by consensus but, as one can imagine, on many occasions a deadlock prevailed, which could sometimes be broken only by the deciding vote of the chairperson. The UNTSO leader tried to be an impartial arbitrator but was nevertheless often criticized for not voting in support of each party.[5]

The majority of complaints heard by UNTSO related to: weapons firing; aircraft over-flights; the presence of troops in the DMZ; border crossings ranging from deadly raids to innocent sheep wanderings; and illegal plant cultivation. To give a sense of some of the challenging incidents that concerned UNTSO in its early days, Table 6.1 lists major events during 1955 that worried General E. L. M. Burns, the UNTSO Chief of Staff from 1954 to 1956. These incidents are drawn from his book *Between Arab and Israeli* (1962). UNMOs seeking to investigate such incidents would routinely invite military representatives from both sides to accompany them, but mostly they worked alone or with an escort from one side, since the parties regularly refused to work with each other.

Many problems were resolved in the MACs when the parties worked harmoniously, but over time the number of unsettled complaints became overwhelming. In October 1966, in the Syria–Israel MAC, for instance, there were 35,500 pending complaints from Israel and 30,600 from Syria. Managing the list became impossible. These and other warning signs of looming war emerged in early 1967.

For over 60 years, UNTSO has been sending regular reports to UN headquarters in New York describing the situation in the field. For the first few decades, if certain violations of agreements or Security Council resolutions were severe, the Chief of Staff could cable special reports directly to the UN Secretary-General, who could inform the Security Council. The Council could, in turn, issue condemnatory statements or resolutions, but it rarely took decisive action. Before the 1956 and 1967 Arab–Israeli wars, the number of violations increased significantly, as did the number of UNTSO protests. UNTSO also sent some warnings about the rising risk of war at other times,[6] but UN actions were not always enough to prevent renewed warfare. UNTSO did de-escalate many flare-ups that could have turned into wars.

An example of the United Nations' capacity to de-escalate a conflict was provided by UNTSO. In July 1955, the Jordanian army rushed troops to reinforce its positions on the West Bank after hearing reports of a possible Israeli attack on Jerusalem. The UNTSO head, General Burns, sought out Israeli Foreign Minister Golda Meir to discuss this "war scare". Mrs Meir was able to reassure him that there was no concentration of Israeli troops in the Jerusalem sector, confirming the information

Table 6.1 UNTSO investigations: Major examples from 1954/55

Incident	Description	Comments	Date
Kibbutz Ein Hashofet sheep Gaza raid	Sheep were taken by Jordanians. Israeli PM asked UN to help find a peaceful solution Two Israeli platoons attacked a military camp; 36 soldiers and 2 civilians were killed in the most serious clash since the armistice	Sheep were returned to kibbutz after 12 days of UNTSO mediation Serious escalation of fighting	27 September 1954 28 February 1955
Mortar fire on a kibbutzim	UNMOs observed that Egyptians began the shooting by firing on an Israeli jeep	Based on UNMO reports, the UNTSO commander convinced President Nasser that he was receiving inaccurate reports about incidents on the Gaza border	30 May 1955
First *fedayeen* attacks	Palestinians trained and supported by Egypt killed around a dozen Israeli civilians and soldiers near Gaza, a sudden increase in violence	UNMOs found and interrogated a wounded infiltrator and directly verified Israeli allegations of Egyptian complicity in planning the attacks	25–28 August 1955
Khan Yunis retaliatory raid	Israeli armoured unit destroyed police station and partially damaged the nearby hospital, leaving approx. 36 dead	Six UNMOs had been detained in Beersheba by the Israeli authorities to prevent them from seeing preparations for the attack	31 August – 1 September 1955
Ketsiot kibbutz near El Auja DMZ established. Local Bedouin killed	Israel claimed this was a new civilian settlement in this strategic area of the Negev desert. Egyptians claimed it was a military settlement. Kibbutz members did not engage in farming but wandered around the DMZ looking for "archaeological specimens". UNTSO commander allowed police to protect the kibbutz but Israel used undercover military forces as police instead	UNMOs inspected kibbutz and noticed unmarried occupants and lack of farming but found no weapons. They further learned from an Israeli deserter (soldier) in Egypt that its inhabitants were all soldiers, as later confirmed. MAC called the new settlement a breach of the armistice agreement, but an Israeli appeal put the decision in limbo. The UN Security Council did not act. On 26 October, Egyptians raided one of the "civil police" posts	28 September 1955

Israeli raid on Egyptian police posts	Egyptians had created checkpoints a few metres inside the DMZ. They later threatened to fire at anyone approaching the checkpoints, including UNMOs. Israelis objected to the checkpoints	Israelis invaded an Egyptian police post at El Kuntilla, killing 5 Egyptians and taking 30 prisoners, who were not returned until after the 1956 War	28 October 1955
Total number of dead owing to aggression near Israeli–Arab borders	In 1955 on the Egypt–Israel front alone: 47 Israelis killed, 118 wounded; 216 Egyptians and Arabs killed, 188 wounded	Not all incidents reported could be investigated; e.g. the backlog since 1953 built up to over 2,100 cases in the Jordan–Israeli MAC	1955

that Burns had received from his own UN military observers. He then conveyed the Israeli assurances to the commander of the Jordanian army in Amman. The commander agreed to withdraw his reinforcements on condition that further inspections by UNMOs confirmed the Israeli assertion. Apparently, the false alarm was sounded by apprehensive Jordanian agents who merely watched traffic on certain roads into Jerusalem. It was easy for UNMOs to disprove the allegations through careful counts and surveys. In the end, the Jordanian forces were withdrawn, something confirmed by UNMOs, thus bringing the immediate threat of escalation to an end. By 1956, however, UNTSO could not prevent a new war between Egypt and Israel, though Jordan and other Arab nations stayed out of it.

A new and stronger type of UN operation was created in 1956 on the initiative of Canadian Foreign Minister Lester B. Pearson in order to separate Egyptian and Israeli armies. The new UN force also helped France and Britain save face, since they had deployed their forces to gain control of the Suez Canal. UN forces assumed the positions of these departing forces.[7] UN Secretary-General Dag Hammarskjöld, in a historic report (UN Secretary-General 1956) to the General Assembly, set out the basic principles that were to guide this operation and future traditional peacekeeping. The first interpositional peacekeeping force, the United Nations Emergence Force (UNEF), was born out of crisis, as would be many other peacekeeping forces. General Burns was transferred from UNTSO to serve as the commander of this new type of UN force and Lester B. Pearson won the Nobel Peace Prize in 1957 for its creation.

After the 1956 War, Israel refused to take part in the Egypt–Israel Armistice Commission, though it participated in the three other MACs. Thus, no joint consultative machinery was functioning to discuss and resolve armed incidents between Israel and Egypt, though a Joint Commission chaired by a UN representative was eventually set up in 1975. UNEF reported on violations and, if warranted, protested to the relevant authorities. Soon after Israel's withdrawal from Egypt in 1956, UNEF established six observation posts (OPs) along the Sinai border and over two dozen observation posts inside the perimeter of the Gaza Strip.

The peacekeepers used binoculars at their observations posts and on patrols. "Dual-use" aircraft performed both resupply and reconnaissance flights (UN Secretary-General 1961). The Canadian-provided aircraft patrolled the international frontier on average four times a week but only in daytime. The aircraft had no onboard sensors, although hand-held cameras were probably carried by observers on board. The air patrols were linked by wireless communication to reconnaissance units on the ground, so suspicious activities seen from the air could be checked by ground patrols.

During critical times, the two UN missions, UNTSO and UNEF, passed vital information to New York. The missions served as the eyes and ears of the United Nations in the Middle East. For instance, UN Secretary-General U Thant first learned about the outbreak of war on 5 June 1967 in a cable from the UNEF Commander at 0300 hrs.[8] An early warning of impending hostilities had come a few weeks earlier when the UNEF Commander was requested by the commander-in-chief of the Egyptian Armed Forces to withdraw all UN troops along the border. As a result, U Thant went on a peace mission to the Middle East but, before he arrived in Cairo, Egyptian forces had taken over UNEF positions commanding the Strait of Tiran and therefore access to the Red Sea and southern Israel. Thus the die was cast, and Israel's pre-emptive strike soon followed, touching off a full-scale though short war – the Six Day War of 1967.

The Security Council has frequently looked to UN field missions for immediate information. During the Six Day War, the Council demanded a cease-fire from the warring parties in its Resolution 235 of 9 June 1967 and asked the Secretary-General to "report to the Security Council not later than two hours from now" (para. 3) about the parties' acceptance of a cease-fire, which came the next day. Secretary-General U Thant had employed the UNTSO Chief of Staff to maintain contact with the parties and to keep track of the escalating conflict. The Secretary-General sometimes had to express his regret to the Security Council that he could not meet its information requests because UN observers could not remain stationed in the "hotspots" or were not there to begin with. In addition, member states, including those on the Security Council, were not sharing the intelligence acquired through their secret sources, including surveillance satellites.

After the Six Day War, a victorious Israel denounced the four armistice agreements and the MACs ceased to function effectively. UNEF, which had been withdrawn under Egyptian insistence, was not reinstated. But UNTSO continued to carry out a variety of tasks (including monitoring), with varying degrees of cooperation from the parties. For instance, UNTSO personnel who were stationed in over a dozen observation posts along the Suez Canal reported on the daily exchange of fire across the canal in 1969–1970 – though they were little able to prevent it – in what was known as the "war of attrition".

UNTSO was able to notify the Secretary-General of the outbreak of the Yom Kippur War (known as such because it began at the time of the Jewish holiday of Yom Kippur) on 6 October 1973, a war that caught both Israel and the United States by surprise. United Nations observers on the Israeli side of the canal were equally surprised when they were quickly overrun by advancing Egyptian forces.

The end of the Yom Kippur War gave rise to the second UN Emergency Force (UNEF II). With that mission, the norm of not using soldiers from the Permanent Five members of the Security Council was ended. To boost the effectiveness of UNEF II, the UN Secretary-General accepted offers of troop contributions from both superpowers: 28 American and 36 Soviet observers were deployed in this operation under the operational control of the Secretary-General.

The first of several Arab–Israeli agreements after the Yom Kippur War was signed on 11 November 1973 at kilometre-marker 101 on the Cairo–Suez road by representatives of the two parties and by the UNEF II Commander, General Ensio P. Siilasvuo of Finland. United Nations peacekeepers began to replace Israeli soldiers at checkpoints. The second agreement, signed a few months later (on 18 January 1974), facilitated a further withdrawal. As Israeli forces withdrew, UNEF II forces were given temporary hold of territory before they handed it over to Egyptian forces.

The Second Sinai Disengagement Agreement (Sinai II, 1975) established a large buffer zone in which military forces were entirely prohibited. In addition, two areas of limited forces and armaments on each side of the buffer zone were created. These zones were monitored by UNEF II and access points to the buffer zone were controlled by UN peacekeepers. The agreement stipulated that UNEF II would carry out an inspection within 24 hours of a request from either party and would promptly furnish both parties with the results of each inspection. The agreement established a Joint Commission to consider any problem arising from the Agreement and to assist UNEF. The Commission met under the chairmanship of General Siilasvuo. A "US Proposal", attached to the agreement, provided for the establishment of an early warning system in the Giddi and Mitla passes, which were vital crossing points for any large military operations across the Sinai. Unlike the peacekeeping operations, these stations relied heavily on technology, including arrays of ground sensors, as described by Michael Vannoni (1998). The system consisted of three US watch stations and stations on either side operated by Israel and Egypt. In the early warning zone, UNEF provided escorts between the US watch stations and the surveillance stations of the parties. The Sinai II agreement (Annex, Art. 2B) provided that:

At each watch station ... United States civilian personnel will immediately report to the parties to the basic Agreement and to the United Nations Emergency Force any movement of armed forces, other than the United Nations Emergency Force, into either Pass and any observed preparations for such movement.

In addition, the watch stations sent weekly and monthly summary reports to the parties and the United Nations.

In the reduced forces areas, UNEF II conducted fortnightly inspections, accompanied by liaison officers from the respective parties.[9] The Force employed a system of checkpoints, over two dozen observation posts and mobile patrols by land to monitor the situation and to intervene in cases of violation. It also kept track of over-flights that might be violations of the agreement. Observation of over-flying aircraft was done by eye (not radar). The Joint Commission received a number of complaints alleging violations but it never became paralysed as did its predecessor, the Egypt–Israel MAC.

In the 1979 Treaty of Peace between Egypt and Israel, the continued stationing of UN forces and observers was envisioned to "supervise the implementation of the security arrangements" (Egypt–Israel 1979). But, because of the opposition of the Soviet Union to the Treaty (in solidarity with the Arab states), it was not possible to get such a force approved by the Security Council. Instead, a Multinational Force and Observers (MFO) was established outside the UN system by a 1981 Protocol to the Treaty to carry out the envisioned tasks. The MFO is funded primarily by the two parties and the United States. The mission, however, employs military and civilian observers and other personnel from over a dozen countries. In accordance with the Protocol, the United States supports the mission by conducting high-altitude surveillance flights to take photographs of the Treaty zones and provides narrative reports of the interpreted raw data to the two parties and the MFO. The United States provides similar assistance to the UN force on the Golan Heights. The technologies employed by this non-UN mission are described later in this chapter.

At the end of the 1973 war, Israel also occupied a portion of Syrian territory: the Golan Heights. UNTSO observers set up cease-fire observation posts at the most salient points in the area but tensions remained high, and artillery, rocket and tank fire intensified in early 1974. In May of that year, Syria and Israel finally signed an Agreement of Disengagement, with a Protocol on the establishment of the United Nations Disengagement Observer Force (UNDOF). The cease-fire and separation of forces were verified by UNDOF. The UN force delineated and marked the lines bounding the area of separation in cooperation with the forces on the two sides and then began its supervision of the demilitarized areas. It continues to do so by means of static positions, 24-hour observation posts and mobile patrols. Fortnightly inspections of the area of limitation of forces are carried out in the 10, 20 and 25 km zones on each side of the area of separation. Liaison officers from the respective party accompany the UNMOs on their inspections. After an inspection, the findings are simultaneously communicated to both parties but not made public. The United States provides UNDOF with valuable overhead reconnaissance, presumably from satellites, to assist with the detection of vehicles and weapons or troops illegally within the UN-monitored territories. Although UN monitoring has generally proceeded smoothly, both sides have at times placed impediments on the movements of UN personnel.[10]

Lebanon

Reliable reporting is a cornerstone of all peacekeeping. Good observation devices are essential.
                    Lt Gen Gustav Hägglund, UN Force Commander in Lebanon[11]

On its northern border, Israel had considerable peace until the Palestine Liberation Organization (PLO) developed bases in Lebanon in the mid-1970s. After a PLO commando unit struck near Tel Aviv on 11 March 1978, Israel sent its first invasion force into Lebanon. Within a few days, Israel occupied almost the entire region south of the Litani River, that is, the bottom fifth of the country. The UN Security Council then established the United Nations Interim Force in Lebanon (UNIFIL) on 19 March 1978 "for the purpose of confirming the withdrawal of Israeli forces, restoring international peace and security and assisting the Government of Lebanon in ensuring the return of its effective authority in the area".[12] As had frequently happened at the creation of a new operation in the Middle East, many of UNIFIL's initial peacekeepers and commander, Major General Emmanuel A. Erskine, were drawn from UNTSO, which also had several of its own observation posts in Lebanon. Israeli forces withdrew from southern Lebanon by 13 June 1978, as verified by UNIFIL, but the Israel Defense Forces (IDF) turned over most of their positions not to UNIFIL but to the de facto forces of what was later to be called the "South Lebanon Army" (SLA), Christian militias led by Major Saad Haddad, a renegade officer of the Lebanese National Army. To the extent possible, Lebanese gendarmes (internal security forces of the Lebanese government) assisted UNIFIL in its work at checkpoints and in both its security and humanitarian activities.[13] The situation, however, was not satisfactory, and there was frequent SLA/Israeli fighting with Lebanese government and PLO forces.

A second and larger Israeli invasion occurred in June 1982. UNIFIL attempted to block advancing forces but in most cases was quickly displaced.[14] Israeli forces partially withdrew in 1984–1985 after providing advance notification to both the Lebanese government and the United

Nations. UN forces started patrolling in the vacated areas. However, Israel continued to claim and occupy a "security zone", a strip varying from 2 km to 20 km along the border. In addition, through the SLA, Israel indirectly controlled a larger area including over 70 military positions. In the area in which it operates, UNIFIL tried to protect civilians and provide humanitarian and medical assistance as well as maintaining checkpoints and observation posts. When Israel withdrew completely from Lebanon in 2000, the United Nations verified its withdrawal.

In 2006, after the capture of two Israeli soldiers by Hezbollah, a 34-day war was fought in Lebanon. The UN peacekeeping operation was greatly strengthened after the end of the war. UNIFIL was tasked with helping the Lebanese army find illegal weapons south of the Litani River. To prevent the introduction of new weapons, the expanded mission included a Maritime Task Force, the United Nations' first. European countries became major contributors to the mission, bringing a more robust capability with a substantial amount of technology (described in Chapter 8).

Iraq and its neighbours

Iraq initiated costly wars against two of its neighbours: Iran in 1980, and Kuwait one decade later. The actions proved disastrous for Iraq. But the aftermath included the establishment of two UN operations to help foster peace on those two Iraqi borders.[15] The first war, with Iran, lasted eight years, ultimately ending after significant UN mediation. Iraq's 1990–1991 war lasted nine months, with the actual fighting lasting only 100 days and ending in military defeat for Iraq by a UN-mandated US-led coalition. A peacekeeping operation was forced upon Iraq as a measure to protect Kuwait.

The Iran–Iraq war was extremely brutal, characterized by the use of chemical weapons and "human waves" across battlefields, as well as by barbaric attacks on civilian targets, including missile targeting of cities. The UN Secretary-General was able in 1984 to gain the agreement of both parties to cease temporarily the attacks on purely civilian population centres. He was also able to deploy small inspection teams that were seconded from UNTSO and based in Baghdad and Tehran to verify the undertaking, dubbed the nine-month truce in the "war of the cities".[16]

It was, however, several years before the war-weary parties became serious about peace and accepted proposals from UN Secretary-General Javier Pérez de Cuéllar. Security Council Resolution 598 (1987) of 20 July 1987 was a watershed in UN history, not only because it clearly demonstrated a new cohesion in the Security Council but also because it showed how the Security Council can present a detailed plan for peace that is subsequently accepted (albeit a year later) and carried out by the parties. In accordance with the resolution, and following the dispatch of an advance technical mission to the area, the United Nations Iran–Iraq Military Observer Group (UNIIMOG) was established on 20 August 1988, the day the cease-fire came into effect. UNIIMOG's mandate was "to verify, confirm and supervise the cease-fire and withdrawal" of forces. UNIIMOG established the agreed-upon cease-fire lines and supervised the withdrawal to, and confinement behind, internationally recognized boundaries between Iraq and Iran. At its peak, UNIIMOG employed about 400 peacekeepers, including 350 UNMOs. The Secretary-General had planned to employ, as well, several fixed-wing aircraft and a squadron of helicopters for observation and transport. But, because Iraq objected, the United Nations could employ only the helicopters belonging to the two parties, which greatly inhibited their freedom of aerial movement and observation. UNIIMOG covered the cease-fire lines, which extended over 1,400 km of varied terrain, using patrols by foot, vehicle and even mule-back in the mountains. The waterways and marshes between the two countries were also monitored, mostly by boat.

UNIIMOG frequently received complaints of alleged cease-fire violations and investigated nearly all of them. The first nine weeks of the mission saw the greatest number of complaints (1,072) but the frequency declined as the cease-fire stabilized. Although most complaints were relatively minor, such as small arms firings, some violations needed to be addressed urgently, including the establishment of new forward defended locations, the deliberate flooding of plains, the seizure of prisoners and mining in no-man's land. The allegations of disputed deployments into the other side's territory were the most serious. Although there was no joint commission to look at and resolve problems, UNIIMOG tried to persuade the parties to return to the status quo, eventually succeeding in most cases. Thanks in part to the strains imposed upon Iraq in the impending 1991 Gulf War, Iraq withdrew from 23 of the 29 disputed locations and Iran withdrew from 13 of 17 such positions. By the time UNIIMOG was withdrawn, the Secretary-General was able to declare with satisfaction that all forces had withdrawn behind internationally recognized lines. UNIIMOG was less successful in arranging an exchange of information about unmarked minefields and creating an area of separation (for example, a demilitarized zone) between the armies. Furthermore, the mission had to be ended because Iran refused to accept a continuation of its mandate, perhaps because Iraq was militarily weak after losing the Gulf War. In view of this, the Secretary-General ended the mission at the end of February 1991.

In contrast to its slow response to the 1980 Iraqi invasion of Iran, the Security Council reacted to the 1990 invasion of Kuwait with great speed and resolve.[17] The first resolution was passed the same day as Iraqi armed forces crossed into Kuwait. The Security Council condemned the invasion and called for an unconditional withdrawal. After its defeat in the Gulf War, Iraq was made to accept the mammoth Resolution 687 of 3 April 1991, which established the United Nations Iraq–Kuwait Observation Mission (UNIKOM) in addition to other bodies, including the United Nations Special Commission (UNSCOM), which was charged with inspecting and overseeing the disarmament of Iraq's weapons of mass destruction (WMD).[18] UNIKOM was mandated to monitor a demilitarized zone between the countries, which covered the entire 200 km length of the border to a depth of 10 km on the Iraqi side and 5 km on the Kuwaiti side. It was also tasked with verifying the withdrawal of all parties from the zone.

UNIKOM set up observation posts and checkpoints on the main roads into and out of the DMZ between Iraq and Kuwait to monitor cross-border movements, which had to be declared to UNIKOM in advance by the two sides. UNIKOM also conducted land and air patrols in the DMZ and monitored the Khawr 'Abd Allah waterway between the two countries. On-shore observation posts were equipped with ground surveillance radar to spot boats moving up the waterway day and night. Patrol boats in the water and planes in the air also helped with the monitoring. DMZ violations were of four main types: incursions by military personnel on the ground; over-flights by military aircraft; police carrying weapons other than personal side arms; and the firing of weapons other than side arms.

UNIKOM was also mandated to observe and report any hostile acts mounted from one side against the other, and did report such an attack when Iraq launched a quick military strike in January 1993 to seek the unauthorized retrieval of Iraqi property from Kuwaiti territory. On receiving the UN Secretary-General's report (1993c) after the attack, the Council authorized the Secretary-General to further strengthen UNIKOM by adding a mechanized infantry battalion to the 300 military observers already deployed. The new force was not authorized to initiate enforcement action but it could use heavy weapons in self-defence, which was defined to include active resistance to any attempts to prevent by force the mission from carrying out its mandate. The infantry battalion served as a "force mobile reserve" capable of rapid deployment anywhere in the mission area. In practice, the infantry was used to reinforce patrols, to provide security at UNIKOM installations and to act as a deterrent in locations where incidents were deemed likely or possible. During the demarcation of the boundary, UNIKOM witnessed incidents and expressed concerns about the deployment of Iraqi forces north of the DMZ. UNIKOM found itself frequently involved in the detection and prevention of unauthorized border crossings by civilians and the repatriation of individuals. Although there was no joint commission for the parties to discuss incidents and problems, UNIKOM maintained liaison with both parties at all levels. UNIKOM was unique in several ways, including that all five permanent members of the Council agreed to provide military observers to the operation.[19] After 1994, the number of incidents and violations was limited until US forces entered the demilitarized zone in preparation for the US attack on Iraq in March 2003.

Sophisticated aerial reconnaissance and other technologies were used in the context of a UN field operation in Iraq. However, the mission was not to maintain the peace but to uncover and destroy Iraq's WMD. The UN Special Commission in Iraq, UNSCOM, employed high-flying American U-2 aircraft with wide field-of-view cameras to cover large areas and high-resolution cameras for detailed pictures. Germany supplied three helicopters with hand-held and gyroscopically stabilized photographic equipment capable of providing a ground resolution in centimetres. These helicopters also possess ground-penetrating radar to locate cavities, metal objects and shallow buried wires. Other helicopters are equipped with forward-looking infrared systems for night vision that can also be used to determine whether buildings are in use; these same helicopters also carry gamma-detection equipment to detect and identify nuclear radiation. Suspicious sites identified from the air could be checked by ground teams. Although the crews of these aircraft were nationals of the United States and Germany, UNSCOM had control over when and where they flew (UN Secretary-General 1995: 94). The analysis of the U-2 data was done by UNSCOM personnel in combination with intelligence agencies, including (controversially) Israel's Mossad (Ritter 1999).[20] UNSCOM benefited from the support of intelligence agencies but this came at the cost of negatively affecting its impartiality. Its successor, the United Nations Monitoring, Verification and Inspection Commission, was more careful, employing only international civil servants rather than personnel on loan. Large numbers of weapons were destroyed, but neither body could confirm that Iraq was not harbouring any WMD. There was enough residual doubt for the Bush administration to use WMD as the justification for the US-led invasion of Iraq in 2003, although without convincing the Security Council or gaining its authorization.

Non-UN case: Multinational Force and Observers (MFO)

Another mission to benefit from US technology was (and remains) the Multinational Force and Observers (MFO), a multinational (non-UN) force stationed in the Sinai since 1982. Although it has proclaimed itself "low tech by design", it has a strong sense of technological capacity and uses information drawn from technologies. The creators and current staff of the MFO are well aware of the possibilities for monitoring technologies because the Sinai Field Mission (1975–1979) was deployed in areas they currently patrol, including the Giddi and Mitla passes. The force is strongly US-backed so it retains a keen awareness of the potential for monitoring technology. It recognized its own deficiencies and explained why it was not making more use of sensor technologies. From the MFO's own literature (Multinational Force and Observers 1997), one can find a number of factors:

- the force acts primarily as a "confidence-building measure" in which political symbolism and commitment are most aptly demonstrated by the physical presence of peacekeepers; thus, the emphasis is on a person-intensive mission rather than a technology-intensive one;
- the fortunate existence of a consensual and "low-intensity" environment since the signing of the 1979 Treaty of Peace between Israel and Egypt gives rise to a "minimal expectation of initiation of hostilities between the parties or threats directed at the peacekeepers themselves"; situational awareness is therefore not critical for safety reasons;
- the sophisticated surveillance carried out by the United States using high-altitude over-flights and satellites is done in a manner complementary to the peacekeeping force, though not part of it; so wide-area surveillance need not be carried out;
- advanced national technical means for early warning and intelligence are retained by the parties, especially Israel, and they rely primarily on these, rather than on the MFO;
- the main funders (the parties) have "fostered aggressive management cost-cutting" and a push for a steadily declining budget; the main management achievements over the period 1988–1996 are listed as decreases in the budget (–33 per cent), in personnel (–21 per cent), in the aircraft fleet (–50 per cent) and in the vehicle fleet (–44 per cent). In such an environment, any large new budget item would need to be justified as a necessity, not a convenience.

In traditional UN operations most of these conditions also apply, including inadequacy of funding, but in multidimensional operations they are much less pertinent. The intensity of conflict or tension between the parties in areas of modern UN operations and the threat level to peacekeepers in general are much higher. Unfortunately, the United States has rarely backed up a UN mission with the kind of continuous surveillance and intelligence support that it has provided to the MFO. Finally, the parties monitored in most UN operations do not have the kind of early warning capability possessed by the Israelis and the Egyptians. Thus, the fact that the MFO is, like the United Nations, at present personpower

Table 6.2 Technologies employed by the Multinational Force and Observers

Device	Manufacturer	Code
Night-vision devices		
Goggles	Universal Audio Visual	AN/PVS 5-A
Scope	Optic Electronic	AN/NVS 900
Scope	Arab International Optronics	AN/NVS 700
Scope	Questar 89	
Scope	Varo Inc. Electron Devices	AN/PVS 502
Global Positioning System		
Magellan		M/NAV 1000 M5
Global receiver	Trimble Navigation	Trim Pac 2
Radar		
Nautical radar	Racal Decca	BT-502
Ground surveillance radar	US Army owned	AN/PPS-5
Explosive Ordnance Disposal Detachment		
(US Army owned equipment)		
Mine detector	Poland Industries	AN/PSS-11 (for depths to 18 in.)
Mine detector	Foerster Instruments	MK-26 (for depths to 6 ft)
Mine detector, radiographic (portable X-ray)	Golden Engineering	MK 26
EOD robot	Remotec	ANDROS MK 5
GPS global receiver	Trimble Navigation	Trim Pac 2
Emergency locator beacon		
Radio set	ACR Electronics	AN/PRC 90-2

Source: Selected equipment listed in Multinational Force and Observers (1997: 9).

intensive and not technology intensive does not obviate the many reasons why monitoring technologies are useful in modern UN operations, especially as technology costs continue to decrease and capabilities increase.

The MFO is quick to point out that, in its case, "low tech does not mean no tech". It has employed a variety of technologies, as listed in Table 6.2, even in the 1990s. Night-vision devices, purchased from the US Army and commercial sources, are of the second-generation type and have been used primarily for site protection. Radar is used on Italian vessels to assist in the monitoring of the Gulf of Aqaba and the Strait of Tiran. Because the Sinai is awash with landmines, detection equipment is essential. The MFO uses both conventional metal detectors and a radiographic (X-ray) detector. Global Positioning System (GPS) is an obvious utility as peacekeepers move about the barren desert, where there are few permanent landmarks and waypoints. The Explosive Ordnance Disposal Detachment (EOD) uses GPS to assist in providing coordinates of hazardous locations. EOD also employs a robot, owned by the US Army, for the disposal of landmines and explosive ordinance, which is frequently brought to the MFO camps by local Bedouin for safe disposal.

The MFO maintains the general policy that it should own the equipment it actively uses, except in cases of weapons and capital assets such as aircraft. In addition, specialized equipment is sometimes obtained on loan from the United States. Through ownership, the MFO can guarantee interoperability and standardization in its equipment. This approach also helps provide cohesion and unity in the force and eases training. The benefits for the United Nations of such a policy would be the same.

The MFO concludes in its 1997 report: "In a world of quickening technological changes, improved and new technologies may well be of service to peacekeepers if they meet the tests of propriety, practicability and affordability. As noted there is limited information and opportunity for interested peacekeeping professionals and those who will be the architects of new peacekeeping mandates to pursue these topics" (Multinational Force and Observers 1997: 8). The present book is an attempt to help fulfil this need.

In the twenty-first century, two missions in the Middle East exhibited some technological innovation: UNIFIL and the United Nations Peacekeeping Force in Cyprus (UNFICYP). In particular, UNFICYP deployed cameras for remote viewing after a reduction in personnel was forced upon it. This shows that in peacekeeping, as in life, necessity is the mother of invention. The Cyprus case is worth considering in detail because of the lessons to be learned from its pioneering initiative.

Cyprus: Tradition meets modernity

In February 2008, UNFICYP became the first UN mission to use remote unmanned cameras (closed-circuit television, or CCTV) to monitor conflict areas.[21] Other missions had used CCTV for security around UN buildings and similar purposes, but not to monitor a tense zone between armed opposing forces. As a quintessential traditional peacekeeping operation, UNFICYP was an unlikely pioneer in monitoring technology, but this success story is worth considering in detail.

UNFICYP was created on 4 March 1964[22] to quell fighting between Greek and Turkish communities in areas across Cyprus, an island that is considered part of both the Middle East and Europe. UNFICYP divided the island into seven sectors. The UN force focused on places where Greek and Turkish communities were clashing. The capital, Nicosia, was an area of heavy fighting that quickly became split between the Greek and Turkish Cypriot sides. The division in Nicosia was characterized by a "Green Line", a term derived from the colour of the line drawn on a map of a British general showing the positions of the two sides. Gradually, UNFICYP restored stability and by May 1974 it was able to reduce its original 1964 strength of 6,411 to 2,341 personnel.[23] Sadly, this glimmer of hope was short-lived.

In July 1974 a sudden coup d'état by Greek Cypriot National Guard forces advocating *enosis*, or the union of Cyprus with Greece, triggered an invasion from Turkey in support of the Turkish minority. The war caused massive displacement of peoples, in effect dividing Cyprus in two, with Turkey controlling the northern third and the Greek Cypriots controlling the southern two-thirds. The war extended the "Green Line" across the entire island from east to west, spanning 180 km and separating heavily armed opposing forces (OPFORs) that faced each other across a buffer zone ranging in width from 7 km in rural areas to a few metres in Nicosia. Constant UN control of this buffer zone became crucial to prevent aggressive moves forward by either side. Patrolling continued to play an important role, as before the 1974 war, but now it was focused entirely on the Green Line as opposed to the areas in Cyprus where Greeks and Turks had lived in close proximity. Such areas were no longer "hotspots", in part because the war had triggered a massive population redistribution that left the south of Cyprus almost entirely Greek and the north entirely Turkish.[24] Volatility in the buffer zone required UNFICYP not only to patrol vigorously but also to erect and permanently occupy a long string of observation posts (OPs).

OPs proliferated after the 1974 war because they played a crucial role in UNFICYP's monitoring function along the buffer zone. UNFICYP delineated forward positions of the opposing forces at the cessation of hostilities and strove to maintain these adjacent cease-fire lines. This involved detecting and if possible preventing moves forward by either side. Clearly the advantage of OPs over patrols was that they achieved constant surveillance of a segment of the buffer zone, making it possible to immediately detect a move forward within sight of the post. The OPs also helped to enhance stability. Especially during the aftermath of the 1974 war, there were many areas along the Green Line where shouting, rock throwing and shooting incidents between the opposing forces occurred frequently. To have several "shot" (firing) reports a day in the Canadian area of responsibility (Sector 3, which included Nicosia) was not uncommon. Areas of such sensitivity required a constant "Blue Beret presence" to prevent escalation from shouting to shooting. Even with the presence of a UN post, however, it was not uncommon for the small group of UN soldiers at the post to be unable to contain a difficult situation. They would have to call a UN patrol to the area to help restore stability. The constant monitoring and pacification carried out by permanently manned OPs all along the Green Line were indispensable after the 1974 war. By June 1975, UNFICYP had 148 OPs (UN Secretary-General 1975: 6) and the OP tradition had become a dominant aspect of the force's modus operandi.

Although this style of peacekeeping proved successful, the peace-making – or negotiation of a settlement – was painstakingly slow and a political solution remained elusive. Frustrated with this slow progress, several countries in the early 1990s, including the major troop contributor Canada, announced that they would withdraw or significantly reduce their contributions to UNFICYP. This prompted the Secretary-General to warn that UNFICYP would cease to be viable by June 1993 without new contributors (UN Secretary-General 1993a: 2). The strength of the force's military component fell from 2,040 in November 1992 to below 1,000 in mid-June 1993 and the Force Commander had to implement an emergency contingency plan that was to have a significant impact on the future of UN monitoring in Cyprus.

On 1 December 1992, UNFICYP's military component consisted of 2,040 troops manning 151 OPs, of which 51 were permanently (that is, constantly) manned (UN Secretary-General 1992: 3–5). Six months later, only 37 OPs were permanently manned. This reduction of 14 permanently manned observation posts was necessitated by a drop of 570 military personnel, bringing UNFICYP's strength to 1,470 (UN Secretary-General 1993b: 2–4). Only two weeks later, in mid-June 1993, the strength of UNFICYP dipped to below 1,000 (UN Secretary-General 1993a: 2) and the number of permanently manned OPs was again reduced – this time by 16 – leaving only 21 posts permanently manned.[25] Even after the force level was increased thanks to Argentina's offer of a line battalion of 375 troops, raising the strength of UNFICYP to 1,168 personnel by November 1993 (UN Secretary-General 1993d: 7),[26] the OP manning levels were not increased to their previous levels (UN Secretary-General 1993d: 4).

UNFICYP learned from the force reduction experience imposed on it in 1993 that there was no need to permanently occupy so many OPs to maintain stability. UNFICYP began to place greater emphasis on *patrolling* as a means of monitoring, as well as housing its military personnel within the buffer zone itself. The situation in Cyprus had grown more stable, allowing the operational transition to fewer constantly manned observation posts. Thus the mission learned a lesson in 1993 on ways to substitute for permanently manned OPs, a practice it would consider again over a decade later.

In 2004, after a breakthrough in negotiations, UN Secretary-General Kofi Annan presented a *Comprehensive Settlement of the Cyprus Problem*, or the Annan Plan (UNFICYP 2004a), to both Cypriot communities for approval by referendums. The Turkish Cypriots accepted it by a margin of almost two to one, but the Greek Cypriots rejected it by three to one.[27]

This rejection of the Annan Plan by the Greek side precipitated a dramatic change in UNFICYP. Given the collapse of peacemaking, Secretary-General Annan initiated a review of peacekeeping in the country. Based on the findings of the review team, he recommended a one-third reduction in the military component of UNFICYP from 1,224 to 860 personnel. He observed that the security situation on the island had become "increasingly benign over the past few years" and that a recurrence of fighting was "increasingly unlikely" (UN Secretary-General 2005). An adjustment in the force's approach to monitoring, observation and surveillance was envisaged in the Secretary-General's Report of 24 September 2004:

> A further shift in emphasis from *static to mobile surveillance* would be appropriate at this stage, resulting in savings in personnel and resources. Better use of *technology* could also improve the Force's effectiveness, including closed circuit television and improvement in information technology. Additional helicopter hours would also be required. (UN Secretary-General 2004: 7, emphasis added)

This new Concept of Operations, termed "concentration with mobility", was opposed by the Greek Cypriot government, which argued that the military situation had not changed and that UNFICYP was already thinly spread on the ground (Ker-Lindsay 2006: 413). Nevertheless, the Security Council, by its Resolution 1568 of 22 October 2004, accepted the Secretary-General's recommendations and by February 2005 the force level was reduced by 300 military personnel. The Force Commander, Major General Herbert Figoli of Uruguay, enunciated a plan to deal with this downsizing or operational challenge, which he entitled the "UNFICYP 860 Concept of Operations", or "Force 860" for short. He wrote:

> I intend to place less reliance on static observation posts and to shift our emphasis to more mobile surveillance. Increased patrolling on the ground and in the air, combined with *greater use of technology such as closed circuit television*, will enhance the monitoring activity of the force. Patrol programs will be more efficiently directed to areas where presence is needed, rather than routine patrolling everywhere. I am prepared to accept some risk in quiet areas. (Figoli 2004: 1, emphasis added)

The successful transition to a smaller force demonstrated the creativity of UNFICYP's leaders and the professionalism of its peacekeepers.[28] Under the new concept, the average number of daily patrols rose from about 50 to 200 between February and April 2005. The number of permanently manned OPs was reduced from 17 to merely 2. Patrol bases were reduced from 21 to 9 and UN camps decreased from 12 to 4 (UN Secretary-General 2005: 4).

The technological contribution: Closed-circuit television

The plan was to introduce "greater use of technology such as closed circuit television" (Figoli 2004: 1) to monitor areas considered "hotspots". Motion-initiated camera systems "would produce the necessary evidence to prove to the OPFORs the UN's allegations of [OPFOR] ill discipline which to date have been denied by the OPFORs because of the lack of corroborative evidence" (UNFICYP 2004b: 1, paras 1–4).

Table 6.3 is my estimate of the cost of a manned versus camera-based OP.[29] It is based on UN and UNFICYP cost figures for personnel and the actual CCTV system deployed with a remotely controlled camera. Rounded numbers and US dollars are used for this estimate.

The total cost for one manned OP is estimated at about $170,000 per year, whereas the cost for a camera system is roughly $15,000 in the first year and $160 for subsequent years. Thus, a camera system is over 10 times cheaper in the first year and 100 times cheaper in subsequent years. With more substitutions, the cost savings would be that much greater. However, if a large number of cameras is deployed (for example, more than a half-dozen), additional watchkeeper(s) would be needed in the Joint Operations Centre (JOC) to keep an eye on the additional screens. Roughly one watchkeeper is required for every half-dozen cameras. Still, the personnel requirements for additional watchkeepers would be far lower than for human observers at additional OPs.

Financial and personnel requirements are not the only consideration in a manned/unmanned comparison. The loss of the human presence in the immediate conflict zone is a significant drawback, although it was a necessary trade-off in UNFICYP's case.

In a camera-based system with no local human presence, the United Nations needed to be responsive. After a violation is spotted by the watch officer in the JOC, a call is made to the OPFORs' local liaison officer, ideally as soon as the violation occurs. For more serious violations, the mission's liaison officers or response forces are on standby to achieve a quick response. The response force is closely linked to the JOC, which can provide live information and guidance.

It took UNFICYP several years to implement the camera plan. The initial concept and the Statement of Requirement (UNFICYP 2004b: 2; 2005) envisaged surveillance of 10 "flashpoints" in the Nicosia city centre, using 16 cameras equipped with infrared filters, transmitter-receivers and,

Table 6.3 Cost estimates for manned versus unmanned observation posts

Components	Costs	Comments
Manned OP		
Personnel: 8 (2 persons/shift × 3 shifts + 2 persons on leave/medical)	$96,000 (8 × $1,000 × 12 months)	UN pays troop-contributing countries $1,024/month for each soldier (specialists more)
Welfare, rations	$73,000 ($25/day × 8 persons × 365 days)	$9,125/year/person
Binoculars and night-vision goggles	$2,500 ($26/month × 8 persons × 12)	$26/month from COE Manual (observation and identification)
Total	$171,500 per year	
Unmanned OP		
Camera: 1 (purchase and installation)	$15,000	Based on UNFICYP contract for one camera to replace each OP. Includes camera, link to control station and maintenance for one year. For some positions, two or more cameras might be needed in future
Maintenance (after first year)	$150	Based on a five-year maintenance contract
Electrical costs	$10	Negligible in cost for posts near electrical sources (as in UNFICYP)
Staff	0	No additional staff employed at the Joint Operations Centre to view the six or so cameras equipped with motion sensors
Total	$15,010 for first year $160 for following years	Contract for five years

at the JOC, a multiplexer, large monitor and DVD recorder. Six cameras were finally installed in the buffer zone by contractor personnel under UN escort in February 2008. The JOC equipment was installed at the same time. The Standard Operating Procedures for the camera system were developed that year (UNFICYP 2008b).

The United Nations chose sensitive areas of the buffer zone to deploy the cameras in parts of Nicosia's city centre where the OPFORs were closest and where violations had been most frequent. The camera system was spread over 1.5 km along the narrowest part of the Green Line. This area, in the centre of crowded Nicosia, is a no-man's land, providing stark evidence of the 1974 war. Majestic but uninhabited and decaying buildings, some pocked with bullet holes, remain frozen in time, an eerie reminder of the intense fighting that brought a once bustling city centre to a dead halt.

The camera system had to be secure, even though there were few intruders along this demilitarized strip. The camera domes were made of vandal-proof (though not bullet-proof) plastic. The United Nations also stipulated that the data stream had to be secure. The contractor[30] used microwave communications to connect the cameras to the JOC of Sector 2, manned by soldiers of the British contingent. The Pan Tilt Zoom cameras incorporated a motion sensor, so that movements within the camera's field of view could be highlighted for the watch officer.

Once installed, it was important for the camera concept to succeed that the OPFORs not resist the new system. The UNFICYP Commander who developed the concept in 2004 had already explained its utility to his senior OPFOR counterparts. Then, when the system was made operational, the Commander, in whose downtown area of responsibility the cameras were installed, also invited the local commanders to separately visit the JOC for a briefing on the system and to view it first-hand (Duncan 2008a). The two half-hour visits were successful, with no opposition coming from the parties.

CCTV in practice

The utility of the camera system was quickly demonstrated in the first few months after its installation. Many "serious" violations were spotted almost immediately. Two cases illustrate the functioning of the camera system.

Greek National Guard Post 50 (NG50)

Soon after a UN camera was installed near NG50, the JOC watch officer observed Greek National Guard soldiers, some armed with rifles, inside the buffer zone.[31] The dispatch of a peacekeeper led to the departure of the National Guard soldiers. The UNFICYP Sector 2 Commanding Officer wrote to his National Guard counterpart that the violation had been "captured on CCTV". He requested a National Guard investigation and explanation, adding: "I am sure you would agree that had this event been observed by the TK [Turkish Forces], a very serious situation could have resulted" (Duncan 2008b).[32] The Guard commander agreed that the soldiers had gone out of the prescribed areas. He assured the United Nations officer that he had re-issued "clear orders" to his soldiers to avoid a repeat of this specific incident. Overall, violations at NG50

"decreased dramatically since the introduction of the CCTV camera".
Previously, though, "the UN had no way of observing a violation unless a
patrol happened to stumble across it happening".[33]

Ledra Street Crossing

Ledra Street runs through the centre of Nicosia's old city. It was the first
street to be barricaded when inter-communal fighting broke out in December 1963. Then, after the 1974 invasion and partition, it became the
dividing line in the city centre and was the site of much OPFOR antago-
nism and grandstanding. After a thaw in relations in 2007–2008, a public
transit point was opened at the Ledra Street Crossing (LSX).[34] The public opening in April 2008 was a symbolic victory for peaceful coexistence.
Moreover, the LSX gained great practical value by facilitating traffic between the Turkish and Greek zones of the island's largest city. Nevertheless, the first days of the opening presented significant challenges for the
United Nations.

On the morning of its opening on 3 April, the crossing was still conten-
tious. The Turkish Republic of Northern Cyprus maintained that most of
the crossing area was in its territory and insisted on a right to enter. This
fact was disputed by the United Nations, which insisted that, as part of
the agreed confidence-building measures, the crossing area was to be demilitarized, that is, unmanned by any forces. The United Nations' video
camera was installed above the centre of the crossing. The CCTV showed
Turkish Cypriot Police (TCP) officers entering the area before the opening of the crossing. Such trespassing was to repeat itself, but, according
to the UNFICYP soldier who watched the CCTV tapes, "once the TCP
realised that the camera was watching over this area for violations, the
offenses became almost non-existent".[35]

CCTV problems and limitations

Although UNFICYP has pioneered CCTV observation of conflict areas,
the actual system in Nicosia took years to be implemented and the area
coverage is still quite modest. Whereas 100 cameras are used for monitoring UN premises, only 6 are used for hotspots along 1.5 km of the Green
Line. Furthermore, one of the six cameras remained non-functional for a
half year after installation owing to a communications-relay problem.

Microwave beams are used to transmit the signals from the existing
camera stations to the Sector 2 Operations Centre. Sometimes, because
of tree foliage along the route, the microwave signal from a camera becomes disrupted or the video link is lost or its quality degraded.[36]

Another problem is that the OPFORs do not tolerate filming behind
their cease-fire lines. Thus the current CCTVs must be pointed across the

breadth of the buffer zone and the view of the cease-fire line must be limited to forward positions only.

If the conflict intensity between the OPFORs had been higher, it is unlikely that CCTV systems could have been used to replace observation posts completely. Clearly, the relatively peaceful atmosphere made possible the technological component of the "concentration with mobility" concept. When the Green Line had seen more violence, for example the shooting incidents of the 1970s and 1980s, the opposing forces would likely not have tolerated the installation of cameras and might even have destroyed them with gunfire. Adversaries firing bullets at each other are unlikely to want a video witness to their actions. For the United Nations, however, a combination of both technology and peacekeepers allows the benefits of both to be leveraged. Technology could serve as a force multiplier. In a hostile situation, peacekeepers could providing the human eyes and the cameras could provide the evidence for later.

Helicopter reconnaissance

Aerial observation is a highly effective monitoring tool that was already in UNFICYP use before the introduction of "Force 860". The Argentine helicopter unit "UN Flight", based at the former Nicosia International Airport, took observers on flights 24/7 upon request from the sectors. Helicopters provide a "bird's eye" view of the terrain[37] and are also equipped with a surveillance pod housing electro-optical and forward-looking infrared (FLIR) cameras that can take gyro-stabilized video footage day and night.[38]

Camera imagery from helicopter flights has been given to the parties as reliable and impartial evidence of violations. Digital cameras held by peacekeepers on helicopters have recorded evidence of violations such as: unannounced military exercises and terrain briefings; illegal road/fortification construction, farming, hunting and motor-biking; and suspicious activities needing further investigation on the ground. Air patrols have also viewed other activities, including ships of doubtful origin off the Cypriot coast, public demonstrations in Nicosia and even lost UN patrol cars.

Lessons from UNFICYP

As a stereotypical "traditional" peacekeeping mission, UNFICYP was an unlikely candidate to deploy surveillance technology. Yet tradition met modernity in the UNFICYP mission, whose innovative actions were borne of necessity as it was forced to downsize after 2004. The adaptive actions were pioneering. Unattended camera systems at hotspots in a demilitarized zone were introduced for the first time in UN peacekeeping history.

Though it took four years to implement the creative CCTV solution in Cyprus, the utility and cost-effectiveness of fixed video cameras in conflict zones have been clearly shown by the UNFICYP experience. The examples described above highlight the significant advantages of cameras, especially to record violations and present evidence to offending parties. In addition, cameras can maintain a 24-hour watch, whereas patrols can observe violations only if they happen to be there at the time.

Manned observation posts allow for a constant watch and may permit a quicker response because some soldiers are already *in situ*. Under the "concentration with mobility" concept, responders are kept on standby at some distance. This sacrifice of reaction time is compensated for by the greater mobility of forces and reduced cost. As a rough rule of thumb, a camera system is 10 to 100 times less costly than a manned OP.

As shown in UNFICYP, cameras can incorporate motion detectors that trigger alarms and watchkeeper attention. Even more sophisticated hardware and software are available to spot potential violations. Furthermore, the cameras can be equipped with acoustic recorders to catch violations such as the shouting of verbal abuse that might result in an escalation of conflict. In addition, the United Nations could set up speakers to address the parties from the Joint Operations Centre for an immediate verbal response to violence.

In Cyprus, the level of violations is low in comparison with other missions. UNFICYP catches 600 or so violations a year,[39] but none have proved life threatening for over a decade. The daily body count in some UN mission areas exceeds the daily count of violations in Cyprus. All the more reason that the UNFICYP experiment with surveillance cameras carries a valuable and transferrable lesson: remote monitoring can help deter, detect and document violations and prevent the death of civilians and peacekeepers. In larger missions, where the stakes are greater, the benefits of early warning and rapid response are even greater. The United Nations would be wise to develop the positive lessons from UNFICYP into broader policies and wider practices.[40] In an age when technology has been widely used to enhance war-fighting, it is only appropriate to make greater use of technology for peacekeeping.

Generalizations on monitoring in traditional peacekeeping

From this sweep through the history of peacekeeping operations in the Middle East, several relevant features can be identified:

- all missions gained the initial consent of the host state prior to the deployment of the force;
- monitoring was a key task of all missions;
- almost all UN monitoring was done in accordance with a cease-fire or peace agreement between the conflicting parties;
- most agreements set up bodies (joint commissions) of the parties to deal with observed violations and anomalies in implementation, with the United Nations often serving as the chair;
- the degree of access and cooperation varied considerably between missions and between parties;
- within most missions, the degree of success varied over time.

The survey of these missions reveals that technology was little used in the traditional missions, except in recent times by UNFICYP and UNIFIL. The human eye, sometimes aided by binoculars, was the primary instrument of surveillance for decades in traditional peacekeeping. The many challenges facing the mission were described.

A review of the wider peacekeeping history also reveals many monitoring failures, some of which could have been avoided had the United Nations possessed better monitoring systems and superior technological means. Failures of early warning occurred in places where the UN forces were stationed, including: the 1973 Yom Kippur War, the 1982 Israeli invasion of Lebanon and the 1990 invasion of Kuwait. The outbreak of the 1950 Korean War is another classic example in UN history where aerial monitoring could have been extremely useful.[41] The lack of monitoring capability also contributed to UN peacekeeping failures and weaknesses in Lebanon (1958), the Congo (1960–1964),[42] Namibia (1989–1990, especially in early April 1989), Rwanda (1994) and Eastern Zaire (1995–1996 during the aborted peacekeeping operation). Did modern multidimensional missions do better? The large number of peacekeeping missions in the twenty-first century provide colourful examples of both successes and failures in the field. They also highlight the use of some modern technologies in the field.

Notes

1. The current missions in the Middle East are the United Nations Truce Supervision Organization, the United Nations Peacekeeping Force in Cyprus, the United Nations Disengagement Observer Force and the United Nations Interim Force in Lebanon.
2. Except where otherwise noted, the information is taken from United Nations (1996).
3. In the early 1960s, David W. Wainhouse prepared, for the United States Arms Control and Disarmament Agency, a thorough description of the field monitoring operations belonging to the United Nations as well as to the League of Nations, the Organization of

American States, the Organization of African Unity and other international organizations. His results were published in the monumental work by Wainhouse (1966).

4. The first head, Count Folke Bernadotte, was assassinated by an Israeli terrorist group in Jerusalem on 17 September 1948. After his death, the Chief of Staff became the military head of UNTSO. The tradition of calling the head of UNTSO the Chief of Staff continues to this day.

5. General E. L. M. Burns of Canada, who served as UNTSO Chief of Staff, commented: "Unfortunately, both sides were only too ready to charge partiality or prejudice against senior personnel of the UNTSO when an adverse decision was given, especially when the case was one in which much blood has been spilled, and emotions were aroused. Allowances have to be made for such emotions, otherwise it would be intolerable for officers to have their honor impugned by assertions in the Press that they had made decisions to curry favour with one side or another in order to 'hold on to their jobs.' Chairmen of MACs in particular have often been attacked like this and, in the cases that come within my knowledge, always unjustly" (Burns 1962: 46).

6. On 14 September 1956, about a month before the 1956 war began, General Burns wrote to UN Secretary-General Dag Hammarskjöld to warn him that "if hostilities between the disputants in the Suez Canal question should break out, Israel ... might provoke a situation where she could attack in the El Arish-El Quseima-Rafah area". Still the exact timing of the Israeli invasion of Egypt on 29 October caught the UNTSO Chief of Staff off guard. Even the mobilization of the Israel Defense Forces on 27 October (along with a deceptive cover story) and UNMO reports of increased Israeli activity were not sufficient indicators. It was not until General Burns was on his way for a swim in the ocean that he noticed first hand "signs of mobilization beyond anything previously seen". On the morning of 29 October, he warned the UN Secretary-General that unrestricted warfare might begin, as it did that evening. The first confirmatory news was from an UNMO who had been forcibly expelled from his observation post. As fighting intensified, all but essential UNTSO personnel were evacuated (Burns 1962: 178–179).

7. The background to the conflict is as follows: Egyptian President Gamal Abdel Nasser nationalized the Suez Canal and escalated the conflict in July 1956. France, the United Kingdom and Israel plotted a course of military action. On 29 October, Israeli forces began invading Egypt across the Sinai Peninsula. The next day, France and the United Kingdom issued an ultimatum to both Egypt and Israel to withdraw their forces 10 miles from each side of the Canal. Israel, whose forces had not yet reached that point, accepted, but Egypt refused. Then France and the United Kingdom deployed their forces with the declared intent "to separate the belligerents", which the world immediately recognized as a thinly veiled plot to gain control of the Suez Canal. The United States opposed the intervention by the former colonial powers. The Security Council was deadlocked. This is when Canadian diplomat Lester Pearson made his proposal for a UN force that helped de-escalate the situation.

8. Under-Secretary-General Ralph Bunche deemed the 0240 hrs cable of 5 June 1967 expedient enough to wake the Secretary-General at his home in order to tell him the UNEF Commander's news: several Israeli aircraft had violated the airspace of the United Arab Republic (UAR); heavy fighting was reported by UNEF personnel in Rafah camp; the UAR authorities had informed the UNEF Commander of a large-scale Israeli air raid throughout the UAR.

9. The Treaty provides that UNEF "will conduct inspections in order to ensure the maintenance of the agreed limitations within these areas" (Article III(2)(b) of the Protocol of 10 October 1975, which forms an integral part of the Sinai II agreement).

10. For instance, Israel prevented the movement of a Polish unit on the Israeli side because Poland had no diplomatic relations with Israel. This was objected to by the Force

Commander, as were all infringements on UNMO freedom of movement, but it was not until after the establishment of diplomatic relations between Poland and Israel that the problem was resolved. See United Nations (1996: 80).

11. Quoted in Bash (1995: 66).

12. Security Council Resolution 425 (1978) of 19 March 1978, para. 3.

13. UNIFIL found the gendarmes especially helpful as interpreters and liaison officers with the local population. The gendarmes were also responsible for investigating and handling civil offences reported to UNIFIL.

14. Nepalese peacekeepers guarding the Khardala bridge refused to relinquish their posts and defences for two days. Only after partially destroying the steadfast Nepalese position could Israeli tanks cross the bridge. See United Nations (1996: 101).

15. After the end of the Gulf War, Iraq was made to accept the findings of an Iraq–Kuwait Boundary Demarcation Commission, which based its 1993 final report on a 1963 treaty between the two countries.

16. This was an innovative use of UN military observers during the actual conduct of a war. UNTSO observers were stationed in the capitals of Iran and Iraq to observe the moratorium arranged by the Secretary-General on military attacks against civilian centres (UN Secretary-General 1984).

17. The UN Security Council did not take up the question of the 1980 Iraqi invasion against Iran for over a month, and then only at the urging of the Secretary-General, whereas within a month of the Kuwait invasion it had passed a series of half-a-dozen resolutions, the first one coming in less than a day. Furthermore, after the 1980 attack the Security Council refused to identify Iraq as the aggressor. Presumably, the negative image of Iran held by the international community (especially the United States) following the seizure of the US embassy in Tehran in 1989 was to blame for the erstwhile (and undeserved) favouritism.

18. The other two missions were the Iraq–Kuwait Boundary Demarcation Commission, which oversaw the delineation of the border between the two countries, and the United Nations Compensation Fund, which was created to administer compensation (to be obtained from Iraq) to those who suffered direct losses from Iraq's illegal actions.

19. There are a number of features in the establishment of UNIKOM that suggest how stronger peacekeeping missions might be created in the future (when the Council members give their full support to a mission). First, the mission was created for an indefinite period, not requiring the traditional six-month extensions, when the Secretary-General usually has to justify the mission mandate to an often sceptical Council. Secondly, the mission could not be ended unilaterally by the host states. It would require the concurrence of all permanent members of the Council to terminate the mission. Thirdly, the Security Council encouraged the Secretary-General to consider the need for rapid reinforcements in emergency contexts.

20. The fact that U-2 aircraft images were passed to the Israel intelligence agency was confirmed in my meeting with UNSCOM Chairman (1991–1996) Rolf Ekeus in The Hague on 17 April 2009.

21. This chapter draws heavily from a more detailed study made by A. Walter Dorn and Robert Pauk (2011). Pauk served as a peacekeeper in Cyprus and a consultant and research assistant on the Monitoring Technology project that made this book possible.

22. UNFICYP was created by Security Council Resolution 186 (1964).

23. The first figure is for June 1964 and is from UN Secretary-General (1964: 2). The second figure is for May 1974 and is from UN Secretary-General (1974: 4).

24. UNFICYP estimates that 165,000 Greek Cypriots fled the newly created northern Turkish sector for the southern Greek-controlled territory and 45,000 Turkish Cypriots left the southern Greek sector for the Turkish north. The United Nations High

Commissioner for Refugees gives slightly higher figures of 200,000 and 65,000 respectively. See the Internal Displacement Monitoring Centre website, at <http://www.internal-displacement.org> (accessed 11 January 2011).

25. Only 21 OPs remained permanently manned, another 3 were manned during daylight hours only, and another 19 were manned periodically. All of these were used for overnight accommodation of UNFICYP military personnel. (UN Secretary-General 1993d: 4)

26. The Security Council changed the financing of the force, which precipitated Argentina's offer.

27. There was much bitterness over this outcome, especially since the Greek Cypriot President, Tassos Papadopoulos, had campaigned against acceptance. His government had not even allowed some key supporters of the plan to appear on the national television station. See Ker-Lindsay (2005: 118; 2006: 412).

28. It should be noted that in March 1993, in the face of an impending manning shortfall, the Secretary-General had warned that, if the force fell to 850 personnel, it would cease to be viable (UN Secretary-General 1993a: 2).

29. The UNFICYP Force Signals Officer (J6), Lieutenant Commander Alberto Cohen, helped develop this table while I was on a DPKO-sponsored visit to UNFICYP in January 2009. His help and insight are much appreciated.

30. The contractor was the Nicosian firm City Watch Security Systems. The camera specifications to which the contractor agreed are: horizontal resolution of 480 lines for colour imaging and 570 in B/W mode (especially for night operation); 30 frames per second; 4× optical zoom; motion detection/activation and tracking facility; electronic map showing positions of cameras; watchdog function for operating system failure and a universal power supply.

31. The Greek National Guard troops are not permitted to loiter in the buffer zone, but at certain spots National Guard sentries can pass through the zone briefly to reach another National Guard post. This was allowed in order for the National Guard sentries to avoid civilian houses and lanes while carrying weapons and live ammunition. The UN agreement grants this right of transit in small groups only. Rifles can be carried but not fitted with magazines or bayonets (UNFICYP 2008a).

32. In 1983, a Cypriot National Guard soldier was shot dead by the Turkish Forces near the post and Friezenburg House. Throughout the rest of 1983, the United Nations observed incidents of the two sides shooting at each other's OPs.

33. Electronic communication to me from WO2 Provan, Continuity Operations Warrant Officer at Sector 2 Headquarters, Wolseley Barracks, 22 January 2009.

34. On the Turkish side of the crossing, documents (for example passports) must be presented to border control agents. On the Greek Cypriot side, no stop is required since the Republic of Cyprus sees Cyprus as one country and the border as artificial and not legal or officially recognized. Some Greek Cypriots feared the opening of the crossing might increase acceptance of two separate states within the federal boundaries of the Republic of Cyprus.

35. Electronic communication from WO2 Provan, 22 January 2009.

36. The United Nations was unable to trim or remove the offending tree in this particular instance because it forms part of the Turkish Forces' cease-fire line and permission was not given. In addition, the camera was put out of action owing to a power surge from a lightening strike on a building nearby. Written communication from WO2 D. A. Provan, UNFICYP Sector 2, 23 January 2009.

37. "UN Flight" has Bell 212-IFR and Hughes 500D helicopters, based at the United Nations Protected Area helicopter landing site. The Argentine unit has flown over 15,000 hours since 1974. It usually flies at an altitude of 200–400 metres. A helicopter can fly

from one end of the buffer zone to the other in under two hours. Planned UNFICYP II requirements listed that the aerial units should have the "capability to serve two separate areas simultaneously with basic FLIR for surveillance". The surveillance safe range was specified as "5 km [distant] or 3,000 feet above ground level".

38. The Inframetrics camera pod was brought to "UN Flight" in 2003–2004. The pod has a 7× zoom capability and its imagery is recorded on super-8 film. The FLIR has proved useful for surveillance of landing zones at night but in 2008 the FLIR was under-used (only one night flight per month, on average).

39. For instance, in a six-month period in 2008 (May–Nov), the number of military violations and other incidents was 352 (UN Secretary-General 2008a: 4).

40. The United Nations is showing evidence that it recognizes the need. The July 2009 "New Horizon" paper (DPKO and DFS 2009: 27) identifies "critical shortages" in "observation/surveillance, including high resolution; night operations capability; data management and analysis". It also notes: "Moving from a troop-intensive to a more agile mission structure and approach will depend on the feasibility of sourcing the very enabling capabilities that are currently difficult to obtain. Rebalancing numbers of personnel with more mobile capacities or technological solutions may change cost structures; it will not necessarily lower them" (2009: 28).

41. The United Nations Commission in Korea (UNCOK) in 1950 had a mandate to monitor the security situation in South Korea. It was greatly delayed in deploying military observers, and only two had arrived by the time war broke out. It is perhaps for this reason (too few military personnel) that the United Nations does not consider UNCOK as a peacekeeping mission. However, these two Australian UN military observers did conduct a reconnaissance trip along the 38th parallel (the dividing line between North and South after World War II), returning to Seoul on 24 June 1950. Their report to UNCOK fails to mention North Korean preparations for an imminent attack. Indeed, if their jeep had so much as received a flat tyre in the final days of their trip, they probably would have witnessed first hand the onslaught by thousands of North Korean troops as the invasion of South Korea began in the early hours of 25 June 1950.

42. See Dorn and Bell (1995).

7

Multidimensional peace operations: Cases

Traditional peacekeeping is appropriate after a conventional war fought by armies and once a cease-fire with well-defined cease-fire lines has been established. This has been rare in the post–Cold War world,[1] where most of the fighting is not of an international but of an internal (*intranational*) character. Hence, modern peacekeeping forces need to be deployed throughout a territory and in the population centres rather than in no-man's land. Intensive negotiations prior to and during an operation need to occur with the host state and any conflicting parties. Resolving a conflict after (or during) civil war also involves a commitment to peacebuilding, meaning the development of the physical, psychological and governmental infrastructure for a sustainable peace. This entails a larger set of tasks and a wider set of players, including police and civilians. It also means that technology needs to be applied in novel fashion.

The UN missions examined in this chapter illustrate the huge political and technical challenges of twenty-first-century peacekeeping. Two of the cases are large and needy missions in Darfur and the Democratic Republic of the Congo (DRC), regions shown on the Africa map in Figure 7.1. The Haiti mission is also analysed for some of its efforts at technological innovation. Some recommendations are made to improve capacity in these three missions.

Unlike the United Nations, the North Atlantic Treaty Organization (NATO) has deployed highly sophisticated technologies in its peace operations in a systematic manner to great advantage. The two NATO cases also examined in this chapter, in Bosnia and Kosovo, provide a reference

Keeping watch: Monitoring, technology and innovation in UN peace operations, Dorn, United Nations University Press, 2011, ISBN 978-92-808-1198-8

Figure 7.1 Locations within Africa of Darfur (Sudan) and the DRC, where the two largest UN missions are operating.
Note: The square around the eastern border of the DRC indicates the perimeter of the map provided in Figure 7.2. Graphic art by R. Lang and H. Chilas.

point, perhaps at the high end, of how field missions could be equipped and deployed in the difficult regions where peacekeepers find themselves.

Darfur: Technology to the rescue?[2]

The world watched in horror as the situation in Darfur became the world's worst humanitarian crisis in 2003.[3] The mass murder, organized rape and a scorched-earth campaign were quickly and rightly condemned as "crimes against humanity", "ethnic cleansing" and even "genocide" (Gryzb 2009: 3–25). In Darfur's brutal civil war, the Government of Sudan (GoS) supervised a campaign against rebel groups. It sponsored militia attacks on farmers and villagers of non-Arab descent to force them to flee the region. About 3 million people became refugees abroad or internally displaced persons (IDPs) within Sudan. The majority of these were in camps in Chad near the border with Sudan. Civilian fatality estimates vary: the GoS claims a death toll of 10,000 whereas numerous non-governmental organizations believe it exceeds 400,000.[4] The United Nations commonly reports 300,000 deaths (Holmes 2009).

Such diverging and unsubstantiated numbers point to the history of insufficient situational awareness of the region. Indeed, most aspects of the Darfur conflict are disputed. Confusing and conflicting accounts arise in the absence of effective monitoring and reporting mechanisms. Verifying information, viewing events and confirming facts pose an ongoing challenge for the United Nations in civil wars. Nevertheless, there was sufficient documentation of crimes against humanity to lead the International Criminal Court (ICC) to issue arrest warrants against members of the Sudanese government, including President Omar al-Bashir. Information, testimony and imagery provided by the United Nations are expected to be important sources of evidence at ICC trials, if and when the accused are captured and brought to The Hague.

From 2003 to 2007 an overstretched African Union Mission in Sudan (AMIS) proved highly inadequate to stem the violence and protect Darfur's civilians. Moreover, between 2005 and 2007 the GoS tried to discourage international support for the deployment of a more robust UN peace operation, even after the Darfur Peace Agreement (DPA) of May 2006 was signed. The latter was a step forward but it failed to achieve a cease-fire largely because of insufficient cooperation and compromise from both the government and rebel groups.

Confronted by the urgent humanitarian needs, intense public pressure and diverse political interests, the United Nations finally secured a conditional compromise for a hybrid UN–African Union (AU) peacekeeping force known as the United Nations–African Union Mission in Darfur (UNAMID) in 2007. The Security Council established this first hybrid UN–AU operation in Resolution 1769 (2007) and gave it an extensive mandate, including: to ensure the security and freedom of movement of humanitarian workers; to support the DPA; to prevent armed attacks; and, significantly, to protect civilians.

With these enormous challenges, UNAMID had many monitoring requirements. Some were specified in the mandate, including: verifying cease-fire agreements, especially the DPA; monitoring the border situation; overseeing militia (Janjaweed) disarmament and the police in places

Table 7.1 UNAMID in numbers

Strength (uniformed personnel)	23,100
Troops	16,900
Military observers	250
Police	4,800; 1,800 in Formed Police Units
International civilians	1,130
Local civilians	2,560
UN volunteers	420
Largest troop contributors	Nigeria, Rwanda, Egypt and Ethiopia
Cost	$1.6 billion (annual)
Fatalities	61

Source: Statistics obtained from United Nations (2010).
Note: Numbers as of 30 April 2010, rounded to three significant figures.

such as IDP camps. Other monitoring tasks were implicit in the mandate, including early warning to prevent armed attacks and using intelligence to protect UN personnel, humanitarian workers and civilians. Though the Security Council gave the mission substantial resources, few technological measures were brought to the field.

UNAMID in Darfur

UNAMID is one of the largest peace operations in history, comprising approximately 26,000 multinational participants (see more detailed figures in Table 7.1). A vast support effort and a large budget sustain the mission (United Nations 2010).

Such a huge deployment is difficult even in the best of circumstances, but Darfur presents enormous challenges. Academic commentators Jones, Gowan and Sherman (2009) adroitly observed:

> The Darfur operation has encapsulated virtually all the obstacles to effective peacekeeping ... It is deployed in a vast space, lacks sufficient forces to handle that space, is overshadowed by international differences over its role, has no credible peace process to maintain – and does not enjoy the genuine consent of either the host state and many non-state actors.

Still, UNAMID has made a difference in Darfur. Reports have confirmed the positive impact of the UN presence, patrols, police centres and quick-impact projects (UN Secretary-General 2009a, 2009b). The number of fatalities decreased after UNAMID's arrival to a small fraction of the number in 2003–2004. However, the situation remains tense and conflict remains unresolved, with many refugees and IDPs unable to return home.

Though the UNAMID mission is large, it must cover a territory that is both vast and inhospitable. Darfur occupies the western quadrant of Sudan and covers an area only slightly smaller than Spain (DPKO 2007). The terrain is arid and typified by large desert areas. The region has two contrasting seasons: one very dry and prone to sand-storms; the other wet and prone to flooding. Transportation within Darfur can be exceptionally slow and difficult owing to the lack of supportive infrastructure such as roads, railways and airstrips. People move on sandy, unpaved desert trails, with only a few dirt roads connecting cities and towns.

Long distances separate the headquarters of the mission, El Fasher, from the sectors and the sub-sectors.[5] Re-supply lines begin at Port Sudan and extend as far as Nyala in southern Darfur, a distance of 2,200 km. Necessitating massive logistical efforts, the geography both exposes and frustrates operational movement and observation.

In spite of UNAMID's large number of troops, the dispersal of its personnel to 55 deployment locations in three provinces renders UNAMID unable to monitor developments in Darfur without modern surveillance technology. But the enormous investment in personnel and finances has not been matched by a corresponding investment in surveillance and monitoring means. The large majority of troops in UNAMID come from the developing world, especially Africa, where technology is not advanced. But there are even more important factors that explain the lack of technological and other resources in the mission.

The origins of the quagmire

The great difficulties in acquiring the necessary monitoring tools are directly related to the political tension that has existed since the creation of the mission. Resolution 1769 was premised upon several compromises that are familiar in peacekeeping operations.

First, the Security Council was not unanimous on the appropriate or effective response to the conflict. Two of the five permanent members (Russia and China) opposed a strong approach that might infringe on the sovereign rights of the GoS (Gaouette and MacKinnon 2007). The United States, in contrast, having explicitly described the atrocities in Darfur as "genocide", wanted to give at least the impression of substantive action through a robust peace operation. Given the risk of a veto, the Security Council resolution that established UNAMID was a compromise between competing great powers, unfortunately resulting in a mandate that negated the prospect of prompt action to stop the Sudanese government.

Second, UNAMID was not authorized within a strictly binding interpretation of Chapter VII or one that identified the GoS as a belligerent, subject to enforcement action. Chapter VII is often invoked as the strongest response, allowing for the use of force (sometimes specified as "all necessary means") to fulfil the objectives of the UN Security Council. Instead of being granted explicit authority to stop, stem, prevent and deter, UNAMID was largely confined to contributing, supporting, facilitating and encouraging cooperation between the parties.

Third, to acquire host-nation consent from the GoS, Resolution 1769 fully recognized the latter's sovereign rights and authority. This essentially gave Khartoum control over many aspects of the UN operation. UNAMID's mandated objectives for civilian protection were permitted only to the extent that they were "without prejudice to the responsibility of the Government of Sudan" as well as "within its [UNAMID's] capabilities" (para. 15(a)).

Desperate for action, the world generally responded favourably to Resolution 1769. Sadly, events soon proved that even the compromise resolution was based on "best-case" analysis. Within its first year the UN Secretary-General complained about violations in the Status-of-Forces Agreement (SOFA), restrictions on UNAMID's freedom of movement, and even ongoing fighting and widespread violence (UN Secretary-General 2008b: 8). Though the resolution explicitly entailed protection of civilians – a vital albeit tough task – UNAMID continued with insufficient tools to monitor and promote civilian safety.

Sudan: An uncooperative host nation

The GoS only reluctantly consented to UNAMID, not wanting its military and paramilitary activities curtailed during a civil war. When pressured by the international community, it argued that the presence of Western forces would represent a "re-colonization" of the country. Consent for the operation remains conditional, with strong restrictions and limitations imposed on UNAMID's presence, activities and equipment by the host country.

The GoS repeatedly restricted UNAMID's freedom of movement, blocked its patrols,[6] delayed and denied passage of goods and supplies through Sudanese ports and airports, rejected night flights, threatened movement, and refused the use of or confiscated effective tools and equipment. The United Nations encountered enormous problems in deploying specific equipment that did not obtain GoS approval.

Few, if any, UN peace operations have deployed to a less cooperative host nation.[7] The political leadership of the Government of National Unity is characterized by extreme sensitivity bordering on paranoia. Sudanese officials view the United States, Western objectives and monitoring technologies with deep suspicion.

The GoS blocks UNAMID observation when GoS military or paramilitary forces are carrying out operations or preparations that the government wants to hide from the world. It is precisely those activities that the United Nations has the greatest need and responsibility to monitor. In this "cat and mouse" game, it is crucial that the UN peacekeepers have the proper tools to uncover clandestine and night-time operations. Human rights violations should be spotted, documented and stopped. To take preventive action, the United Nations needs an early warning capability, detailed information and the ability to see through distorted information. Sudanese government officials have, for example, declared that the war is over while they simultaneously organize an offensive. Image evidence would bolster future criminal trials or a potential "truth and reconciliation" commission.

Given the desire on the part of the GoS to conceal its activities, new UN systems for surveillance and monitoring were not being permitted. In April 2009, Sudanese officials suspended all UN Medevac/Emergency flights in southern Darfur after learning that night-vision equipment had been installed on a helicopter. Although informed that such equipment was necessary as a safety measure for night rescue and landing, Sudanese officials refused, claiming that the apparatus could be used for intelligence-gathering during over-flights of national installations (UNAMID 2008). This prohibition was lifted only after many months.

UNAMID typifies a larger "commitment-capacity gap" (Langille 2002a) within UN peacekeeping, in which the mandates are not matched with the necessary capabilities and resources. In Sudan this is compounded by the Sudanese demand that the mission be primarily an African one. The AU troop-contributing countries (almost all of them developing countries) do not have the capacity of the vetoed developed countries that sought to participate in the mission. UNAMID's troops – primarily from Nigeria, Rwanda, Ethiopia, Egypt, Gambia and Ghana – lack experience with modern technology for surveillance and monitoring, though South Africa has some excellent night-vision capabilities. Western police and defence officials view advanced technology as an essential tool in security and military operations but others lack familiarity with it. In the words of one UN official, "night-vision goggles were as far as the AU would go".[8]

UNAMID's technological capacity

The initial plans developed at UN headquarters for the UNAMID operation in 2007 included a substantive package of surveillance and monitoring assets.[9] Along with military observers and liaison officers, there were to be reconnaissance units, long-range patrols, systematic information-gathering units, unmanned (uninhabited) aerial vehicles for surveillance, and other aerial reconnaissance means. Unfortunately, the diverse constraints made most aspects of those plans unfeasible. Only six pilots were assigned to the three observation aircraft of UNAMID's air reconnaissance unit. Peacekeepers on patrols and within convoys were seldom equipped even with night-vision binoculars.

When asked in 2008 to provide a list of its shortfalls in monitoring and surveillance technologies of low/medium cost, UNAMID officials identified the following needs (UNAMID 2009):
- digital cameras and laptops for UN military observer teams; and
- night-vision devices;[10]
- aircraft fitted for observation, including unmanned aerial vehicles (UAVs) with live feed;
- dedicated ISTAR cell (for Intelligence, Surveillance, Target Acquisition and Reconnaissance).

UNAMID could use these to monitor broad areas of land as well as to detect, identify and recognize groups (including those beyond their weapons range and at night) and to protect convoys and patrols.

Although most UNAMID activities are conditional upon approval from the GoS, certain technological steps could be taken to sidestep this problem. Some recommendations for this case are offered here and generalized later for UN missions more broadly.

Satellite surveillance

Satellites can provide significant "information power" to help keep the peace. Moreover, it is legal to observe any territory from space without national approval. Satellite surveillance can be conducted despite GoS efforts to conceal its activities. Furthermore, national and commercial satellites are beyond GoS authority, and UNAMID's computers, on which imagery can be stored, are legally inviolable.

UNAMID's vast area of operations requires satellite surveillance. Analysts within UNAMID, perhaps in the Joint Mission Analysis Centre, could discern friendly civilians from armed and dangerous belligerents. The latter could then be watched, identified, tracked and, if necessary, approached and warned so as to prevent violent crimes. Patrols could be directed and dispatched based on satellite reconnaissance. Remote towns, villages and camps could be monitored daily to ensure better protection.

Numerous commercial imagery satellites are available. Old images, taken a month earlier, typically cost $3,000 per scene and can be of high resolution (down to 0.5 metres) and wide area (300×500 km^2), which is important for mapping. For real-time imagery, the cost is greater and specific contracts with commercial satellite controllers would be required. Moreover, UNAMID would have to develop a system for rapid image requests and analysis. The organization may have to rely on a member state or a coalition of states working in a group.

Improvements are in sight as the political environment shifts toward better cooperation and assistance to peacekeeping operations in general, and to the Darfur mission in particular. There is more enlightened leadership among at least some permanent members of the Security Council. The United States, which has the most advanced satellite reconnaissance system in the world, has re-engaged in peacekeeping in a fashion not seen in over a decade and the Obama administration has proclaimed Darfur a priority. On some occasions, US analysis of Darfur imagery has been shared with UN officials. Other permanent members such as France and the United Kingdom also have excellent satellite systems. European satellite imagery has been offered to the United Nations in the past, although not in real time. A standing arrangement with the European Union Satellite Centre (EUSC 2010) near Madrid in Spain could be developed.

As interest in Darfur and the United Nations increases, it is to be hoped that states may share their satellite information, either as a voluntary contribution as a member state or as a multilateral contribution from a "Friends Group" of sympathetic and proactive nations working together to support a specific UN initiative. Such an effort might be encouraged through the sort of partnership envisaged in the 2009 "New Horizon" agenda of the Department of Peacekeeping Operations (DPKO) and the Department of Field Support (DPKO and DFS 2009). One or more supportive nations might convey real-time information to DPKO and UNAMID via one of several secure UN communication systems.

Furthermore, the United Nations could carry out its own analysis of satellite imagery by acquiring the appropriate hardware and software. The United Nations could also expand the current lists of required resources under the UN Standby Arrangements System (UNSAS)[11] and Contingent-Owned Equipment (COE) to include imagery analysis software and hardware.[12]

"Google Earth" is already used for Darfur mission planning both at UN headquarters and in the field. Furthermore, Google developed a partnership with the United States Holocaust Memorial Museum to provide overlays on its Darfur maps to show villages destroyed, mostly between 2003 and 2005.[13] The "Crisis in Darfur" display also offers high-resolution satellite imagery released by the US Department of State. Although imagery for recent atrocities is not available even months later, the Google Earth application does provide a strong database in which the United Nations could enter its own information about the evolving situation in Darfur.

Portable cameras and camcorders

Imagery can deter and document armed conflict, as one US photographer in Darfur was able to demonstrate.[14] Day and night patrols in UNAMID would benefit from the use of portable digital camcorders. Some of these should be capable of night-vision and GPS location. These cameras could be provided to selected UN workers and possibly to local civilian leaders, who could document nefarious activities – surreptitiously if need be. Photographing atrocities could endanger the photographer, so protection measures are crucial. Locals might still be unwilling to take such imagery.

Camcorders on UN personnel would enable peacekeepers to record and relay any development within eyesight to their sector and mission headquarters. Both still images and video links could be included in UN reports. Scenes from the field are a powerful means to convey conditions and activities by both "good" and "bad" actors.

Small, mobile units within UNAMID would also benefit from night-vision camcorders. Along with other night-vision devices (such as goggles), these could be a critical enabler for peacekeepers, allowing the United Nations to "take back the night" from the attackers, smugglers and criminals who use the cover of darkness to carry out their crimes. Almost all UN patrols take place during daylight.

Whether used during the day or the night, a recording capacity could deter and identify belligerents. An ambush on the afternoon of 8 July 2008 that killed 8 peacekeepers and injured another 22 illustrates a recurring problem.[15] During the three-hour fire-fight it was possible to discern uniforms similar to those of the Sudanese army, heavier weapons than normally encountered, approximately 80 armed men in 40 vehicles and fighters on horseback, a characteristic often associated with the Janjaweed. UN officials had circumstantial evidence, but no means to verify the identity of those responsible.

Had a few brief moments of this ambush been recorded by a camcorder, images could have been sent to UNAMID and UN headquarters via cell phone link, possibly in near real time. Senior officials would then have had a picture of the emergency situation and might have been able to deploy a quick response team. Moreover, with a digital record of the event and the individuals involved, the United Nations would then have had evidence for the Security Council and the ICC, since attacks on peacekeepers are violations of international law.

Many peacekeepers already have personal cameras, so a modest upgrade might not be objectionable to the GoS. If shared (with instructions) among troop and police formations and used primarily on patrols and convoys, then the "intelligence" objection might dissipate. Because these camcorders are designed to be user-friendly, users would not need to have specific training or a high level of technical competence. Digital camcorders with a high-zoom lens, night-vision capability and GPS locator are now available commercially for under $1,000. Acquiring several hundred cameras of this nature would save lives and substantially improve the security situation within Darfur.

Closed-circuit television networks

Like commercial camcorders, closed-circuit television (CCTV) and digital video networks (DVNs) have vastly improved in quality and decreased in cost.[16] In the developed world, they are increasingly used to enhance public and personal safety by providing continuous coverage of areas ranging from parking lots to home interiors to military bases.

The United Nations uses CCTV/DVN for camp and facility protection in many of its missions and could also place unattended camera systems in hotspots in Darfur where peacekeepers cannot stand guard 24/7. Examples include refugee camps, town squares or main streets where violence occurs or where armed groups are known to assemble. In addition, motion detectors with solar-powered illuminators could be activated when persons enter the area, thus reassuring innocent persons and deterring would-be aggressors. In more high-risk areas, the motion sensors could also trigger a camcorder, allowing intruders and violations to be watched, videoed and, if need be, intercepted.

Incidence reports from UNAMID demonstrate the need to develop a CCTV network for IDP camps and certain towns, as well as for UN facilities in Darfur. Such a system could complement efforts to ensure an ongoing UN presence in various camps. A CCTV system might deter Sudanese forces from repeating anything similar to their August 2008 attack on the Kalma IDP camp in Nyala (BBC News 2008; Roberts 2008). At that time, UNAMID had to wait while verifying reports of the attack on the camp of 80,000. Only then did it respond with a police and military patrol to investigate the incident after it had happened. Had UNAMID been able to view the arrival of 50 military vehicles outside the camp, it could have responded faster to protect the civilians.

Case conclusion

Technology will not rescue Darfur but it could improve UNAMID's situational awareness and its ability to spot and reduce violence. Darfur demonstrates the need to think creatively. The scale of the problem necessitates comprehensive and coordinated responses. It is evident that there are new and increasingly cost-effective technological options to help this mission and others.

Other missions have made considerable progress in ways that UNAMID was not able to achieve. Though similar problems were encountered in another large UN mission in Africa, notably in the DRC, that mission has made more technological progress. The use of advanced surveillance packages on helicopters has proved to be a key enabler in the DRC, though the mission still suffers a "monitoring technology gap" in other ways, despite the long and chequered UN peacekeeping experience in the Congo.

Congo: Jungle monitoring and the Mi-35 attack helicopter

We are fully aware of your long-standing limitations in gathering information. The limitations are inherent in the very nature of the United Nations and therefore of any operation conducted by it.

UN Secretary-General U Thant to Lt Gen Kebbede Guebre,
Force Commander, Congo, 24 September 1962[17]

In 1960, the United Nations embarked on what would become its most ambitious mission of the Cold War: the Opération des Nations Unies au Congo (ONUC, 1960–1964). The organization's first multidimensional mission had the goals of preventing secessionism, providing security in a country filled with warring factions and simultaneously helping the newly independent state to establish itself. The ONUC leaders soon recognized that the mission required a dedicated information collection and analysis system. In 1961, a Military Information Branch was created under the leadership of Scandinavian military intelligence officers to gather information using an unprecedented number of sources and methods. These included information gained from UN patrols and supply flights, dedicated reconnaissance aircraft, wireless-message interception (with code-cracking capabilities), interrogations of captured mercenaries (conducted in accordance with the Geneva conventions), and informants (some of them privately paid). Most of these early experiences in multidimensional peacekeeping were forgotten over time and only uncovered from archival sources some 30 years later (Dorn and Bell 1995).

The United Nations had to relearn many of the lessons from ONUC after it re-engaged in the DRC some 35 years later. In 1999, the United Nations was back in the Congo with an operation of a similar name, Mission de l'Organisation des Nations Unies en République démocratique du Congo (MONUC), dealing with similar problems. In 2010, the mission was officially succeeded – essentially a renaming – by the Mission de l'Organisation des Nations Unies pour la Stabilisation en République démocratique du Congo (MONUSCO).

This case offers a detailed look at the monitoring problems and challenges that MONUC/MONUSCO has faced, and how the mission came to exemplify modern multidimensional peacekeeping. The same types of challenges and actors have come up repeatedly, with varying levels of intensity, in many post–Cold War missions around the world: from Bosnia to East Timor, from Cambodia to Central America, and from Sierra Leone to Nepal. MONUC/MONUSCO shows that, as the United Nations struggles to deal with these monitoring problems, some of the solutions can be enabled by technology.

> Monitoring is an extremely demanding and sensitive task, especially in the security conditions of the Democratic Republic of the Congo. (MONUC 2008a: para. 3)

> The troops at all levels require intelligence on the locations, capabilities and intent of the various armed militia groups and their leaders who might derail the [peace] process ... The lack of timely and accurate intelligence, surveillance assets and night-vision devices (NVD) at the tactical level severely hampered their ability to effectively pursue their tasks. (Joint Assessment Mission, DPKO 2005b)

MONUC/MONUSCO is one of the largest and most costly peace operations, with some 25,000 personnel (including 18,800 military) and a budget of over \$1 billion annually.[18] The mission has been challenged by jungle warfare since its creation in 1999 and by the lack of a responsible national military or government. The current government appears motivated to avoid the democracy that gave it power in the UN-sponsored elections of 2006. The mission must cover a vast forbidding terrain in a country with little local infrastructure – fewer than 500 km of paved roads in a territory (2.3 million km^2) the size of Western Europe. Figure 7.1 shows the location of the DRC within Africa. Figure 7.2 shows the tense region of North Kivu and South Kivu, in the eastern Congo, which borders on Uganda, Rwanda and Burundi.

The Congo operation is a "flagship mission" of the United Nations under constant challenge. It covers the spectrum of mandates and functions of multidimensional peace operations. Its tasks have included:

- helping implement peace agreements;
- managing delicate political negotiations to reach power-sharing agreements among conflicting parties;
- overseeing a referendum and elections in 2006 (the largest elections in UN history, with over 25 million registered voters);

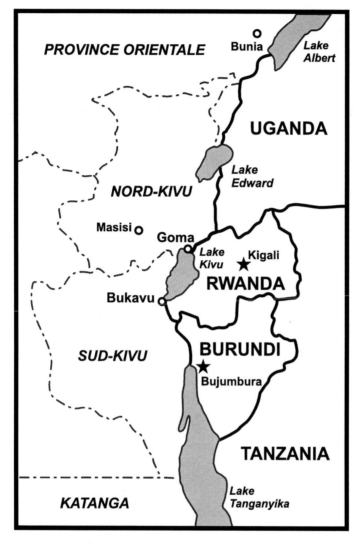

Figure 7.2 Map showing the Kivu provinces on the eastern border of the DRC and the neighbouring countries.
Note: Graphic art by R. Lang and H. Chilas.

- disarmament, demobilization and reintegration (DDR) of ex-combatants, as well as repatriation of foreign combatants;
- human rights monitoring in a country filled with violations;
- de-mining and removal of unexploded ordinance;

- security sector reform across the range of governmental agencies; and
- other nation-building tasks across the spectrum of development and governance.

As a robust mission operating in dangerous areas, it also finds itself engaging in combat against militia who oppose the government and continue to attack towns in the eastern DRC. This trend towards UN robustness began in earnest after traumatic experiences in the Ituri region of the eastern DRC.

In 2003, MONUC found itself in the centre of widespread violence in Ituri. Neighbouring Uganda and Rwanda had deployed their military forces into the region and were arming militia groups under their control while extracting precious minerals from Ituri. Massacres were common as fighters from rival ethnic groups, who shared the marketplace during the day, hunted each other at night. The international media exhibited the Ituri tragedy on the world's TV screens and front pages. Some experts called the situation in the eastern DRC "genocide in slow motion". The UN peacekeepers, barely able to protect themselves, felt helpless and powerless in the face of this level of violence because they were widely blamed for not protecting innocent civilians. In addition, two UN military observers were hacked to death in Mongbwalu, north of the Ituri capital, Bunia, on 13 May 2003. In the field and at UN headquarters, staff feared worse to come as the ethnic rivalries grew increasingly bitter. Uganda and Rwanda, claiming they played a pacifying and peacekeeping role, agreed to withdraw their forces only after the stern demands of the government of the DRC and the Security Council.

At this precarious time, the United Nations sought help from the European Union (EU). Under the aegis of a tough (Chapter VII) Security Council resolution, the EU launched Operation Artemis. The French-led force quickly took control of Bunia, forcing the fighters to leave and calming the region as a whole. This tough action showed both the United Nations and the world that force combined with intelligence could play an effective role in peacekeeping in such volatile regions. Robust peace operations could work.

As MONUC took over responsibility from the European force in September 2003, it managed to acquire observation and attack helicopter units from India that proved their worth. They were initially not permitted to fly at night for safety reasons, and were too few in number to cover the vast territory effectively. The infiltration routes for arms and fighters from neighbouring countries were not monitored.[19] Although some rebel leaders were apprehended and sent to the ICC after 2005, many others were roving the land with their bands. The United Nations was unable to keep track of their movements or prevent their pillaging and human rights abuses. The mission itself was subjected to attacks and kidnappings. Many cordon and search operations proved fruitless. Over time and of necessity, the mission began increasingly robust operations under Chapter VII of the UN Charter.

A first in the history of peacekeeping, MONUC's "Eastern Division" was established in early 2005 to run operations in the lawless eastern provinces of DRC. Commanding three brigades and a plethora of specialized units from attack helicopters to riverine and Special Forces, the Eastern Division is changing the nature of UN military operations from a traditional, more static and reactive form of peacekeeping to robust and offensive operations alongside or in support of local military forces.[20]

MONUC created its Eastern Division with Security Council support in 2005 to bring more law and order to the Congo's "wild East". It was the first time a peacekeeping operation had included a division-sized component. The plan was to bring illegal armed groups, both local and foreign, under control through DDR programmes and, if all else failed, to confront them forcefully. MONUC's new robust Rules of Engagement permitted combat action to prevent militia attacks on civilians. But a number of hard-line militia leaders, supported by breakaway factions of the DRC army, continued their abuses and illegal mining activities. They intimidated the local population, attacked villages and clashed among themselves and with the troops of the country's armed forces (the Forces Armées de la République Démocratique du Congo, FARDC). These government troops were themselves frequent perpetrators of human rights violations.

Despite having 13,000 UN troops in the east, MONUC's monitoring and reaction capacity was far from satisfactory in the vast and volatile territory. The leaders began to call for more sophisticated technical means, beginning in 2005.

At UN headquarters, the Military Planning Division of DPKO sought to find ways to fill the surveillance gap.[21] In April 2005, the Military Division sent a Joint Assessment Mission (JAM) to the DRC to identify "the exact nature of the surveillance assets" that were needed. The JAM made a candid assessment of the capacities and needs of MONUC, concluding that "the force never had any structured information collection assets other than the eyes and ears of the soldiers and military observers on the ground" (DPKO 2005b: 2). It recognized a "total lack of tactical mapping at all levels" and that MONUC had "no airborne *imaging* capability at all, and no night surveillance capability". The JAM suggested that "a stock of NVD could also be available for loan to the contingents that either have few or do not have such devices in national inventories to meet the operational requirements".

Neither the DRC government nor MONUC had the resources to track aircraft, let alone control them, in the country's airspace. Commercial aircraft travel in the east depended on the limited air traffic control provided from neighbouring countries. To complicate matters, hundreds of landing strips, built in the era of Congo's dictator Mobutu, were available for arms smuggling with little chance of detection – the United Nations could not afford to place UN military observers at such a large number of landing strips. The JAM therefore recommended the acquisition of three mobile surveillance radars, with an effective range of 150–250 km each, "to provide timely warning to enable airborne operations against smugglers".

To monitor and prevent the movements of militia both from and to neighbouring countries, the JAM also recommended that DPKO arrange for human-portable ground surveillance radars to supplement foot and vehicle patrols. The Uruguayan riverine units patrolling the lakes on the country's eastern border (Lakes Kivu, Albert, Edward and Tanganyika) were unable to detect or interdict arms smugglers. The JAM recommended mobile maritime radars and NVDs capable of detecting smugglers who used makeshift canoes and small motorboats.

In urban environments such as Kinshasa, the JAM concluded that MONUC needed surveillance helicopters to provide warnings about dangerous crowd movements in cities, especially since the government placed large areas of the city out of bounds to MONUC. Thus JAM recommended urban aerial surveillance. The JAM also recommended an electronic intelligence capacity, to locate, track and monitor the cellular/ satellite phone usage of militia leaders. This was controversial because such a system would be capable of monitoring a range of calls and callers, including DRC government officials. So it would need to be well regulated.

The JAM noted the need for detailed aerospace imagery, since the printed maps of the DRC were old and large scale. Often MONUC staff had to draw their own maps by hand. The JAM recommended that a contributing country be approached to provide accurate (1:50,000) maps, which the Netherlands soon did. The JAM also envisaged that imagery from satellites and aircraft could help with terrain familiarization, operational planning (for example, the placement of troops in cordon and search operations) and general surveillance and oversight. Such near-real-time imagery, however, never became available to MONUC. The JAM recommendations and the current status of implementation are summarized in Table 7.2.

To accentuate the problem, MONUC suffered numerous fatalities. For instance, in February 2005, a Nepalese officer engaged in providing protection to human rights investigators was fatally shot as he tried to board a departing helicopter. A subsequent investigation showed that MONUC lacked even a basic awareness of the attacking militia's position, strength, equipment, mobility, logistical resources, commanders, command structure, organization and intent.[22]

Engaged in a robust peace operation without the full complement of tools, MONUC's Eastern Division commander strongly supported the conclusions of the JAM. In June 2005, Major General Patrick Cammaert (2005b) declared a "critical shortfall in dedicated surveillance and intelligence-gathering assets with sufficient reach to provide commanders with accurate, timely and comprehensive intelligence". He identified an urgent requirement for "an aerial surveillance platform with the ability of near real-time enhanced video, geo-coordinated reference data, thermal imagers, and compatible downlink for communications down to the tactical level". In response, UN headquarters approved a $5.83 million budget item for an "airborne surveillance system" for MONUC for 2006/2007, and initiated a bidding process.[23] But, to the frustration of the mission leaders, UN headquarters could identify no compliant or suitable bids from industry.[24] The story became worse after several failed attempts to contract UAVs for the mission.

Despite the setbacks, MONUC has enjoyed more capacity and some remarkable success. It has engaged in extensive cordon and search operations and has employed mobile operating bases and surgical operations using special forces equipped with night vision. With enhanced capabilities for night flying, its attack helicopters were able to support many ground initiatives to prevent militia atrocities. In November 2006, it was able to halt an attack on the town of Goma. Also in 2006, MONUC supervised the largest and most complex elections ever overseen by the United Nations, allowing millions of voters to go to the ballot boxes in relative peace. Monitoring technology was making a difference in the difficult conditions of the rebellious Eastern DRC.

MONUC's Mi-35 attack helicopters: Robust surveillance and targeting platforms

The Mi-35 attack helicopter (AH) has become a symbol of robust UN peace operations. It is a powerful surveillance and weapons platform. Used by MONUC since 2004, the four attack helicopters of the Indian Aviation Contingent, based in Goma, are equipped with state-of-the-art surveillance systems. Though the sensors are designed for target identification and engagement, they are also used extensively for area reconnaissance in support of ground troops in the eastern DRC. An image of an Mi-35 in flight is provided in Figure 7.3.

Table 7.2 Surveillance asset requirements of MONUC: The JAM recommendations and subsequent action

	Condition 2005	Recommendation	Action
Mapping	"A total lack of tactical mapping at all levels throughout the Force"	"Approach member states for release of existing maps or mapping data covering the East DRC … MONUC's GIS to update it"	Netherlands provided 1:50,000 maps; Geographical Information System (GIS) Unit used the data
Aerial surveillance	"With the exception of one flight of Indian Alouette III helicopters, MONUC has no dedicated aerial surveillance capability. It has no airborne imaging capability at all, and no night surveillance capability"	"The provision of day and night aerial surveillance assets would have an early and positive impact"; UAVs for local surveillance and over-watch of operations.	UAVs deployed temporarily (2006) in western DRC by the European Union Force during election period; UAV contractor bid process aborted in 2010
Airspace surveillance	MONUC needs a capability to monitor/control the airspace in eastern DRC. However, "there is no functioning airspace coordinating authority in the DRC, and MONUC does not have the resources to control the airspace in the East"	"Deploy three mobile air surveillance radars on wheels for temporary surveillance of selected airspace"	Discussions ongoing to provide airports with radar sets for dual use (transport/aerial surveillance)
Ground surveillance	"Ground surveillance radars would provide some capability to monitor major infiltration routes through the border and the plains … none of the units are equipped with adequate NVD"	Provide "man-portable ground surveillance radars … a stock of NVD could also be available for loan to contingents"	No action

Lake surveillance	Illegal smuggling and movement of militia are "unquantified due to limited surveillance assets"	Provide optical surveillance and NVDs, mobile maritime radars for lakes	Improved equipment obtained
Urban surveillance	"MONUC requires a capability for crowd warning and movement monitoring ... MONUC has no police surveillance patrols by helicopters fitted with adequate sensors"	Redeploy urgently "surveillance helicopters to Kinshasa, or, when required, to support crowd control operations"	Helicopters temporarily redeployed in 2006 during critical periods
Other	Commercial satellite imagery (CSI) needed at 1–15 metre resolution	Establish structure of acquisition, distribution and funding of CSI	GIS Unit orders CSI routinely but response is not fast enough for current operations
Intelligence organization and process	MONUC "never had any structured information collection assets other than the eyes and ears of the soldiers and military observers on the ground ... The lack of timely and accurate intelligence ... severely hampered MONUC"	"Create a proper intelligence organization ... produce a force intelligence directive"	Established G2 (army intelligence), JOC and JMAC; "Force Intelligence Directive" produced
Electronic intelligence (ELINT)	No collection	"Conduct directed surveillance of specific high value targets"	ELINT unit supplied temporarily by the Netherlands in 2006–2007
Human intelligence (HUMINT)	"All units are exclusively reliant on HUMINT collection ... some positive results achieved"	Much more structured approach needed. Provide: linguists at higher levels and better vetting of translators, classified environment and debriefing teams for detainees and militia soldiers, funded HUMINT collection in a managed, auditable fashion	Some progress on structuring HUMINT and funding sources

Figure 7.3 Mi-35 helicopter gunship used in robust peacekeeping.
Source: UN photo by C. Herwig.

The helicopter's great value in the DRC has been demonstrated many times, especially when the rebel group known as the CNDP (Congrès national pour la défense du peuple, or National Congress for the Defence of the People) attempted to attack Goma in 2006 and in 2008. In both cases, the Mi-35 helicopters proved essential in repelling CNDP advances. The helicopters aided the ground troops of MONUC and the Congolese army (the FARDC) by determining the exact locations of the rebels and, when necessary, aiming rockets or machine-gun fire directly at them.

The CNDP's first major advance on Goma in November 2006 brought the rebels to a town called Sake, some 20 km west of Goma. At this critical juncture, the small fleet of UN attack helicopters was able to maintain an over-watch, continuously updating the United Nations on the positions of friendly forces and militia in the area. In one prominent case, the CNDP established a camp near the cell phone (Celtel) tower on a ridge west of Sake. The attack helicopter used its onboard sensors to scan the Celtel tower ridge, finding 60–100 renegade troops at the upper camp. It observed that the forces were exchanging fire, using machine guns and rocket-propelled grenades, with FARDC troops at a lower camp (MONUC 2006a).[25] With onboard sensors, the crew could relay information about "tubular" and "tripod-mounted" structures that appeared to be rocket launchers and mortars, respectively, in the CNDP-held area

(MONUC 2006b). On other flights the helicopters observed rebel militia clearing areas of growth and engaging in construction. They also reported on deserted villages and civilians fleeing violence (MONUC 2006c). The helicopters informed MONUC about the presence or absence of rebel movements along important roads, especially ones used in the rebel advance towards Goma, and in advance of UN patrols (MONUC 2006d).

The helicopters were usually not on offensive missions so the militia were not much deterred from their activities and even ignored the presence of helicopters overhead (MONUC 2006e). But during the intense periods, when the United Nations had warned the CNDP not to advance, the militia would often disperse after spotting or hearing the approaching attack helicopters. During ground battles, on-scene UN commanders observed that rebel firing would usually stop after the arrival of an Mi-35, though not always.

In addition to a colour television camera, the helicopters had fourth-generation forward-looking infrared (FLIR) cameras and the crew were equipped with special goggles for night flying, which was permitted in special circumstances. The night flights detected some hidden militia camps operating with the intent of overwhelming and threatening Goma. Since the militia often moved forward at night to prepare for dawn attacks, the FLIR provided crucial intelligence on developing threats. For instance, on 26 November 2006, an attack helicopter detected a vehicle plying the Sake–Goma road with its headlights off. Closer tracking revealed that this vehicle was shuttling between two towns, stopping on the road as large numbers of armed personnel emerged from their jungle cover at the road side to meet the occupants. The helicopter concluded that renegade militia were hiding off the Sake–Goma road in order to group for an assault towards Goma. The Indian battalion patrols in the vicinity were advised accordingly and they were able to confirm the deduction by making contact. This vital information could then be passed to the brigade headquarters located in Goma in order to mount joint operations to repel the attack (MONUC 2006f). The Mi-35 helicopters provided area domination and surveillance on the Sake–Goma road, and helped end the militia advances towards Goma in the autumn of 2006.

The CNDP once again threatened Goma in the period September to November 2008 and, once again, the Mi-35 provided early warning and a potent means to repel the rebel advance. Local UN ground commanders sometimes called for helicopter backup after being attacked. Such was the case on 19 September 2008, when both FARDC and MONUC positions were assaulted near the town of Masisi, some 70 km north-west of Goma. The attack helicopter quickly made radio contact with the local MONUC commander of the Contingency Operating Base (COB), who relayed the supposed position of the rebels on the Kahungole ridge. The nearby FARDC identified their own positions using smoke and white flags. The rebel positions were confirmed by the helicopter crew using visual observation and sensors of the Mi-35 upgrade. The helicopter carried out dummy dives to warn and deter the CNDP elements. After the COB commander reported that CNDP cadres were continuing to threaten UN forces, the helicopter fired a warning shot. When rebel firing continued, salvos of rockets were launched on the CNDP position. This finally caused the CNDP to pull back and stop shooting. The mission was accomplished without any collateral damage and fratricide thanks to the accurate firing by the attack helicopters.

The weapons on the Mi-35 are "slaved" to the sensors, meaning not only that the sensors serve as sites for the guns but that the guns automatically point towards the target in the middle of the sensor screen (the cross-hairs). Obviously, for precise fire, the sensors must be extremely accurate at a considerable distance. The helicopter pilots do not want to come too close to the target for fear of being hit by a rocket-propelled grenade or automatic rifle fire. Though armoured, the helicopter does have vulnerable spots. Greater stand-off distances are safer, so high-resolution sensors are needed. The exact resolution and capabilities of the sensors are national (Indian) secrets, but the system in the Mi-35 upgrade is at the cutting edge of most modern militaries.

Despite UN warnings and defensive actions, several thousand rebel troops attempted for over two months to seize Goma again in 2008. On 27 October 2008, an Mi-35 helicopter following the Goma–Rutshuru road observed thousands of people streaming towards Goma. It learned that UN and FARDC troops were under fire from the CNDP in the vicinity of the Kibumba COB. As usual, once the helicopter reached the target area, it established radio contact with the local UN commander, who attempted to describe the general location of the rebels. Soon, rebel fire was also directed at the helicopter. Tracer rounds from the CNDP enabled easy identification of the CNDP locations from the air. The rebels were in trenches on the periphery of a captured FARDC location atop Hehu hill, approximately 4 km north-east of the UN base. The CNDP cadre had dug the trenches into the ground so well that, even at the highest magnification, the TV camera could not show the rebel soldiers but only the flashes from their weapons.

Once the UN ground commander had confirmed that all FARDC troops had vacated their former post and that no civilians were in the area, the helicopter dived towards CNDP forces and fired rocket projectiles. While pulling out from the dive, tracer rounds were observed streaking just below the aircraft. Subsequent dives were done from different heights and angles to minimize the possibility of bullets hitting the aircraft, although helicopter armour had withstood bullets before. A total of

28 rocket projectiles were fired at the rebels. Although the rockets hit the general area of the target, it was not possible for the AH crew to determine the extent of the damage owing to the need to turn away immediately after firing. During the dives, pilots saw muzzle flashes from the trenches[26] but they could not determine the success of their fire, despite the sophisticated sensors on board the helicopter (MONUC 2008b).

On 28 October 2008, as the rebel offensive continued, an Mi-35 crew was briefed by senior MONUC officers, including the Indian Brigade commander and the Deputy Chief of Staff (DCOS) Forward. The officials shared intelligence on CNDP cadres concentrating in the jungles near the Nyiragongo volcano for an attack on Goma in the night. The attack helicopter arrived in the general area and established radio contact with a MONUC Forward Air Controller (FAC). The DCOS was the on-scene commander. The FAC directed the helicopter towards the location of the "negative elements", as they were called. The helicopter also received information from FARDC troops on CNDP positions, although communications with FARDC troops proved technically problematic owing to incompatible radio sets.[27] Nonetheless, the attack helicopter identified the ground target and carried out a dummy dive as a warning. The FAC delineated the Forward Line of Own Troops and gave explicit details on the disposition of UN ground troops. He also confirmed the absence of friendly troops and civilians in the vicinity of the target area. The attack helicopters assessed the appropriate attack direction, having to keep clear of the line of fire of a FARDC tank and two army vehicles fitted with heavy-calibre automatic weapons, which were sporadically engaging the rebel target. After receiving confirmation from the FAC, the helicopter fired warning shots at the rebel positions. The FAC confirmed that the target was correctly identified. The helicopter then engaged the target during two more passes. The accuracy of the fire was confirmed by the FAC after each pass and the helicopter orbited the target area to carry out a damage assessment.

The helicopter fired again as the government ground troops commenced their assault on the target. This fire had to be accurate because of the forward movement of the FARDC troops. The helicopter carried out a final live pass, engaging the target with four rockets. Henceforth, the proximity of FARDC troops to the target meant no more helicopter attacks could be mounted. Approaching the end of its 1.5 hour flight endurance, the helicopter was replaced on station by another Mi-35. The helicopter crew remarked in its After Mission Report (MONUC 2008c):

> The operation was successful in stopping CNDP advance and stopping their concentration, preparatory to attack on Goma. The AH support was decisive in stopping the FARDC from falling back, boosting their morale and thus

encouraging them to advance and attack the CNDP positions and reclaim lost ground. This was possible due to the co-location of the ground FAC and FARDC officers [so] the operation and the AH support could be coordinated.

The helicopter and ground actions achieved this tactical success, but the CNDP continued its advance from other directions. The next day, 29 October 2008, an Mi-35 was dispatched along the Goma–Rutshuru road. About 10 km north of Goma, the attack helicopter observed DRC troops and army vehicles, including tanks and BMPs,[28] moving in retreat towards Goma. The on-scene commander, again the DCOS, informed the Mi-35 crew by radio that the army was withdrawing after a battle with the rebels. Furthermore, the CNDP rebels were advancing in company strength along the road towards Goma. Both UN and FARDC troops were being fired upon with small arms and mortars from about 2–3 km north of the DCOS position, which also marked the Forward Line of Own Troops. The DCOS approved a helicopter engagement with the CNDP rebel cadre north of his position. The AH pilots identified the positions from which the rebels were firing. After ascertaining that there were no civilians in the area, the attack helicopters engaged them with four 57 mm rockets. The mission report did not give a damage or casualty assessment. The attack helicopter then reconnoitred the area north using the onboard scanners, but could not spot any movement. The DCOS asked for a scan of the Rwandan border for possible military elements. No such elements were located (MONUC 2008e).

The limits of joint and combined jungle warfare were also shown when an Mi-35 sought to engage CNDP elements near Kibumba at the base of the Nyiragongo volcano on 29 October 2008. After hearing reports of fire on FARDC troops, the crew spent 30 minutes scanning the target area with its TV camera, seeking to spot any movement or arms fire. Finally it found seven or eight men approximately 3 km west of the FARDC location moving towards the forest at the base of the volcano. Before engaging, the attack helicopter needed to obtain reassurance that there were no FARDC soldiers in the area. Because the FARDC commander took seven or eight minutes to confirm that the men were of the CNDP rebel cadre, the rebels were able to disappear in the jungle and the attack helicopter lost its ability to track and target them.[29]

The Mi-35 attack helicopters had other limitations as sensor and weapons platforms. They could remain on site for a maximum of 1.5 hours before returning to refuel. They were also limited by poor weather conditions, which sometimes forced them to return early. Nevertheless, in the crucial test of September–November 2008, they proved to be a key enabler to repel aggression. The rebel attack on Goma was thwarted, and the United Nations protected a major population centre, something it had failed to do in other missions. This success served as a lesson of robust peacekeeping.

From the remote jungle of Africa to the dense urban slums of the Caribbean, the United Nations has made progress in the twenty-first century to incorporate some intelligence and advanced technologies into some of its missions.

Haiti: Intelligence-led peacekeeping

The first peacekeeping operation in Haiti, the United Nations Mission in Haiti (UNMIH, 1993–1996), was illustrative of the organization's poor intelligence capacity during the 1990s. UNMIH took over responsibilities from the US-led Multinational Force several months after the end of the Haitian junta. An American officer was appointed as the UN Force Commander, the first time a US officer had held such a role since the Korean War. Being double-hatted as commander of US Forces Haiti and the UN commander, he could oversee the overlap of the two missions' functions, including intelligence. A "U2" (intelligence) position was created in UNMIH to parallel the J2 of US Forces Haiti (J2 being a standard military term for joint services intelligence). Even though the U2 was a US marine officer, the U2–J2 relation proved awkward at first, since the United Nations had no intelligence experience, no technical means, no Standard Operating Procedures and little actual intelligence to offer. A US Army report later remarked that "the United Nations has nothing written or any policy regarding intelligence/information operations" (Center for Army Lessons Learned 1995: para. 2.4).[30]

A decade later, the United Nations was back again in Haiti after President Jean-Bertrand Aristide was ousted in 2004. The new mission was able to learn from earlier UN missions and its own mistakes.[31] In the Haitian slums, where pistol- and machete-wielding gangs dominated the populace through murder, intimidation, extortion and terror, the United Nations Stabilization Mission in Haiti (MINUSTAH) managed after three years to establish law, order and government control by "taking on" the gangs in a series of military and police "search and arrest" operations during 2006–2007. The achievement was made possible by using "intelligence preparation of the environment", a procedure similar to NATO's "intelligence preparation of the battlefield". Intelligence proved to be key in finding and arresting violent criminals. Technology was a considerable aid.

The case shows that human and technological intelligence are complementary. Intelligence remains a controversial and sensitive matter within the United Nations, but in this mission and others in the twenty-first century the organization finally discovered the value of peacekeeping intelligence. After four decades (1950s–1980s) of ignoring and even deriding the concept and a decade of struggling to find a place for it (1990s),[32] the United Nations finally began to systematically include dedicated intelligence bodies in its field missions.[33] In 2006, the United Nations' DPKO adopted a policy that a Joint Mission Analysis Centre (JMAC) and a Joint Operations Centre (JOC) should be established in all peacekeeping operations to conduct all-source information-gathering using military, police and civilian personnel (DPKO 2006a). By that time, several field operations (including MONUC)[34] had already begun to carry out "intelligence-led operations",[35] that is, those driven in timing and objectives by intelligence or to gain intelligence. The operations were sometimes commanded or controlled by one of the intelligence sections of the mission, such as the JMAC or the J2/U2. Such operations enormously improved the capacity of the intelligence-shy United Nations to meet some of its most challenging mandates.

The UN Stabilization Mission in Haiti was one of the pioneers of intelligence-led UN operations in the twenty-first century.[36] This approach allowed the mission to gain ascendancy over the gangs who controlled large sections of several Haitian cities, particularly the capital, Port-au-Prince.

The gangs perpetrated terror and chaos. Politically motivated murders were widespread, and kidnappings, not previously prevalent in Haiti, became increasingly systematic as the gangs targeted the middle and upper classes to extract ransoms. The gangs also set up choke points on main roads, including the strategic Route Nationale 1, to extort bribes from cargo trucks, taxi drivers and motorists. In Cité Soleil, the capital's worst slum, gang leaders controlled food and water distribution to the 300,000 people living there, imposed "taxes" on vendors and terrorized citizens. Hundreds of shots could be heard daily and dead bodies were often found at daybreak. The police had been unable to even enter Cité Soleil to conduct investigations for years. After Jordanian peacekeepers were shot dead in 2005, members of that contingent would not leave their armoured personnel carriers. Heavy gunfire prevented peacekeepers from helping the people they were supposed to protect. In fact, the United Nations could not even secure its own freedom of movement because gang members would fire on UN troops and then escape through a labyrinth of alleys and shacks.

The United Nations challenged the gangs in 2005 by launching operations to overwhelm their strongholds. Though these were successful, the United Nations' efforts were often thwarted by corrupt police who warned the gangs of an impending operation. Accordingly, the operations were not always surgical and there was evidence of collateral damage, which led to complaints by human rights groups. Then, in February and April 2006, the UN-supported elections brought President René Préval to power. He tried to negotiate with the gangs, but they only increased their demands and widened their illegal activities. After many school children were kidnapped and killed in early December 2006, he gave the green light to the United Nations to intervene militarily in gang strongholds.

From December 2006 until March 2007 the United Nations renewed operations against the gangs. This time the United Nations devoted great energy to intelligence-driven planning. This meant acquiring information about gang leaders and their hideouts through a wide variety of means. The United Nations also relied heavily on its enormous advantage at night with image intensifiers and night-sights and concealed its plans from local police until just prior to an operation. The result of this technological and intelligence-oriented approach was that the main gang leaders were arrested in the first few months of 2007. Indeed, after the 9 February 2007 Operation Jauru Sudamericana and the arrest of a number of prominent gang members, gang resistance subsided almost immediately. The United Nations easily established new strong points and started patrolling previously inaccessible routes. Joint patrols by UN and Haitian police and MINUSTAH soldiers secured a previously hostile area. Traffic on Route Nationale 1 flowed freely, no longer obstructed by gang checkpoints set up for the extortion of bribes.

Although Haiti remained a very troubled country, the enormous success of MINUSTAH provided a highly instructive example of how intelligence and technology could aid a UN mission in restoring order, security and the rule of law. What follows is a detailed examination of what technological means and methods of acquiring intelligence were employed by MINUSTAH, and how they led to the success of the mission.

Imagery intelligence

Imagery intelligence was a key tool for MINUSTAH. Photos of the gang members and their leaders assisted in their identification and arrest. During search operations, soldiers and police officers used such photos to screen individuals leaving cordoned-off areas. For instance, in Operation Nazca in the Belecour district practically all the men of working age were stopped by the Brazilian battalion (BRABATT) and United Nations Police (UNPOL) (MINUSTAH 2007a). A dozen suspects were identified and arrested through this dragnet operation.

Aerial imagery allowed MINUSTAH to produce useful intelligence and up-to-date maps. Both JMAC and operational units conducted over-flights. Aerial images were often included in the "target packages" for soldiers and police seeking to apprehend gangsters. Such imagery helped the force determine the best access routes and potential obstacles in the slum of Cité Soleil. From helicopters, gang members were photographed digging ditches to block the advance of the United Nations' armoured personnel carriers. The juxtaposition of "before and after" pictures showed the expansion of such ditches over several days (MINUSTAH 2005: 7). Aerial imagery combined with ground proximity reconnaissance allowed the force engineers to determine, before an operation, the best locations to stockpile sand and stones for filling holes. Imagery could be used to identify any "no-go" or "slow-go" zones for armoured personnel carriers.

Heliborne images also showed a gang member on a rooftop in shooting position with a weapon and a possible spotter at hand. MINUSTAH was able to map out dozens of potential sniper positions using aerial images. Also identified were weapons storage sites, hiding places for the victims of kidnappings, the goods from car jackings, the rebel leaders' bases and dwellings where the leaders were known to sleep.

Because the Force Commander preferred night operations, heliborne reconnaissance was also done at night, probably to the consternation of residents. During one observation flight with night-vision goggles and forward-looking infrared, gang members were seen escaping after firing on a UN patrol. As the bandits withdrew to their base, the United Nations counted about 30 gang members. The escape routes were identified (MINUSTAH 2007b). Several potential hiding places, such as shelters under bridges, were also identified using oblique photography from the air.

During the actual operations, the United Nations usually flew a helicopter at a safe altitude of 500 metres or higher for reconnaissance as well as for command and control. On 9 February 2007, during Operation Jauru Sudamericana, gang members put out white sheets on the streets surrounding their headquarters to indicate surrender, but aerial observers spotted gang members moving into position to fire at UN troops. Some gang members were even donning new clothes (including women's clothes) to provide cover. The ground troops were alerted by the heliborne observers and could avoid the deception of fake surrender and the potential exposure to sniper fire. MINUSTAH did not, however, equip its helicopters with weapons to fire from the air, fearing this might lead to civilian casualties in urban areas.

Signals intelligence

The mission continues to lack a very important source: signals intelligence (SIGINT). This reflects the general hesitation by the United Nations, which has sought to uphold privacy and respect national laws. Still, precedents exist in UN peacekeeping for signals interception, for example in the UN Operation in the Congo (ONUC, 1960–1964). But, given the lack of institutional memory in the world organization, peacekeeping officials were not aware that such intelligence-gathering had been done until it was described in the academic literature. The successor operation in the Congo, MONUC, also employed signals intelligence in 2006–2007 during the operations of its Eastern Division.

For tactical operations in Haiti, the ability to listen to the cell phone calls of gang members would have greatly aided the United Nations' ability to challenge, incriminate and apprehend them. To overcome fear of broad telephone surveillance in the national and international community, the United Nations could in the future limit such monitoring to "tactical SIGINT", meaning the surveillance would be confined to current operations and for specifically approved targets. But UN headquarters has remained sceptical of signals intelligence as a means of information-gathering.

Once having arrested a gang member or seized a gang stronghold, the United Nations could certainly examine seized cell phones to record numbers called and determine the network of associates. This would require deeper analysis, so JMAC later purchased new software (for example, i2 analytical tools) for this purpose.

Since 2007 and following the 2010 earthquake, the gangs in Haiti do not possess the power they once did to rule districts, but they often work perniciously in the drug, crime and kidnapping business. The population remains traumatized by 15–40 monthly kidnappings, including of children. The mission had made this a priority until the January 2010 earthquake. Special equipment could still be of great help. During negotiations with kidnappers, the ability to locate the cell phone transmissions of the latter would be extremely valuable. A means to "triangulate" cell phone signals could help the United Nations and the Haitian National Police to seize hostage-takers and free their victims.

Other technologies

MINUSTAH was probably the first UN force to operate a UAV. The small prototype was in the mission for only a short time, however. When the Brazilian battalion that brought it was rotated out, the UAV was also withdrawn. Still, it proved useful for distributing leaflets. Hundreds of leaflets were dropped over Cité Soleil to inform the population that the United Nations did not seek to harm innocent civilians and that UN operations were aimed solely at defeating the gangs.[37] The UAV did not have a significant observation capacity and was not equipped for night

Figure 7.4 The pod containing the FLIR camera, attached to a Chilean helicopter in MINUSTAH.
Source: Photo by H. Lixenfeld.

observation. Some soldiers suggested that a UAV could be used to draw fire from the bandits, thus exposing their positions (MINUSTAH 2007a).

As mentioned, significant aerial observation was conducted from helicopters. The FLIR deployed in some helicopters was particularly useful to observe gang shooters during night operations. The camera also provided a gyro-stabilized platform to take images during daytime. A view of the pod is shown in Figure 7.4. Hand-held cameras with high zoom also proved useful.

The mission ordered commercial satellite imagery from Ikonos and QuickBird satellites, but the resolution was not better than 1 metre and the supplier (Macdonald-Dettwiler of Canada) would typically take over a month to fill the order. Accordingly, the images were not useful to observe current events. Still, the images allowed the mission's Geographic Information System (GIS) Unit to produce detailed maps for commanders, planners and troops. The walls of many headquarters offices are covered with satellite photos and maps of this kind.

In 2008, the low–medium-cost surveillance and communications project run by DPKO (New York) sought feedback from missions on the

Table 7.3 Cameras and other equipment sought by MINUSTAH

Camera types desired	Other technologies desired	Purposes
• Video/still • CCTV (remote places) • Heliborne • Motion detection • Real-time streaming • Thermal vision (incl. cabling) • Satellite imagery	• Radars for ground surveillance and border control and to see through walls • Frequency scanners • Metal detectors • Chemical (gunpowder) sensors • Fingerprint scanner	• UN perimeter surveillance (e.g. high tower installation) • Patrols of borders and port areas • Border surveillance • Hidden weapons/ammunition and drugs detection

technology they sought. MINUSTAH already had fixed video cameras to protect its premises, though none to monitor hotspots. Remote cameras could potentially provide constant monitoring of one or more blocks from UN checkpoints and of "strong points" in Cité Soleil to view what was approaching. In response to the headquarters survey, the mission identified much desirable equipment, as shown in Table 7.3.

As a result of the low–medium-cost project, the mission purchased surveillance materials for patrols and camp protection at a cost of approximately $75,000. These included 121 cameras, spotlights triggered by remotely installed infrared sensors, 5 infrared cameras, "snake" cameras that permit photography around corners, and related recording devices. Motion sensors, CCTV and acoustic sensors were not procured.

In 2008, the Uruguayan Air Force provided a CASA-212 aircraft equipped with FLIR and a hatch for taking hand-held photographs. In 2009, the mission achieved the capacity to send a signal from the Chilean helicopter camera to MINUSTAH headquarters for real-time viewing in the JOC/JMAC.

The crash of the CASA-212 on 9 October 2009, causing the deaths of all 11 on board, dealt a heavy blow to the mission. The earthquake on 12 January 2010 was even more devastating, with about 100 staff killed, including the Special Representative of the Secretary-General and the acting Police Commissioner. In addition, over 4,000 inmates in Haitian prisons escaped, including notorious gangsters whom MINUSTAH had previously apprehended.

As the United Nations tries to pick up the pieces after the earthquake, direct technological observation could help the mission confirm or refute information provided by informers, thus helping to assess the reliability of the human source. The United Nations has not used radars for either aerial or ground surveillance in Haiti. In 2008, however, the mission did acquire sea–surface radar aboard its CASA-212 aircraft and on marine vessels. It has not employed seismic or acoustic sensors. Most significantly, MINUSTAH has not employed signals interception, as mentioned. In these areas, there is much room for improvement.

Night-time operations

Initially, peacekeeping in Haiti, as elsewhere, was daytime work only. In Cité Soleil in 2004, MINUSTAH would hold its posts only during the day, being forced to leave by nightfall to avoid attacks. Night-vision technologies and intelligence-led operations reversed this practice in 2006. Once the United Nations could spot oncoming threats such as shooters, it could engage them more easily than in daytime, when there were many distractions and a greater chance of collateral damage in busy streets.

This night capacity allowed the Force Commander to run combat operations at night, often starting at 0300 hrs.[38] Sometimes he changed the times to confuse the gangs. The night operations allowed the mission to reduce injuries to innocents and increase the element of surprise. The United Nations could use the cover of darkness, something that bandits had habitually done themselves to support their criminal activities. UN forces gained a huge superiority at night simply by using headgear with image intensifiers and night-sights for rifles, along with infrared devices to detect heat. The gangs were practically blind in comparison, allowing the United Nations to take the initiative at a time and place of its choosing.[39]

During night-time operations, thermal imaging (FLIR) on helicopters provided the UN force with a useful view from above. Liaison officers on board employed image intensifiers (monoculars and binoculars) and described what they saw to ground elements such as troops and UNPOL. Heliborne FLIR also helped identify the hideouts of kidnappers and gang chiefs. In one case in early 2006 the gang leader "Belony" Pierre kidnapped three Filipino businessmen shortly after they had visited MINUSTAH headquarters, releasing them only after a ransom was paid. The victims described to JMAC personnel the physical conditions of their captivity, including the position of a water tank and a specially painted wall. JMAC personnel then determined three probable locations from aerial photographs. Jumping on an FLIR-equipped helicopter to overfly these locations, a JMAC officer was able to positively identify the hideout within 10 minutes. This was an invaluable step in the process that led to the arrest and conviction of the gang leader.

Night-vision equipment (NVE) used by MINUSTAH troops is contingent owned. The quality varies considerably between contingents:[40] the NVE used by the Brazilian battalion in Cité Soleil was of high quality, but most other contingents have not been so well prepared.

Border management

In 2008, the Security Council expanded MINUSTAH's mandate to help the government "address cross-border illicit trafficking of persons, drugs, arms and other illegal activities" and in "protecting and patrolling ... maritime borders" (UN Security Council 2008). The mission acquired maritime patrol boats (Boston Whalers) equipped with marine radars. The radars on the boats have a maximum range of 24 nautical miles but the usual range of the radar will be only 12 nautical miles, depending on the sea state and respective radar scatter.[41]

Large anti-drug operations were staged to catch drug lords, including those operating from small islands off the coast of Haiti. The operations typically involved the orchestration of UNPOL, the Haitian National Police and military components (air, marine and ground forces).

The land border with the Dominican Republic is quite porous and subject to a great deal of illegal trafficking. UN patrols were ineffective in identifying and capturing infiltrators. To better spot and stop illicit trafficking, the mission would be wise to consider using tethered balloons (aerostats). These could be positioned along the border as a means to help demarcate it as well as to observe it. Since such aerostats might well be subject to gunfire, rapid replacement and cheaper cameras might be employed. Alternatively, the aerostats could be raised only at night to fly in a more covert fashion with infrared cameras. ,

MINUSTAH does not have an aerial radar capability to keep track of aircraft passage across Haiti's borders. Neither it nor the Haitian government can observe the cross-border movements of suspicious aircraft, except for what can be seen from the radars at Port-au-Prince airport. This is another border management gap.

Because the United States had a great interest in stopping the flow of drugs through Haiti, the Drug Enforcement Administration, a component of the US Department of Justice, provided MINUSTAH with information on possible drug-carrying planes landing in Haiti. This information was often gained from aerial tracking radars based in Florida. But the warning rarely came early enough to allow the UN troops to reach the unofficial landing points, of which there are many, to carry out an interception.[42] Were the United Nations to have its own aerial surveillance radar, it would probably have more success in apprehending smugglers.

Intelligence analysis, sharing and products

Although JMAC has some excellent all-source analysts, there remains a lack of more technical analysis in the mission. For instance, there are no air imagery interpreters. One suggestion is that one or more troop contributors be sought to provide air picture analysts.

In 2006–2007, the crucial JMAC intelligence "products" for anti-gang operations were the target packages. These included personal information on the leaders to assist with their arrest, including the locations where (and with whom) they met and slept. JMAC attempted to assess the gangs' strengths and weaknesses, as well as their tactics, intentions and capabilities. Vulnerability analysis backed up proactive arrests.

In addition to target packages, other JMAC intelligence products are: the weekly intelligence briefing for the Special Representative of the Secretary-General, the weekly intelligence summary, and threat assessments for VIP visits and electoral processes. The JMAC's weekly assessments in 2006–2007 "laid the foundation against the gangs" (Dziedzic and Perito 2008: 8). The documents offered a "unified situation analysis" drawing from military contingents, police officers, civil affairs, UN security, political advisers and others. JMAC also developed long-term strategic assessments and other products for the senior managers, as needed or requested for decision-making.

As in all peacekeeping operations, MINUSTAH produces situation reports (Sitreps) daily and weekly for New York, as well as flash reports on more urgent matters. During the 2006–2007 operations, New York requested the mission to produce after-action reviews, especially as it had to assess how far the mission should go in the use of force, a delicate subject in the halls of the UN headquarters. Press releases were sometimes issued after major operations, particularly the successful ones.[43]

The mission, like the United Nations more generally, has not made the jump from cartography to GIS. Useful data that can be geo-referenced could be placed in a GIS database with access in JMAC and JOC and other appropriate units. But the mission is not making use of the huge commercial advances in databases linked to GIS. Especially since the 2010 earthquake, the mission has the need for an additional set of surveillance tools.

Bosnia: From United Nations to NATO

When we use our night-vision equipment with our thermal imager and distance finder, we actually turn night into day. We like operating at night, because our special equipment gives us a great advantage.

Sgt First Class Mark Overhaart, Recce Platoon,
NATO Stabilization Force, Bosnia, 1999[44]

The United Nations experienced its baptism by fire in multidimensional peacekeeping during the conflict in the former Yugoslavia. The United Nations Protection Force (UNPROFOR) operated from 1991 to 1995 in the midst of fierce fighting, ethnic cleansing and brutal massacres by Serb, Muslim and Croat forces, particularly in Bosnia. The UN mission suffered some of the most infamous failures in UN history for its inability to prevent attacks on United Nations Protected Areas and on the people it was mandated to protect. In the town of Srebrenica, about 8,000 Bosniak men and boys were executed between 12 and 22 July 1995, just days after UNPROFOR troops withdrew in the face of Bosnian Serb threats. UNPROFOR was the largest UN operation up to that time, with over 40,000 personnel at its peak. It employed ground forces from nations with advanced militaries (for example, European countries and Canada, but not the United States), although they were deployed in a traditional peacekeeping posture. UNPROFOR was still poorly equipped for the monumental tasks it was given by the UN Security Council.

In principle, UNPROFOR had complete freedom of movement, but in practice the warring factions set up many obstacles, checkpoints and road blocks that made important areas unobservable. Although aerial reconnaissance was carried out by NATO planes and US drones (Predator UAVs flown from Albania), most of the information and imagery was not shared with the UN operation. Selected US satellite imagery was provided, however, to UN officers who were from NATO countries. Ironically, UN superior officers not from NATO countries were not allowed access, so their subordinates could not share the imagery with them.

The Canadian forces felt a need to deploy additional weapons and equipment to the dangerous mission, well above what the United Nations requested and covered. If only for self-protection, they brought tripod-mounted thermal imagers and night-vision (starlight) goggles but lacked a mobile, vehicle-mounted thermal imager. To compensate, the forces improvised by taking the night-vision sites from TOW anti-tank missile launchers and used them to monitor the movements of the combatants. Furthermore, to conduct night patrols of the zone of separation between Croatian and Serb-Krajina forces, the Canadians put the thermal imagers on their armoured personnel carriers: the M113 carrying TOW Under Armour (TUA).[45] One commentator (Koch 1995: 23) wrote:

> While highly effective at deterring and halting armed incursions by both sides, and at times even breaking up firefights, the necessity of using the battalion's highest-value single asset, the TUA, mounted on its least-reliable platform, the M113, starkly demonstrates to me the equipment shortage.[46]

After many trials and unsuccessful cease-fire agreements, the Dayton Peace Agreement finally brought a durable peace to Bosnia in December 1995. NATO replaced the United Nations as the provider of forces for the peacekeeping operation, or peace support operation in NATO terminology.

NATO's new Implementation Force (IFOR) for the Dayton Agreement learned from the UNPROFOR experience, especially from the mission's failures. IFOR took a much more robust approach towards the former warring factions and deployed a far greater level of force, equipment, intelligence and technology (Schmitt 1995). One analyst described the modus operandi (Wentz 1997: 57; emphasis added):

> Upon arrival in country, IFOR made it very clear to the FWF [former warring factions] at the outset that [it was] different than UNPROFOR and [was] there to enforce compliance with the Dayton Accord, using force if necessary. Checkpoints were bulldozed, roadblocks were shut down, and the FWF equipment and forces placed in cantonment areas and barracks. On 19 February 1996, COMIFOR [Commander IFOR] held a meeting of the Joint Military Commission on board the USS George Washington aircraft carrier. COMIFOR stated that the reason for having the meeting on board the "Spirit of Freedom" was to give the leaders of the FWF a display of the firepower the United States was prepared to use in the enforcement of the Dayton Peace Accord. IFOR's tremendous military firepower was certainly a major deterrent but the military also put a lot of faith in the deterrent power of "*information dominance*". IFOR, through its intelligence operation (supported by significant national contributions, especially from the United States), was able to make it clear to the FWF that *they could monitor them any time of the day or night* and under all weather conditions. The ability to see, understand the situation, and strike with precision no doubt had its effect in deterring aggressive actions on the part of the FWF and maintaining the peace during the IFOR operation.

To achieve "information dominance", the new NATO mission came with a set of monitoring and intelligence-gathering assets unprecedented for peace operations. The aerial surveillance component employed a fleet of diverse aircraft. Apache and Kiowa helicopters provided imagery from video cameras that relayed images automatically to command posts within 90 seconds, a feature not possible with the United Nations' Mi-35 helicopters in the DRC. In addition, the NATO helicopters had thermal radiation (infrared) sensors capable of monitoring troop movements several kilometres away. Aerial surveillance was also achieved with high-altitude U-2 aircraft, P-3 Maritime Patrol aircraft and the RC-135 reconnaissance aircraft. Perhaps most significantly, the sophisticated Joint Surveillance and Target Attack Radar System aircraft provided high-resolution imagery of the ground, including synthetic aperture radar (SAR) images both day and night and in virtually all weather conditions. SAR in the Doppler mode was especially effective at detecting moving targets.

UAVs gathered signals intelligence and provided imagery in near real-time. For instance, a Predator UAV was able to display the faces of people opposing US entry into the town of Han Pijesak. Ground units deployed their own shorter-range UAVs such as the US Army's Pioneer UAV. Remote video terminals allowed soldiers deployed across the mission area not only to view UAV imagery but also to control the onboard camera angle and zoom in order to "zero-in" on desired objects and people.

Complete awareness of the airspace was achieved with Airborne Warning and Control System (AWACS) aircraft. NATO's E-3A Sentry is the "world's only integrated, multi-national flying unit, providing rapid deployability, airborne surveillance, command, control and communication for NATO operations" (NATO 2010a). All flying objects within a radius of over 300 km could be tracked: a single AWACS aircraft could monitor the entire Bosnian airspace.

Troops deployed ground surveillance radar (GSR) to observe both the day and night movements of people to a distance of 10 km and vehicles to 15 km. The GSR was used for desired areas, cantonment sites, intersections and the perimeters of IFOR camps. It was usually positioned in high areas providing a long line of sight for early warning.

The ground troops also deployed ground sensors from the Remotely Monitored Battlefield Sensor System (REMBASS). This provided early warning and compliance data on the former warring factions, including their withdrawal from zones of separation. Like ground surveillance radar, REMBASS was also used for perimeter security of IFOR camps and strategic locations. But, rather than radar, the system employed hand-placed sensors to determine the direction of moving objects. The components of the system, as shown in Figure 7.5, included:

(1) magnetic sensors (for detection of vehicles and personnel carrying ferrous metal such as rifles);
(2) seismic sensors (for detection of targets and their classification as unknown, wheeled vehicle, tracked vehicle or personnel);
(3) passive infrared sensors (for both vehicles and personnel);
(4) radio repeaters (to extend the broadcast range of radio messages from anti-intrusion sensors);
(5) sensor monitoring sets (a dual channel receiver with a permanent hard copy recorder and a temporary visual display);
(6) radio-frequency monitors (to receive, process and display sensor ID codes and detection/classification messages).

To support the array of technologies, US Army Materiel Command established the Bosnia Technology Integration Cell at the start of the mission. It was a "clearinghouse for critical technologies and the 'nerve centre' for tracking and integrating the technology community's efforts to support US soldiers in Bosnia" (Wentz 1997: 367). In addition to surveillance technologies, the Cell also dealt with anti-mine, anti-sniper and

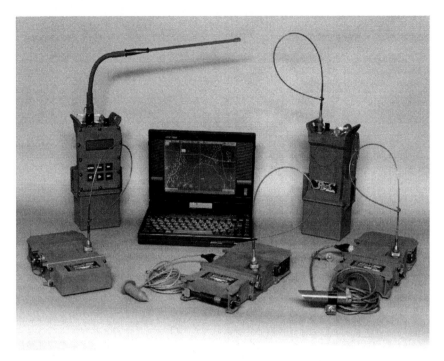

Figure 7.5 Ground sensor ("Improved REMBASS") system components.
Source: L3-communications Systems, used with permission.
Notes: The system has three detectors (shown at the front, left-to-right): magnetic, seismic, and infrared. In the back row are (left-to-right): a hand-held monitor, a laptop computer for programming and display, and a signal repeater. Modern sensor systems are continually becoming smaller and more sophisticated.

communications technologies. The mission could also rely on longstanding NATO bodies specializing in advanced technology, for example the laboratory at the NATO Consultation, Command and Control Agency (NC3A) and its testing establishment at The Hague for prototyping and system integration testing, as well as a 24/7 "Cronos" help desk.

IFOR did experience technological setbacks such as UAV crashes owing to failures of an engine, generator, rocket-assisted launcher and an onboard computer (Wentz 1997: 104). But the purposely redundant system provided a steady stream of information from technologies that helped NATO soldiers gain "information dominance" in order to keep the peace.

When the Stabilization Force (SFOR) took over from IFOR after a year, it built upon the intelligence infrastructure. NATO countries ensured their soldiers were equipped with their best surveillance "kits".

Canada deployed a half-dozen Coyote reconnaissance (recce) vehicles, which had entered into service in 1996 with an impressive suite of sensors. A third-generation thermal infrared camera and a state-of-the-art ground radar were mounted on an extendable mast that could rise to 7 metres. The cameras could allegedly "read the name of a soldier on his uniform within a 6 km range" and the radar could "see a man walking within 24 km" (Thomas 2001). Soldiers from the armoured reconnaissance squadron who saw suspicious movements would call on patrols to spring into action.

The success of the Coyote recce vehicle in NATO missions in Bosnia, and subsequently in Macedonia and Kosovo, encouraged Canada to deploy it to a new UN operation in Africa in 2001. The United Nations Mission in Ethiopia and Eritrea (UNMEE) was tasked with ensuring that these two countries withdrew their forces from a disputed area and a wider temporary security zone at the end of a particularly brutal war. The Coyote's sensor suite, shown on the front cover of this book, helped maintain a 24-hour vigil. Canadian soldiers were able to watch hundreds of soldiers from opposing sides tear down reinforced concrete defences at the front-lines, mostly under the cover of darkness. At points on the former battlefront, the opposing encampments were separated by only 300 metres. Walls of volcanic rock had been constructed 1–2 metres high, topped with "'rock-made' silhouettes matching the size and shape of soldiers" to deceive the opposing side. Now they were moving the rock materials to new defensive positions in the rear (Oberwarth 2001). With the advanced observation technology, the United Nations was better able to prevent possible fire-fights between the sides. The mobile recce units identified heavy weapons in the security zone and confronted intruders. The sides would often send soldiers into "no-man's land" to establish "listening posts" to provide early warnings of any enemy movements at night. Coyote vehicles were also stationed on the front-lines to observe any traffic attempting to skirt UN checkpoints or moving out of towns being inspected by UN soldiers. In addition, the surveillance suites could detect raiders moving into abandoned villages seeking booty or UN camps seeking food. The mission had unprecedented means to spot violations of the peace accords and to confirm each force's withdrawal. One Canadian soldier commented (Oberwarth, 2001):

[S]ince neither side knew or understood the capabilities of the surveillance suite, it forced them to be up-front and honest with our soldiers on the line. Neither force would conduct any activity around our checkpoints without notifying our soldiers of what their intentions were for fear that we may see them and disapprove. This relationship allowed us to curb any planned activities that may lead to a renewal of hostilities.

Table 7.4 NATO bodies mandated to enhance military technology

Agencies
Airborne Early Warning and Control Programme Management Organisation
   (NAPMO)
Air Command and Control System Management Agency (NACMA)
Communication and Information Systems Services Agency (NCSA)
Communications and Information Systems School (NCISS)
Consultation, Command and Control Agency (NC3A)
EF 2000 and Tornado Development Production and Logistics Management
   Agency (NETMA)
HAWK[a] Management Office (NHMO)
Helicopter Design and Development Production and Logistics Management
   Agency (NAHEMA)
Insensitive Munitions Information Centre (NIMIC)
Maintenance and Supply Agency (NAMSA)
Medium Extended Air Defence System Design and Development, Production
   and Logistics Management Agency (NAMEADSMA)
Military Agency for Standardization (MAS)
Military Telecommunications and CIS Agencies
Naval Forces Sensor and Weapon Accuracy Check Sites (FORACS)
Research & Technology Organisation (RTO)

Military advisory groups and committees
Air Command and Control System (ACCS)
Air Defence Committee (NADC)
Air Defence Study Working Group
Air Traffic Management Committee (NATMC)
Central European Pipeline Management Organisation (CEPMO)
Committee for Standardization (NCS)
Committee of the Chiefs of Military Medical Services in NATO (COMEDS)
Committee on the Challenges of Modern Society (CCMS)
Conference of National Armaments Directors (CNAD)
Consultation, Command and Control Board (NC3B)
Consultation, Command and Control Organisation (NC3O)
Electronic Warfare Advisory Committee (NEWAC)
Euro-Atlantic Disaster Response Coordination Centre (EADRCC)
Group of National C3 Representatives (NC3REPS)
Industrial Advisory Group (NIAG)
Information and Systems Management Service (ISMS)
Infrastructure Committee
Maintenance and Supply Organization (NAMSO)
Military Committee Meteorological Group (MCMG)
Pipeline System (NPS)
Research and Technology Board (RTB)
SACLANT Undersea Research Centre (SACLANTCEN)
Science Committee
Senior Civil Emergency Planning Committee (SCEPEC)
Senior NATO Logisticians' Conference (SNLC)
Senior Resource Board (SRB)
SHAPE Technical Centre (STC)
SNLC Movement and Transportation Group (M&TG)

Table 7.4 (cont.)

Standardization Organisation (NSO)
Training Group (NTG)
NATO Secretariat Divisions
Infrastructure, Logistics and Civil Emergency Planning Division
Scientific and Environmental Affairs Division
Scientific Adviser to the Secretary-General

Source: NATO (2005).
Notes: Even this extensive listing is not comprehensive – it does not include some important subcommittees and subsidiary organs or a plethora of NATO equipment depots. Many of the listed bodies are officially prefixed by the word "NATO", as indicated in the abbreviations, but it is omitted here.
[a] HAWK is a surface-to-air missile system.

The robust recce vehicles provided the United Nations with unmatched situational awareness within the UN-mandated zone and helped the mission enforce the terms of the peace treaty (Veterans Affairs Canada 2006). Though few in number, the half-dozen Coyotes showed their worth in the Horn of Africa after their earlier successes in the Balkans.

More generally, the success of NATO operations in the Balkans encouraged the United Nations to take a more robust approach to its peace operations. The need was evident from the stark contrast between the experiences of IFOR and SFOR relative to the poorly equipped UNPROFOR. After a decade of NATO forces in Bosnia, the situation was stabilized to such an extent that NATO could turn over the residual peacekeeping tasks to a European Union Force in 2005. Although the United Nations cannot hope to be as well equipped as NATO, the benefits of robust surveillance platforms to assist peacekeepers in difficult conflict zones were demonstrated by NATO and can continue to serve as a model.

Behind the NATO operation stood a vast military technology infrastructure, including over 40 NATO agencies, institutes and standing committees. The list in Table 7.4 includes bodies involved in research and development and in technology procurement, maintenance, standardization and support. By contrast, the United Nations has only the Communications section in the DFS. Since the Communications section already dealt with sophisticated communications technologies, other technologies, such as night-vision and GPS devices, were also placed under its responsibility. In the future, the United Nations may want to enter into agreements with NATO to make use of some of its technological organizations to enhance peacekeeping.

Notes

1. The only case of a traditional peacekeeping force being created after the end of the Cold War was in Ethiopia and Eritrea where the mission (UNMEE, 2000–2008) separated the two armies after a fierce interstate war (1998–2000).
2. This case draws heavily from a draft paper developed by H. Peter Langille and A. Walter Dorn (Langille and Dorn 2011). Dr Langille served as a consultant and research associate on the Monitoring Technology Project that helped make this book possible. His assistance and the UNAMID case-study drafting are gratefully acknowledged.
3. This claim about Darfur was first made on 5 December 2003 by UN Under-Secretary-General for Humanitarian Affairs and Emergency Relief Coordinator Jan Egeland. See UN News Centre (2003).
4. One authority, Eric Reeves (2009: 152–182), estimates in excess of 450,000 civilian deaths between 2003 and 2006 from the Darfur crisis.
5. For example, the ground movement time between the Mission HQ in El Fasher and the Sector HQ in El Geneina is three days; between El Geneina and Al Daein it is two days and between El Fasher and Tine it is three days.
6. Sudan blocked UN patrols on 42 separate occasions in the first 11 months of 2009, according to UN reports.
7. The unreliability of the consent of the parties and frequent violations of the SOFA are repeatedly referred to in the Secretary-General's reports on UNAMID. See, for example, UN Secretary-General (2008c: 7).
8. Personal interview by Dr Peter Langille with an anonymous official in the UN DPKO, 2009.
9. It proved difficult to document the specific surveillance and monitoring systems in the UNAMID mission for several reasons, according to researcher Peter Langille. Firstly, UN officials from different departments and offices provide contrasting accounts. Secondly, people in DPKO have legitimate concerns about sharing relatively sensitive information on aspects of UNAMID. Disclosure might be damaging. Experience has provided no basis to establish trust in the host nation or other belligerents. Finally, this apparent gap between capacity and need must be a source of extreme frustration, even embarrassment, to those working for the United Nations.
10. Specific types of night-vision device listed by UNAMID for the low–medium-cost project were: monocular for patrol teams and sentries, helmet-mounted for vehicle driving, weapons-mounted for sites, thermal imaging for long-range patrols, convoys and force protection.
11. Through UNSAS, the United Nations solicits conditional pledges from member states to contribute specific resources within agreed response times. The UNSAS provides DPKO with a list of national assets that may be available. In principle, this allows DPKO to find resources more quickly and allows member states to respond more quickly and precisely when they receive UN requests. In practice, however, member states have not lived up to their commitments and the UNSAS list is outdated.
12. The COE arrangement allows for the leasing of national military equipment for the duration of the nation's deployment to a specific UN operation.
13. The "Google Earth" program can be downloaded free from <http://www.google.com/intl/en_uk/earth/index.html> (accessed 7 January 2011). The Darfur map can be found under the heading "United States Holocaust Memorial Museum: Crisis in Darfur" at <http://earth.google.com/intl/en_uk/outreach/cs_darfur.html> (accessed 7 January 2011). For other information, see <http://earth.google.com/outreach/cs_darfur.html> (accessed 7 January 2011).

14. The "CNN effect" demonstrated the influence of the camera on both crisis awareness and peace operations. It is also noteworthy that the most influential pictures of the conflict in Darfur were taken by a US cease-fire monitor working with the African Union force, former Marine Captain Brian Steddle. His photos captured international attention on his return from Darfur in 2005. They document a variety of war crimes and remain within an exhibit at the US Holocaust Memorial Museum. Available at <http://www.ushmm.org/genocide/take_action/gallery/video> (accessed 13 January 2011).

15. This ambush on a UNAMID Protection Force convoy of 14 vehicles occurred about 100 km south-east of El Fasher near the village of Umm Hakibah. Various reports point to the attack being a joint operation of Sudanese armed forces and the Janjaweed. For example, see Reeves (2008).

16. For purposes of illustration solely, a complete CCTV system for a residence (including four outdoor cameras with night vision, four indoor cameras with motion detection, an eight-channel security observation system with internet remote viewing, and monitor) can be purchased for under $1,000. A larger 48-camera kit designed for a school may cost approximately $15,000. A single outdoor camera that provides high-resolution colour images over 100 metres and night vision (image intensification) at 100 metres may cost approximately $500. Naturally, costs rise with higher-quality images and if systems are hardened (ruggedized) for security purposes.

17. Quoted in Dorn and Bell (1995).

18. MONUC had, on 30 April 2010, a strength of 20,819 uniformed personnel consisting of 1,223 police (mostly in "formed police units", in which police officers arrive in pre-formed national units rather than as individual appointments), 712 military observers and 18,884 troops. It also had 991 international civilian personnel, 2,749 local civilian staff and 634 United Nations Volunteers (see <http://www.un.org/en/peacekeeping/missions/monuc/facts.shtml>, accessed 13 January 2011). The total number of personnel is approximately 25,000. Only UNAMID was larger. The number of military in MONUSCO decreased in 2010, and the future of the mission is in question because of the DRC government's call for its withdrawal.

19. The Security Council requested MONUC "to inspect, without notice as it deems necessary, the cargo of aircraft and of any transport vehicle using the ports, airports, airfields, military bases and border crossings in North and South Kivu and in Ituri" and authorized the mission to seize illegal arms and related materiel (Resolution 1593 of 12 March 2004, supplementing Resolution 1493 of 28 July 2003).

20. Summary of Peacekeeping Best Practices study, DPKO Intranet, 30 November 2006.

21. The Military Planning Division recommended the establishment of a "Technical Assessment Mission" on 23 July 2004. The Joint Assessment Mission visited the DRC from 11 to 19 April 2005. It was composed of representatives from DPKO and several troop-contributing countries. DPKO (2005b).

22. To fight against the militia in Ituri or elsewhere such data would be essential for military operational planning. "The Board recognizes that neither the staff of the Brigade nor the battalion were organized to conduct such Intelligence analyses. Furthermore, MONUC sources of information are very limited and do not have any early warning or air surveillance capacity to gather information" (MONUC 2005).

23. The request was advertised by the UN Procurement Division (MONUC 2007).

24. MONUC leaders felt the firm Airscan, which had earlier approached them to provide such a service, would have been satisfactory, but the firm was deemed non-compliant in New York because some of its services had been used by governments in South America and Africa in conjunction with human rights abuses (see International Labor

Rights Forum, <http://www.laborrights.org/end-violence-against-trade-unions/colombia/news/11403>, accessed 13 January 2011; also see O'Brien 1998).

25. MONUC After Mission Reports for Mi-35 activities in 2006 and 2008 were provided to me by the mission with the permission of the Chief of Staff Forward.

26. Despite firing 28 rocket projectiles at the dug-in CNDP forces, the attack helicopter still found itself under persistent counter-fire. It seemed only a direct hit on the trench could cause attrition. The crew reported (MONUC 2008b): "CNDP cadre never moved out of the trenches and continued to direct steady, controlled and disciplined counter fire at AH till the very last. This is indicative of the minimal effect that AH firing could achieve against militiamen that were well dug in. This needs to be considered in the planning of subsequent operations, especially when viewed in conjunction with the vulnerability of AH to ground fire in such circumstances and the counter productive effect of AH being hit."

27. The attack helicopter crew later suggested that the ground troops be provided with intercom sets for direct communication with the attack helicopter, since this is normally a mandatory requirement for the attack helicopter when it seeks to provide fire support to ground forces. In another sortie, the attack helicopter had to communicate with ground forces via a UN Lama helicopter that was also in the area.

28. The BMP (Boyevaya Mashina Pekhoty) is a Russian-made infantry fighting vehicle, combining the features of an armoured personnel carrier and a light tank.

29. Even though it had lost sight of the confirmed CNDP fighters, the attack helicopter fired in their general area repeatedly with 28 rockets. The success of these shots could not be ascertained owing to thick vegetation in the area. The crew remarked in the After Mission Report: "A golden opportunity to engage CNDP cadre in the open and thus helping stem their advance was lost due to the long channel of communication between on-scene Cdr [commander] and AH." It also recommended that, as far as possible, the commander should be on-scene "to provide accurate and timely intelligence and guidance to AH" (MONUC 2008d).

30. By contrast, the J2 of the US Forces Haiti created a Sensitive Compartmented Information Facility, used a Multispectral Imagery processor and benefited from the Joint Deployment Intelligence Support System for assessments and operational planning. By contrast, the United Nations had "the human eyeball".

31. This case draws heavily from my paper in the journal *Intelligence and National Security* (Dorn 2009).

32. See Smith (1994) and Dorn (1999).

33. See, for instance, Ekpe (2007); Shetler-Jones (2008).

34. In MONUC, for example, the G2 (army intelligence) at the regional (Eastern Division) headquarters in 2006 was given control over the movements of soldiers in the field tasked to obtain information about dangerous rebel groups hiding in the jungle (personal observation while on a visit to MONUC, Kisangani, December 2006).

35. The term "intelligence-led operations" originated within the policing community ("intelligence-led policing") in the 1990s.

36. The United Nations Interim Administration Mission in Kosovo was another twenty-first-century mission that pioneered intelligence-led operations, especially to deter, target or capture the "spoilers" of the peace process and criminal elements. See Lovelock (2005: 144).

37. This UAV was shot in its wing with one round while dropping leaflets at low elevation, but it was not seriously damaged. In Operation Humaitá of 31 January, 400 pamphlets were launched in four over-flights of the Bois Neuf neighbourhood (BRABATT situation report, 31 January 2007). One of the flyers used by MINUSTAH was directed at gang members: "IF YOU ARE ARMED, SHOW YOURSELF AND HAND

OVER YOUR WEAPONS. TURN YOURSELF IN. YOUR RIGHTS WILL BE RESPECTED."

38. Personal interview with Major General Carlos dos Santos Cruz, Force Commander, at MINUSTAH Headquarters, Christopher Hotel, Port-au-Prince, 18 December 2008.

39. In some night operations in Haiti, a clear view of the surroundings was needed, if only briefly, so illumination grenades launched from 81 mm mortars were sometimes used, especially at the start of an operation.

40. The evolution of NVE has resulted in four generations of technology. Typically, a person can be "seen" on a full moon night at the following ranges (metres): 1st generation – 250; 2nd generation – 500; 3rd generation – 650; and 4th generation – 725. Generations 3 and 4 typically require export licences. In MINUSTAH, night-vision goggles were from Lunos (Gen II and III tubes), Litton M 972 (Gen II+, developed in the late 1980s), New Noga Light, N-Vision Optics GT 14 and Leica Vector. Night-sights for weapons included Raytheon NightSight, Litton M994, OIP Sensor Systems IRBIS (6X) and Simard KN252.

41. The Raymarine C70 radar package includes a multifunction display and RD218 radar scanners (2 or 4 kW). Adding a GPS option allows for radar navigation and on-screen maps. Radar target tracking is possible and sonar devices allow for underwater scanning. The package costs less than $3,000.

42. Personal interview with the Chilean Commander, Cap Haitien, 21 December 2008.

43. Examples of UN press releases: "In notorious area of Haitian capital, UN troops clear house used by gang members", 24 January 2007; "UN peacekeepers launch large-scale operation against criminal gangs", 9 February 2007; "Haiti: UN peacekeepers extend crackdown on criminal gangs", March 2007; "So far in 2007, more than 400 gangsters seized in UN-backed crackdown in Haiti", 27 March 2007 (available through the UN News Centre, <http://www.un.org/apps/news/>, accessed 13 January 2011).

44. Quoted in Paulsen (1999).

45. TOW stands for tube-launched, optically-tracked and wire-guided missile system.

46. The article also describes the tripod-mounted thermal imagers: "The eight-power NODLR [Night Observation Device, Long Range, with 8× magnification] clearly identifies vehicles and humans at distances up to 2,000 metres. Its only drawback is the noise from its cooling system, which makes silent observation and listening difficult" (Koch 1995: 23).

8

Current UN standards: Starting from near zero

Simply put, the scale and complexity of peacekeeping today are mismatched with existing capabilities.... New peacekeeping tasks demand new equipment, from night vision and modern communication equipment, to naval vessels. The UN also needs access to new technologies for better situational awareness in the field.

DPKO and DFS (2009: iii, 32)

The UN Department of Peacekeeping Operations (DPKO) and the UN Department of Field Support (DFS), which authored the "New Horizon" study quoted above, have become aware of the technology deficit in the field. At the urging of troop-contributing nations, they sought an evaluation of past, present and future capabilities, which resulted, in part, in the research for this book.

The review of UN history showed that only some missions have used some advanced technologies, usually when they are brought by developed nations. These rare examples were examined in the previous two chapters. Only a small number of simpler monitoring technologies are in regular use. Night-vision devices (NVDs) are present in many missions, but only as short-range image intensifiers, usually of an older (second) generation. The United Nations does not systematically deploy thermal imagers, which are needed for field missions to operate effectively at night. Some technologies that are ubiquitous in the civilian world, such as digital cameras, Global Positioning System (GPS) devices and "Google Earth", have found a regular place in peace operations, but only in a simple form, rarely linked to multi-user databases. The lesson from the

Keeping watch: Monitoring, technology and innovation in UN peace operations, Dorn, United Nations University Press, 2011, ISBN 978-92-808-1198-8

North Atlantic Treaty Organization (NATO) missions in Bosnia is that the potential for technology use is literally sky-high. It is worthwhile to examine the nature of the technology deficit from which UN peace-keeping currently suffers.

The monitoring technology gap

The monitoring technology gap is of several dimensions. First, there is a gap between UN mandates and UN means. The organization's important, ambitious mandates are too often unachieved or underachieved because of the lack of monitoring capabilities, among other reasons. Particularly for the protection of civilians, sanctions enforcement, border surveillance and nation-building, UN missions are under-equipped with the tools needed to cover large territories at a minimum level of disruption to civilian activities. Some missions, such as those in the Democratic Republic of the Congo (DRC) and Darfur, are responsible for vast areas with only a small number of UN personnel. Regular wide-area surveillance by aircraft is greatly needed. Yet this need has not been met in either of these missions, or indeed in any other, although the UN mission in the DRC (MONUC) has some short-range capability (for example, Mi-35 helicopters). In conflict zones with long porous borders that facilitate the smuggling of guns, drugs and illegal resources, border monitoring and control have been mandated. But standard border surveillance technologies, such as aerial observation and ground radars, are not provided to UN missions. Chapter 3 highlighted the need for UN surveillance at night when most violations, atrocities and illegal trafficking occur. However, only a few missions have successfully broken the night barrier. Long-range night-vision and radar technologies are still lacking in almost all UN missions.

The monitoring technology gap is also characterized by a large divergence in the capabilities of different troop-contributing countries (TCCs). A few nations deploy to UN operations with their own surveillance technologies, considered by them as "standard kit", but most arrive with barely enough to receive reimbursement under the United Nations' list of necessary equipment, that is, self-sustainment in the "observation" and "identification" categories under the United Nations' Contingent-Owned Equipment (COE) system. Moreover, the United Nations' COE standards are ill defined and the night-vision specifications are reached by few contingents. The standards for night vision had to be lowered in most missions; otherwise most contingents would have failed to get any reimbursement in the category. The result is that a few contingents with advanced technologies cover their areas of responsibility more efficiently than other contingents do theirs. Closing the gap, especially between contingents from the developing and developed world, also entails better training and equipping. It means procuring more UN-owned equipment and deploying selected surveillance systems on a force-wide basis. Moreover, it means gaining experience. For instance, the United Nations should start to make night observation and patrols standard in most missions.

Some developed nations insist that they will deploy their troops to the field only when they are equipped with their "standard kits" required for force protection, including monitoring technologies such as radars. Unless the United Nations understands, appreciates and utilizes these capabilities, developed nations will be disinclined to participate in UN operations, viewing them as under-equipped and unnecessarily risky. A United Nations that is better able to demonstrate situational awareness and technological competence will be more enticing to developed as well as developing contributors.

The United Nations also experiences a monitoring technology gap in relation to some of its partners, regional organizations and the agencies with which it cooperates. The European Union (EU) and NATO, both well equipped, have deployed forces in cooperation with the United Nations in the past. In Bosnia, for instance, NATO worked closely with the United Nations both before and after the 1995 Dayton Peace Agreement. Currently, the organizations work together in Kosovo and, to some extent, in Afghanistan. In the DRC, a European Union Force assisted the United Nations during the country's successful 2006 elections. In each of these cases, assistance included sophisticated aerial reconnaissance, including from unmanned aerial vehicles (UAVs). But a smooth operational interface with the United Nations was not achieved in those missions, in part because of the United Nations' lack of technological prowess, especially in image analysis and processing.

In some missions, a monitoring technology gap exists between the United Nations and the parties and forces it seeks to monitor. Some conflicting parties have better technology than the UN watchkeepers for keeping watch. For instance, in Namibia in April 1989, the South African forces employed much better night-vision equipment than the United Nations, which contributed to the United Nations' unawareness of the extent of the incursion of guerrilla (SWAPO/PLAN[1]) fighters from Angola into Namibia. This ignorance allowed South African politicians to raise an exaggerated alarm and seize the initiative at the expense of an embarrassed United Nations. Hundreds of guerrillas were killed. During "Operation Storm", launched by Croatia against the self-proclaimed Serb Republic of Krajina in 1995, aerial surveillance by US drones allowed the Croatian army to aim artillery near UN positions in an attempt to stop the disadvantaged UN peacekeepers from preventing or even observing the ethnic cleansing that was occurring around them.[2] In Georgia, the UN mission was not able to get a real-time picture of events during the Russian advance of August 2008, despite the mission's requests to obtain UAVs, which both sides of the conflict possessed. In Haiti, a few gangs and drug groups possessed better night-vision equipment than the United Nations. In the "cat and mouse" game, the mouse is all too often better equipped and so can evade detection.

In summary, the United Nations' technological gap is of several dimensions: between its ambitious mandates and its modest means,[3] between the developed and developing world contributors (the latter forming the significant majority), between the United Nations and some of its partner organizations, and between the United Nations and some of the parties it is assigned to monitor. Most importantly, the gap reveals the inadequacy of the United Nations in protecting its own staff and carrying out effective operations. The world organization needs the ability to provide early warning of attacks in sufficient time to prevent or mitigate them.

Although the monitoring technology gap remains large and is growing, especially as technology advances at a rapid pace, there are positive signs. The United Nations has shown it has the ability to deal with some high tech. Its communications systems are advanced and impressive, especially given the difficult local conditions and remote areas to which the United Nations deploys. For monitoring technology, there are some recent precedents on which to build. The force in Lebanon has deployed several sophisticated radars for both air and ground surveillance. The mission in Cyprus has installed video cameras in six hotspots between conflicting parties. And the Haiti mission has heliborne cameras that transmit imagery in real time to mission headquarters. The mission in the DRC has attack helicopters with advanced observation for target acquisition. These innovations are slowly helping the United Nations to gain experience and knowledge, which deserves to be documented and studied.

The technology gap in the field has been caused in part by UN headquarters, where little attention has been paid to the issue. Moreover, there remains little awareness of military technologies, particularly among the civilian staff. This is reflected in the "Capstone" document (DPKO and DFS 2008), which fails to mention any technology aside from information technology (computer networks). This technological omission is found in all other categories of DPKO materials: training documents, equipment manuals, policy documents and other forms of internal and external knowledge transmission.

A major challenge will be to integrate technology into the information management and decision-making process. A mental shift will inevitably be required based on greater awareness and training.

Peacekeeping training

There are currently no UN training materials to prepare peacekeepers to use modern monitoring technologies. The majority of publications of the DPKO Integrated Training Service fail even to mention, let alone describe, any monitoring technologies, leaving the false impression that these technologies have no role in modern peacekeeping. A few training documents make casual reference to technologies. The *Selection Standards and Training Guidelines for United Nations Military Observers* (DPKO 2002: 27) simply note the use of "binoculars and night observation devices" and "specialized equipment to support monitoring".

Only the *United Nations Peacekeeping Training Manual* provides a rudimentary level of detail: "In addition to illumination, PKOs [peacekeeping operations] use a wide variety of NVE [night-vision equipment] and ground radars" (DPKO n.d.[a]: 27), Contrary to this statement, ground radars have almost never been used in peacekeeping, although NVE is now deployed in many missions. The Training Manual briefly outlines some means to procure equipment in general[4] and recommends a training activity, which would include "day and night observation where troops/observers would be tested on their ability to observe and report on some contrived incidents" (DPKO n.d.[a]: 44).

The Integrated Training Service of DPKO conducted a survey of its field staff and discovered that "technological awareness" was the "core value and competency" that a majority of staff members in the field would most like to strengthen.[5] The result was true for each category of personnel: military (57 per cent), police (56 per cent) and civilian (58 per cent). Such a high demand may lead to the development of training programmes for various technologies.

UN equipment manuals and lists

The Table of Organization and Equipment (TOE) is used to generate appropriate forces and capabilities for peacekeeping operations. It would be a natural place for a comprehensive list of potential monitoring technologies, but the published TOE (DPKO n.d.[b]) merely recommends that military observers be equipped with NVDs. It makes no mention of other technologies. A later draft version of the TOE (DPKO 2006c) is only slightly better, with more specifics on night vision. It recommends one device for every 10 to 15 soldiers, "unless there is a requirement to increase equipage due to mission/threat level". It also suggests the use of GPS devices together with laser range-finders, which can be used to determine distances to faraway objects so their positions can be identified precisely from the GPS coordinates of the observer. The 2006 draft TOE specifies that the GPS units must have an accuracy of 25 metres or more. But this figure is out of date: currently, even inexpensive commercial models ($200–300) offer a precision of 10 metres or better.

Contingent-Owned Equipment shortfalls and standards

Contingents are expected to bring some basic equipment to the field, as outlined in a Memorandum of Understanding (MOU) signed by the United Nations and the TCC before deployment. The MOU is based on the guidelines provided in the *Manual on Policies and Procedures Concerning the Reimbursement and Control of Contingent-Owned Equipment of Troop/Police Contributors Participating in Peacekeeping Missions* [COE Manual] (United Nations 2008).[6] Despite these minimal requirements, many contributors are unable to meet them, particularly troops from the Global South, which currently provides the bulk of peacekeeping operations. These nations have small military budgets and their armed forces lack sophisticated military hardware for monitoring, such as night-vision equipment (NVE). By contrast, the armed forces of the developed nations are usually well equipped but they contribute far fewer troops to UN PKOs. Sometimes they bring more surveillance equipment than was requested by the United Nations.

As an incentive to nations to bring at least the basic equipment, the United Nations developed the COE system. In essence, UN inspectors examine the equipment of a member state while they participate in a PKO. The member state is then reimbursed financially by the United Nations if it meets the requirements in each category of equipment.

The equipment that contingents bring to the field is inspected upon arrival, quarterly and upon departure to see if it meets the standards described in the COE Manual. A verification report is issued after each inspection. The COE Database contains the verification reports from 2001 onwards.[7] The database shows the level of shortfalls in each of the 25 categories of equipment. Table 8.1 indicates the percentage of contingents that were unable to uphold the COE standards. The categories for positioning (GPS), night vision and "general observation" are among the highest on the equipment shortfall list, as shown in Table 8.1. Most night-vision shortfalls are with the developing world contingents.

For comparison, the average shortfall for all equipment types is 7 per cent. Even the 13–16 per cent shortfalls for monitoring equipment should be considered underestimates of the real percentage. This is because COE inspectors have tended to give many contingents the benefit of the doubt, particularly since the COE Manual is vague on observation and identification standards. In addition, some missions reduced the COE

Table 8.1 Equipment shortfalls: Top 10 of the 25 categories

Rank	Equipment	Shortfall (per cent)
1	Explosive ordinance disposal	18
2	Positioning (GPS)	16
3	Night vision	16
4	General observation	13
5	Level 1 medical	12
6	Tenting	11
7	Catering	9
8	Telephone equipment	8
9	HF radio	8
10	Accommodation	7

Source: COE Database, DPKO/DFS, searching over period 2001–2006.

standard of night vision from the COE Manual range of 1,000 metres because few contingents were able to meet it.

The COE Manual itself is deficient, especially considering its importance in setting the standards for equipment from TCCs. Under COE rules, the TCCs are paid according to two classes of equipment that they bring to the field: self-sustainment and major equipment. The self-sustainment list is standard for almost all UN missions, though in some cases the United Nations assumes responsibility for providing some equipment for some nations. There are 25 categories of self-sustainment: from catering to tenting, from communications (within each contingent) to medical capabilities. The two COE categories of interest here are observation and identification.[8] They are only vaguely defined in the 2008 COE Manual, as quoted in Table 8.2.

If equipment does not meet the standard set by the COE Manual, the country is not reimbursed for that particular category of equipment/ capability. But the method used to inspect NVDs rarely includes actual field tests in the dark. Mostly they constitute nothing more than a battery check.

For observation and identification, the COE Manual is deficient in both quantitative and qualitative terms, leading to problems and disputes between contingents and COE inspectors over what is acceptable. The Manual does not provide any formula or means, not even a rule of thumb, to determine how many NVDs or GPS units are needed per military unit. Nor are the types of equipment (goggles, monoculars, image intensifiers or infrared) or capabilities specified. Furthermore, the terms "identify" and "categorize objects" are not defined, so testing is necessarily subjective. Also, for the night-vision category, the COE Manual ignores any consideration of lighting conditions (starlit, moonlit, no-ambient light,

Table 8.2 Contingent-Owned Equipment: Self-sustainment standards and rates (per person) for the observation and identification categories

	Standard	Monthly rate (US$)
Observation		
General	Provide hand-held **binoculars** for general observation use	1.15
Night observation	Detect/identify/categorize persons or items at **1,000 metres** or more; conduct night patrols and intercept missions	24.58
Positioning	Determine the **exact** geographical location	5.78
Identification	Conduct surveillance operations with **photographic** equipment, such as videotape and single lens reflex cameras; process and edit the obtained visual information	1.09

Source: COE Manual (United Nations 2008); emphasis added.
Note: Monthly rates are per person. For a battalion of 800, the United Nations would multiply the specified rate by 800. For NVE, if the battalion meets the requirement for quantity and quality (54 NVE is the standard MONUC adopted), the United Nations will reimburse the TCC 800 × $24.58, or $19,664 per month, for the NVE. The self-sustainment reimbursement rates are often increased by various factors, typically 1–5 per cent, depending on the mission conditions (e.g. environmental, intensified operations, hostility/forced abandonment).

etc.) for the 1 km target range. Similarly, the category labelled "identification" (but better renamed "recording") does not specify the number or quality of cameras/video recorders needed for each military unit.[9] In MONUC, it was decided, after many difficult experiences, to adopt a "force standard" of four NVDs per infantry platoon (usually 20–30 soldiers) and to reduce the required range from 1,000 to 500 metres, because almost no contingent could meet the original COE Manual standard of 1 km.[10] This example highlights the need to establish detailed and rigorous but reasonable COE standards, perhaps by adding an annex to the COE Manual to specify in sufficient detail the standards for observation and identification.

Under the "major equipment" class of the COE Manual, the United Nations *leases* expensive equipment from TCCs as DPKO deems necessary. The listed equipment types are shown in Table 8.3. Here again, the COE standards are inadequate. Without accurate standards for equipment quality and specification of various types, the listed prices can only be considered artificial. The variety and quality of night-vision and radar equipment vary considerably across several generations, with no standards at all being specified (except the requirement for "round-the-clock operability and routine calibration").

Table 8.3 Major observation equipment listed in the COE Manual

	Generic fair market value (GFMV), US$	Monthly wet-lease per person, US$	Percentage (lease/GFMV)
Personal			
Night observation devices – tripod mounted	13,140	159	1.2
Binoculars – tripod mounted	8,586	86	1.0
Area			
Artillery-locating equipment	Special case	–	–
Ground surveillance radar/ system	Special case	–	–
Thermal imaging systems – aerial	133,096	1,895	1.1
Thermal imaging systems – ground	111,260	1,674	1.5

Source: United Nations (2008).

The costs listed for these technologies in the current manual represent prices from the 1990s. Many technologies have come down considerably in cost since then. But even with these old and high prices, the value of the technologies can be appreciated. For comparison, the United Nations pays TCCs $1,028 per soldier per month ($303 more for specialists). For the annual cost of one soldier, the United Nations could purchase a tripod-mounted thermal imaging system or lease over 80 of them.

For the "special case" equipment in the table, TCCs need to negotiate the reimbursement rate with the United Nations. The rate is then specified in the MOU between the United Nations and the TCC. The COE Manual does not even list a number of monitoring technologies (see below for a more extensive list).

When the United Nations purchases its own equipment, it also uses certain guidelines. The *Standard Cost Manual 2003* (DPKO 2005a) lists only three observation technologies under "other equipment" with some old and exorbitant figures:

- binoculars (hand-held – $350; tripod mounted – $6,500)
- infrared system (no details – $50,000)
- thermal imaging system (aerial – $120,000; ground – $72,000)

There are serious deficiencies in this list. In fact, "infrared" and "thermal" systems are the same.[11] Like the COE Manual, the Standard Cost Manual grossly oversimplifies the wide range of available technologies in terms of types (image intensification versus infrared), generations (for example, night-vision equipment ranges from first to fourth generation) and equipment quality.[12] Furthermore, the items were priced in 1995, when the costs were considerably higher. In the cases above, the current costs are 10 times lower (for example, $5,000 for thermal infrared devices instead of $50,000). Finally, like the COE Manual, the Standard Cost Manual is incomplete. It fails to list many types of monitoring technology. These documents need substantial review and improvement. Until recently, however, the relevant departments gave little or no priority to the monitoring technology gap.

Policies and operating procedures

To its credit, DPKO is beginning to grapple with monitoring technology issues at the management and policy level. A draft policy on "Monitoring and Surveillance Technology in Field Missions" was first prepared in December 2008. In the long drafting and consultation process, however, it quickly became apparent that the benefits of such technology can come to full effect only with broader improvements in UN intelligence and information management. Consultations revealed the limits of the political will of DPKO and of member states to address such controversial topics as intelligence, euphemistically called "situational awareness" at UN headquarters. That topic will probably require a separate but linked policy. At the urging of the UN Special Committee on Peacekeeping, the policy on monitoring technologies (DPKO 2010a) is being promulgated.

The draft policy calls for advance technology planning, including a "monitoring and surveillance technologies" analysis in the "pre-deployment" phase. This could be subsequently augmented during the "rapid deployment", "mission start-up" and "implementation" phases.[13] Specifically, the military and police sections of DPKO are requested to draft the Concept of Operations to include a section on "Monitoring and Surveillance Capabilities". In addition, these capabilities should be included in the Force Requirements for proposed missions.

The policy also deals with the thorny issue of host-state consent. Some aspects of technical monitoring (for example, with signals interception) may need host-state approval. But technologies used solely for protection purposes, such as closed-circuit television (CCTV) on UN premises, do not require host-state consent. Neither is consent needed for UN operations engaging in enforcement measures imposed by the Security Council under Chapter VII of the UN Charter.

The policy paper suggested that financial allocations for the technologies should be included in mission budgets and that sufficient training should be provided for use of the equipment. The analysis of the data was to be done in a centralized section, probably the Joint Mission Analysis Centre in each mission. "By default, the work of the UN should be open and transparent", it stated, but information deemed sensitive should be protected and assigned a security classification (for example, "Confidential" or "Strictly Confidential", as per UN Secretary-General 2007).

A "Standard Operating Procedure" document for "Monitoring and Surveillance Technology in Field Missions" was also drafted. The technologies most needed for staff security were to be included among the strategic deployment stocks at the UN Logistics Base in Brindisi, Italy. This should allow the equipment to be deployed faster as part of the basic kit.

The Monitoring and Surveillance Technology policy and Standard Operating Procedure should help to increase awareness within DPKO and improve the standards for technology use. But it took almost two years to draft the documents, showing how difficult it is to bring progress to such issues, even if they can enhance staff security and better decision-making – both of which are central concerns for UN managers.

Safety and security standards

One might expect UN safety and security documentation to contain a thorough consideration of monitoring technology since it is so prevalent in the security industry. However, in the written materials relating to the safety of UN personnel, there is a paucity of such information. The outdated "Security in the Field" pamphlet (United Nations 1998–), meant to provide individuals going on field missions with basic tips, makes no mention of any technology except walkie-talkies and telephones.

After the terrorist bombing in Baghdad of 19 August 2003, in which 22 UN staff members lost their lives and a large section of the mission headquarters was destroyed, the United Nations developed new structures, procedures and equipment lists for a more systematic approach to personnel protection. The newly created Department of Safety and Security (DSS) introduced Minimum Operating Security Standards (MOSS) for system-wide application (DSS 2004). The "baseline MOSS" provides an extensive list of telecommunications equipment, even for its lowest threat level (phase I, precautionary):[14] a "fully operational, independent radio network utilizing UHF, VHF and/or HF equipment" and mobile satellite telephones for each agency's country office. The MOSS also recommends the creation of a communications centre manned 24 hours a day, seven days a week (24/7), in addition to an ever-present emergency communications system.

Under the security system, each country's Designated Official and Security Management Team must develop country-specific MOSS. This includes a Threat and Risk Assessment and a table of equipment, training and structures. The only monitoring technologies listed in the template table for phases I to III (that is, precautionary, restricted movement, relocation phases) are digital cameras and GPS devices, both of which are "mandatory for Field Security Coordination Officers". Only when there exists a threat of terrorism are "Enhanced Protective Measures and Resources" (Annex B of DSS 2004) recommended to "supplement" the baseline MOSS. Included in the perimeter protection and access control measures are: CCTV monitoring and recording of perimeter areas by a 24/7-manned control room and possibly X-ray machines; metal detector archways and/or wands at visitors' entrances. In addition, a vehicle-check mirror is recommended for the driveway entrance.

Thus the DSS documentation deals solely with security equipment for UN facilities and with communications systems for travelling personnel. Realizing that a more proactive approach to security means achieving better situational awareness, the DSS partnered with DPKO in 2006 to look at equipment in the field more generally. The joint Technical Specifications Working Group was mandated "to identify and procure security-related equipment necessary for DPKO-led operations" (DPKO 2006b: 6). The Peacekeeping Operations Support Service unit of DSS was tasked with maintaining awareness of new equipment and recommending equipment priorities in the field. So far, the Working Group has developed specifications for only one type of monitoring technology: CCTV.[15]

This review shows the meagre nature of UN documentation for employing monitoring technology in PKOs. The training manuals, equipment standards and equipment lists are far from adequate for a proactive approach in the field. Many categories of technology have not even been mentioned. What would a more thorough list look like? Table 8.4 is an attempt to provide the answer. It lists monitoring technologies that should find application in peacekeeping and be covered in UN documentation, especially in the COE Manual.

Demand from the field: The low–medium-cost project

In February 2008, I had the opportunity to brief DPKO's Extended Senior Management Team and, at the end of the meeting, the DPKO leadership decided to commence two projects to improve surveillance equipment in UN missions. One project was to conduct a more in-depth study of past, present and future UN capabilities, resulting in an internal report by me which has become part of the present book. In parallel, a low–medium-cost technology project was launched to rapidly address the shortfall for

Table 8.4 Summary of monitoring technologies

	Types	Quantity measured[a]
Video monitors	• video cameras (indoor/outdoor) • web cameras • closed-circuit television (CCTV) • digital video networks (DVN) • aerial & space-based surveillance	Visible light: electromagnetic radiation of wavelength 400–700 nanometres
Night-vision equipment	• image intensifiers (II) • thermal or infrared (IR) imaging	For II: visible light Thermal devices: IR (electromagnetic radiation of wavelength 700–12,000 nanometres)
Motion detectors	• automatic illuminators • alert or alarm connections	Changes in IR or radar or light beam intensity
Radars	• air surveillance radar (ASR) • artillery-locating radar (ALR) • ground-penetrating radar (GPR) • ground surveillance radar (GSR) • synthetic aperture radar (SAR) • marine radars • weather radars • speed enforcement radars	Reflected radio waves* ASR: 2–30 cm ALR: 3–50 cm GPR: 2–10 m GSR: 10–30 cm SAR: 1 mm–1 m Marine: 3–15 cm Weather: 2–15 cm Speed enforcement: 1–2 cm
X-ray machines	• baggage and shipments • portable	Electromagnetic radiation of wavelength 0.03–3.00 nanometres*
Acoustic sensors	• small arms fire detection and localization • movement of persons or vehicles	Acoustic (sound) waves in air or ground
Seismic sensors	• geophones (for personnel/vehicle detection) • seismic arrays (for explosion detection)	Acoustic waves produced by movements in the Earth's surface
Chemical sensors	• explosives detector	Molecular mass or chemical binding properties
Metal detectors	• hand-held wand • mine detector	Electric currents inducted in underground (metal) objects*

166

Pressure transducers		Pressure applied (converted to an electric signal)
Electronic monitors	• intrusion alarms • road monitor • signal-locating equipment • radio scanners / signal monitoring	Electromagnetic radiation (radio waves) of wavelength > 1 mm
Positioning and tracking systems	• Global Positioning System (GPS) • transponders and tags • radio frequency identification	Radio signals from the GPS of satellites

Notes: Other technologies less likely to be used in peacekeeping include: sonar, ultrasound, LIDAR (light detection and ranging), taut-wire fences, IR break-beam detectors, seals and tags. Nuclear detectors (e.g. Geiger counters) are needed only when nuclear materials present a potential hazard.

[a] Items marked with * are "active sensors", meaning that the devices emit a wave and the reflection is measured by them. Infrared devices can be active if they are equipped with an IR emitter to "brighten" the area invisibly; otherwise they are "passive".

low- and medium-cost technologies in selected missions. DPKO sent a Code Cable to 14 field missions asking them to identify the types of technology they possessed and any shortfalls that existed. This resulted in long lists of many needed technologies. The responses expressed the same need for monitoring technologies as found in a previous survey of UN field personnel conducted in 1995. That survey found that the large majority of personnel (90 per cent) thought ground sensors had a place in peacekeeping (see Appendix 6 for a detailed description of the survey). The 2008 low–medium-cost project received responses from the missions themselves. The technologies desired by the missions, listed in Table 8.5, were many.[16]

MONUC requested cameras for its rudimentary glass-domed surveillance (Lama) helicopters. It noted that the more advanced attack helicopter (Mi-35) had cameras for "target identification" but that these were "for national use only". The Indian contingent tended to keep the imagery within its unit, hesitant to share with other contingents in the eastern Congo, especially those from Pakistan and Bangladesh – countries that could be potential future opponents. Unlike the Mi-35, the Lama helicopters have no gyro-stabilized pod for onboard cameras. Imagery was taken from the Lama helicopters but only using hand-held cameras, leading to reduced resolution and greater blur.

The African Union/United Nations hybrid operation in Darfur (UNAMID) stated that it was unable to monitor many events, areas and routes owing to the large distances involved. Furthermore, its staff had no expertise in Intelligence, Surveillance, Target Acquisition and Reconnaissance (ISTAR) to exploit and manage information from numerous sources. So UNAMID suggested that any future ISTAR system or concept should have the following characteristics: simple, robust, reliable, as maintenance-free as possible, having a small logistics trail and a low-training requirement, inexpensive and proven to work under harsh climatic conditions.

The United Nations Disengagement Observer Force in the Golan Heights (UNDOF) identified an "urgent priority" to obtain long-range night vision, otherwise it "could not fulfill its monitoring/observation mandate". It explored the option of borrowing NVE from the United States, though this proved unsuccessful.

The United Nations Interim Force in Lebanon (UNIFIL) noted that only 4 out of its 32 units (in 62 locations) were equipped with surveillance cameras, sensors and/or thermal imaging systems for force protection. The mission wanted to expand its system of Internet Protocol (IP) cameras for the protection of facilities. Whereas Contingent-Owned Equipment from some countries (for example, France, Italy and Spain) was quite advanced, UN-owned equipment was seriously lacking in

Table 8.5 Low–medium-cost surveillance technology shortfalls, as identified by the field missions

Mission (location)	Cameras desired (types)	Other technologies desired	Purposes
MINURSO (Western Sahara)	• digital, high zoom • GIS (GPS-stamp) for aerial photos • CCTV with motion sensor • aerial • night vision (long-range, 3rd generation)	• satellite imagery of Western Sahara and boundaries	• team-site perimeter security • patrolling • mapping (e.g. position of berm and roads network)
MINUSTAH (Haiti)	• video/still • CCTV (remote places) • heliborne • motion detection • real-time streaming • thermal vision (including cabling) • satellite imagery	• GSR for control of border and remote areas • radars (ground surveillance; and to "see" through walls) • frequency scanners • metal detectors • chemical (gunpowder) sensors • fingerprint scanner	• unit perimeter surveillance (e.g. high tower installation) • patrols of borders and port areas • border surveillance • find hidden weapons/ ammunition and drugs
MONUC (DRC)	• cameras for surveillance helicopters • satellite images of specific areas of the Kivus to identify changes	• radars to detect vehicles and personnel, and for tracking of light aircraft • UAVs	
UNAMID (Darfur)	• digital camera and laptop to UNMO teams • night-vision devices (monocular, helmet-mounted, for vehicle driving, weapons site) • aircraft fitted for observation • UAVs with live feed	• dedicated ISTAR cell at Force HQ	• monitor events, areas and routes over large area • detect, identify and recognize groups beyond effective weapons range, especially at night • overmatch opposition • protection of halted convoys and long-range patrols

Table 8.5 (cont.)

Mission (location)	Cameras desired (types)	Other technologies desired	Purposes
UNDOF (Golan Heights)	• night-vision equipment (long-range) • thermal weapons site	• satellite images to update geo-database	• night-time temporary checkpoints • approaches to observation post • spotting violations
UNFICYP (Cyprus)	• improved CCTV system • portable CCTV system with thermal vision • portable sensor system	• portable sensor systems (acoustic/seismic)	
UNIFIL (southern Lebanon)	• surveillance cameras at UN camps and with deployed units • satellite and aerial imagery • night vision (mounted on vehicles and weapons, and non-mounted)	• radars	• day/night security of camps • monitoring specific areas in mission
UNMIL (Liberia)	• aerial reconnaissance (especially at night), UAVs • network cameras • increased bandwidth	• GSR	• security of UN compounds • border surveillance • search for arms caches
UNMIS (Southern Sudan)	• day and night with motion sensors • satellite and aerial reconnaissance	• RFID tags, bar code readers and scanners	• perimeter surveillance for team sites • aid UNMO movements • monitoring and verification, especially at night

Mission		
UNMOGIP (Kashmir)	• laser range-finders • thermal IR binoculars • night-vision equipment • UAVs	
UNOCI (Côte d'Ivoire)	• metal detectors • radars (ground-penetrating, ground, air, maritime) • X-ray machines • GIS tools • sensors (motion detectors, acoustic and seismic sensors)	• arms/diamond embargo enforcement • cross-border surveillance • protecting military positions, guarding storage facilities, securing office and residential areas • elections/DDR (low-intensity operation) • air and coastal observation
UNOMIG (Georgia)	• UAVs • radars	• observation post security, especially in isolated areas
UNTSO (Palestine, including Lebanon)	• Internet Protocol cameras (PTZ) • modern night-vision equipment • intrusion sensors • IR beams	

Source: Responses from the 14 UN peacekeeping missions to Code Cable 0451 of 27 February 2008 sent to heads of mission from Under-Secretary-General Jean-Marie Guéhenno requesting the missions to fill out a survey on current and potential technologies in order to identify where shortfalls exist, as well as a way forward.

Abbreviations: DDR – disarmament, demobilization and reintegration; GIS – geographic information system; GSR – ground surveillance radars; ISTAR – Intelligence, Surveillance, Target Acquisition and Reconnaissance; PTZ – Pan Tilt Zoom; RFID – radio frequency identification; UAV – unmanned aerial vehicle.

comparison. UNIFIL does not possess any of its own satellite or aerial re-connaissance means, radars, radio monitoring, or acoustic or seismic sensor equipment. This was due in part to the fact that it is "not specified in the Force Requirements for traditional types of units". However, the mission had deployed some unusual but necessary equipment, notably electronic countermeasures (jammers) against improvised explosive devices (IEDs). It was seeking to procure radars and forward-looking infrared, as proposed by the Italian Force Protection Company. This use was to be procured by the Communications and Information Technology Service within the DFS,[17] along with smart CCTV technology for the security of Force HQ. In addition, a portable under-vehicle surveillance system was under procurement. As cars drive through a checkpoint, cameras take im-ages of the bottom of the vehicles so operators can search for IEDs. The envisioned system would also include a vehicle plate recognition system.

Some nationally owned equipment in UNIFIL was very advanced, in-cluding the best radars the United Nations has yet deployed: COBRA counter-battery radars, air detection radars (NC130 and NC140) and maritime radars aboard frigates and other ships. UNIFIL was the first mission in UN history to deploy intelligence, surveillance and reconnais-sance companies. COE night-vision equipment was mounted on both vehicles and weapons. Soldiers also carried digital cameras and NVDs, ranging from 35 to 200 NVDs per battalion.

Despite being in existence for over 60 years, the UN mission in Kash-mir (United Nations Military Observer Group in India and Pakistan, UNMOGIP) did not possess any advanced technologies, including night-vision equipment. This limited its effectiveness because most of the oper-ations of the opposing forces – India and Pakistan – occurred after sunset. The mission relied on the personal cameras of UN observers. It requested a vehicle tracking system because it was unable to track its patrols. In the event of serious incidents or accidents, the mission found that it could locate a car only through the local authorities, sometimes preventing a timely rescue. It sought the ability to locate in real time the position of all cars moving along the line of control that separates the opposing Indian and Pakistani forces. The mission reported: "This is an issue which is affecting the quality of work, the safety and security and the motiva-tion of experienced officers we have here."[18]

Political concerns were also raised in the responses from the missions. The United Nations Truce Supervision Organization and the United Na-tions Mission in Sudan (UNMIS) noted that the introduction of new technical and electronic equipment required consultation with the host countries. The United Nations Operation in Côte d'Ivoire (UNOCI/ ONUCI) ventured: "in the sensitive pre-election/ DDR [disarmament, demobilization and reintegration] period and considering [the] suspicious attitude toward ONUCI demonstrated by local political and military actors, the use of surveillance tools may endanger the mission's credibility and impartiality." It might be considered as "intelligence-gathering" and seen to be "contradictory to the organization's established transparency". When parties seek to evade UN detection of their activities, these kinds of allegations are often heard.

Based on the responses from 14 field missions, DPKO then identified seven missions for providing additional technology. These were: the United Nations Mission for the Referendum in Western Sahara (MINURSO), the United Nations Stabilization Mission in Haiti (MINUSTAH), UNDOF, UNIFIL, the United Nations Mission in Liberia (UNMIL), the United Nations Observer Mission in Georgia (UNOMIG) and UNMIS. It tasked the Integrated Operating Teams with helping to procure new technology, which resulted in an influx of equipment into a few of the missions, although some snags were observed such as a lack of current funding and long procurement lead-times. MINURSO received some cameras and GPS for its five team sites. MINUSTAH gained a substantial number of cameras, including infrared and snake cameras to take pictures at night and around corners.

UNMIL reported that it was setting up a CCTV system, though hampered by the rainy season, and it had many other equipment needs. Its lack of monitoring equipment was further highlighted in an audit by the United Nations' Internal Audit Division (2009): "UNMO teams and Sector HQs did not have video camera recorders, sound recorders, night-vision binoculars or goggles, or infrared sensing equipment essential for surveillance and monitoring operations." The lack of state-of-the-art surveillance equipment was bemoaned in the audit and the mission promised to improve its standards.

Unfortunately, the low–medium-cost project was closed in November 2008, after substantial gains were achieved. In addition to the provision of hardware, the project generated greater awareness about monitoring technologies, though many missions had asked for much more than they received. Some missions put desired items into their budgets and identified future benefits of technology (Ostrowski 2008: 4). The project concluded modestly that "there is awareness that more has to be done in the technology field" (Obiakor 2008).

It is recommended that a similar project be launched over a longer time period to include not simply low-and-medium-cost technologies but some higher-cost ones as well. A coordinated and integrated effort will help make the procurement process easier and more effective both financially and organizationally. The project should run over more than one budget cycle so that greater results can be observed. The 2008 project ran for only a short period of time, from February to November, and it was not possible to see how budgets reflected the increases in monitoring technology.

Export permits are needed to purchase some equipment (for example, advanced night-vision equipment), meaning that procurement time might need to be further extended. Some of the newest equipment might not be accessible because of a lack of permission from the manufacturing nation (for example, the United States).

In a positive development, the first Capability Development Officer in the Office of Military Affairs arrived in 2008. Also, the suggestion in the draft policy for "a procedural framework, like development of the COE Manual and possible development of a 'UN Policy on Monitoring' in a holistic approach" (DPKO 2010a), was greeted with hope. Maybe these steps will lead to a sustained effort.

Given the high demand from the field, the modest response from UN headquarters and the low technological standards over the history of UN peacekeeping, one question naturally arises: why the continuing technology gap? In order to close this gap, a wide range of obstacles will need to be reviewed and eventually overcome. For UN technologies to be improved, it is important to understand the weaknesses and deficiencies of the UN system as well as any problems with the technologies themselves.

Notes

1. PLAN (the People's Liberation Army of Namibia) was the military wing of SWAPO (the South-West Africa People's Organization).
2. Some of the reconnaissance provided at the beginning of Operation Storm was probably supplied by the United States. Similarly, in Zaire in 1996, the United States used satellite imagery to draw conclusions that were at odds with UN estimates about the number of refugees. This led the Multinational Force Commander, General Maurice Baril, to conclude: "Some nations who controlled intelligence used it to kill the mission" (personal communication, 21 November 2000).
3. The gap between "mandate and means" is an aspect of the larger "commitment–capability" gap in peacekeeping. See Langille (2002b).
4. The means of acquiring equipment are: a Memorandum of Understanding with member states, a Letter of Assist from member states or contractors, or outright purchase as UN-Owned Equipment. The Training Manual does not mention these provisions, or the deployment of equipment as part of the unpaid National Support Element.
5. Integrated Training Service (2008: 20). After technological awareness, the core values and competencies that most staff wanted to improve were (in order): "commitment to continuous learning", "planning & organizing", "creativity" and "communication".
6. The 2008 COE Manual of 233 pages was finalized by the 2008 Working Group on Contingent-Owned Equipment and published as UN Doc. A/C.5/63/18 of 29 January 2009. The contents of the COE Manual are reviewed every two years by the Working Group.

7. The COE Database is not available to the general public, but information on the COE system can be found at <http://www.un.org/en/peacekeeping/sites/coe/about.shtml> (accessed 5 January 2011).

8. The COE Manual also calls for "early warning and detection systems to protect contingent premises" under the self-sustainment category of "Field Defence Stores". However, this requirement does not necessitate technology under the current UN interpretation. A single sentry would suffice to meet the COE standards.

9. Payments are made per person in a military unit only if the entire unit has the required capability. Payments in each category are "all or nothing". TCCs meeting the requirements in part do not receive compensation. For example, if 50 NVDs are required and the contingent has only 25, the TCC is not reimbursed at all for the category.

10. Isberg (2004). Even with the reduced standard, MONUC COE inspectors estimated in November 2006 that only 50 per cent of the contingents have equipment that can satisfy the requirement.

11. Thermal imaging is usually done by detecting radiation in the middle "far" infrared part of the electromagnetic spectrum.

12. When the United Nations provides night-observation equipment, its standard is much lower than the one specified for Contingent-Owned Equipment: the NVD must have an "effective range" of only 250 metres as per the specifications of the UN systems contract. This inconsistency should be corrected.

13. Mission start-up is further subdivided into three distinct phases: I (initial start-up), II (build-up) and III (consolidation).

14. The security phases are I (precautionary), II (restricted movement), III (relocation), IV (emergency operations) and V (evacuation). See DSS (2004).

15. I do not know the degree of detail in these specifications – email requests to the Peacekeeping Operations Support Service for the specifications were not answered.

16. The low–medium-cost technologies survey also covered radio monitoring, jamming technologies and special communications; GIS systems; and several other technologies.

17. The DFS works closely with DPKO.

18. UNIFIL response to the low–medium-cost survey, dated 5 March 2008.

9

Challenges and problems

To deploy effective and appropriate monitoring technologies to the field, a range of issues and obstacles must be considered, including operational, technical, legal, political, institutional/cultural and financial challenges. Examining the desired characteristics and the practical problems helps identify potential pitfalls and promote potential solutions.

Operational

First and foremost, technologies must be operationally *useful*. They must provide increased situational awareness in important locations and of significant activities. They must not be purchased simply because they are appealing in an abstract sense. Hardware development in some nations is driven by a "technological imperative" – simply because it *can* be done. The United Nations cannot afford to adopt unproven technologies. As shown in previous sections, even the United Nations' limited technological experience demonstrates the utility of many monitoring technologies such as night-vision goggles for night patrolling, aerial cameras to spot advancing threats, satellite imagery for mapping, and tracking systems to monitor UN vehicles.

Fortunately, technology is, in general, becoming increasingly *user friendly*, especially through the use of on-screen icons and menu-driven interfaces. But even user-friendly devices require testing and practice runs to

Keeping watch: Monitoring, technology and innovation in UN peace operations, Dorn, United Nations University Press, 2011, ISBN 978-92-808-1198-8

overcome potential problems. For example, depth perception can be a problem with night-vision equipment but to trained users these problems are manageable.[1]

To be *practical*, technologies must be reliable, accurate and easy to operate by the UN mission, if not plug-and-play. The modern experience with some technologies in UN and other operations – for example, those of the North Atlantic Treaty Organization (NATO) – has also shown that this is achievable, though special expertise is often required. For instance, expert analysts may be needed to recognize target signatures and to discard artefacts in imagery, especially with techniques such as synthetic aperture radar. Technical expertise may also be needed to calibrate equipment and adjust threshold levels, for example, to separate background "noise" from actual "signals" (the classic "signal to noise" problem). To accommodate the extra data from sensors, the United Nations would also need to increase the bandwidth, speed and reliability of its electronic transmission channels (for example, information technology networks).

In harsh peacekeeping environments, for example in hot climates or under rough handling, devices need to be *robust and durable*. Most military equipment is ruggedized to allow for difficult conditions, even combat. Ruggedization may increase the cost of the equipment, but not necessarily by a large factor.[2]

Terrain type and sensor range are key factors in technology selection.[3] In flat areas where the line of sight is long, such as in deserts, open fields and bodies of water (lakes, rivers and oceans), long-range sensors are best. These technologies include radar, high-zoom cameras (still and video) and laser range-finders, preferably on elevated towers or aerial platforms. Conversely, in terrain typified by a short line of sight and many obstacles – as found in jungles, rapidly undulating areas and built-up urban regions – numerous short-range sensors, spaced at regular intervals, might be needed to cover the area. Short-range devices typically include seismic, acoustic, magnetic and infrared break-beam sensors.

Weather conditions also play a role in the choice of sensors. Like human eyes, cameras operating in the visible part of the electromagnetic spectrum can become virtually useless in heavy fog or rain. Other devices, such as radar, are much less susceptible. For night vision, image intensifiers work better when there is more ambient light, for instance from a full moon on a cloudless night. Infrared devices give the clearest signals in cold weather when there is a greater temperature difference between the targets (warm bodies) and the background. Acoustic sensors sometimes have difficulty distinguishing target sounds (for example, rifle fire) from noise caused by thunder, rain or even wind, although automated acoustic analysis can supplement the human ear to identify the types, locations and sources of particular sounds.

The challenge is to achieve technological proficiency among a wide range of peacekeepers. Military, police and civilian personnel in UN missions have a wide diversity of computer and technical skills, especially as the majority come from the developing world. There is a constant and critical need to train and to integrate users. Both actions are needed to make effective use of technology in the organization's daily operations (Schwabe et al. 2001: 97). Without a process of integration, even the most powerful technological system would be ineffective if the intended users cannot take the results and apply them to the challenges of violent conflict.[4]

Some monitoring devices such as video cameras are now widely used consumer items and are designed to be "user friendly". Consequently, there is a reduced training need.[5] The challenge is to integrate video cameras into daily operations so that many can benefit from the imagery.

Interoperability – defined as the ability of one group to exchange information or equipment with another group for a common end – within peacekeeping missions is an ongoing challenge, given the various nations and nationals participating. Interoperability is not simply a technical challenge. Language barriers, different methods, national caveats on the use of force, lack of confidence and trust in the United Nations, and absence of familiarity are all obstacles to effective integration and cooperation.

Monitoring technologies are typically susceptible to false alarms, usually by responding to events the devices are not designed to detect: the "false positives". False alarms may also be caused by equipment malfunctions, poor maintenance, incorrect installation or calibration, improper usage, lack of training and other factors.

Outdoor motion sensors are an example of a monitoring/detection technology that has traditionally been inadequate in discriminating between real targets and nuisances such as wandering animals. One of the most effective means to counter false alarms is through dual technologies, that is, using systems or devices that incorporate at least two detection methods. For example, dual-mode motion detectors use both passive infrared (PIR) and microwave signals. PIR is used to detect the movement of warm objects against a background level. Microwave sensors transmit an electromagnetic pulse and analyse the reflected echo. PIR and microwave operate in different portions of the spectrum. In addition, one is passive, catching only the emissions from the monitored object, and the other is active, sending out a signal and catching the reflection. Consequently, they are not subject to the same types of false alarm. Combined, they usually give a better result. Similarly, "layering" of technologies for short-, medium- and long-distance viewing can result in "smarter" and more effective systems.

Technical

Technical problems are frequently encountered in the field. In remote locations, especially conflict zones in the developing world, challenges include:
- intermittent power;
- unreliable telecommunications;
- computer workstations that are stand alone and are not linked to any network, the Internet or even each other.[6]

The Achilles' heel of most technologies in remote locations is their dependence on reliable electrical power. Peacekeeping missions often operate in areas where a robust electrical infrastructure is lacking. Some areas have intermittent power for only a few hours a day, and other areas have no electrical grid at all. Fixed installations can mitigate some of this using gas/diesel-powered generators or alternative energy sources such as solar panels or more expensive wind turbines.

Mobile devices often rely on small portable generators or batteries. However, the reliance on rechargeable and/or disposable batteries entails logistical and environmental considerations. Older models of many technologies, including night-vision devices, quickly run through many batteries for normal operation. The absence of reliable power may require a cost/benefit analysis before deploying technology that is heavily power dependent. One consideration is the noise and high visibility of generators. In some UN situations, the covert/discreet operation of electrically powered devices may be needed.

A hopeful trend is the increasing use of solar power. Some smaller electronic devices can already be solar charged during travel. Cell phones with built-in solar panels are available. For instance, the "Surge" from US start-up Novothink provides a solar back cover for iPods and iPhones that generates about half-an-hour of talk time for two hours of charging (Donoghue 2009a, 2009b).

Even when power is available, a communications infrastructure is required to link computers, networks, databases and assorted sensors together effectively. Sensor or surveillance technology can be a powerful force multiplier but, for it to be effective, the data must be delivered to human operators and for interpretation and response by leaders.

Developing a communications infrastructure requires a highly skilled maintenance workforce and can be expensive to build and operate if no existing infrastructure can be leveraged or if the cost of bandwidth is exorbitant. Fortunately, the Communications and Information Technology Service of the Department of Field Support runs a communications network that is world class.

Furthermore, commercial cell phone networks have been spreading fast in the developing world. These telephone services, which are multiplying even in conflict-ridden parts of the world, can be extremely useful to UN operations. Most networks are engineered and built to ensure a high degree of reliability, driven by the business competition for market share and profit. As a result, the infrastructure tends to be robust and possesses significant redundancies, so that if one part fails a similar system can take over. A dedicated cell/radio system for tactical purposes can create an "all-informed net" where one station/transmission is heard by all others. Using cell phones can be useful in the policing context when one-to-one communications are sufficient and appropriate.

Cell phone coverage is rapidly expanding in the developing and the developed world (as shown in Figure 4.2). Even in many remote parts of the Democratic Republic of the Congo (DRC), cell phone service is available. This provides an additional means to communicate by voice to officers deployed in the field on operations or patrols. Equally important, it can provide data access and services to those same officers without the need to deploy a complex private data network or to rely on satellite phones, which can be very expensive. As an example, officers can use cell phones or iPhone/BlackBerry® type devices to capture and transmit photos directly from the scene or to exchange text/SMS messages and email for operational purposes, as well as to enter information into centralized databases while deployed.

An advanced smartphone now incorporates a still and video camera, voice recorder, calculator, weather forecaster, and a Global Positioning System (GPS) with maps and provides links to the Internet.

Legal

From a legal perspective, there are relatively few obstacles to deploying monitoring technologies in UN field operations, provided that the equipment serves the purpose of the mission. The UN Charter (Article 105) states that "the Organization shall enjoy in the territory of each of its Members such privileges and immunities as are necessary for the fulfilment of its purposes". The 1946 Convention on the Privileges and Immunities of the United Nations further declares: "The property and assets of the United Nations, wherever located and by whomsoever held, shall be immune from search, requisition, confiscation, expropriation and any other form of interference" (United Nations 1946: Section 3).[7] In the Status-of-Forces Agreement (SOFA), which the United Nations negotiates with the host state, the state almost always recognizes the United Nations' right to import equipment as well as the state's own responsibility to promptly grant all needed authorizations and licences. The SOFA also provides reassurance to the host state:

> The United Nations peacekeeping operation and its members shall refrain from any action or activity incompatible with the impartial and international nature of their duties or inconsistent with the spirit of the present arrangement. The United Nations peacekeeping operation shall respect all local laws and regulations. (United Nations 1990: Article 6)[8]

Because local laws may sometimes include restrictions on certain monitoring – for example, of military activities – a legal dilemma could potentially arise, but experts in the United Nations' Office of Legal Affairs differ over the legal response. For some, the United Nations' fulfilment of its mandate would take precedence under the legal principle of "factual displacement".[9] Others see the host state, no matter how fragile or failed, as sovereign and having the final say in matters of monitoring. In any case, even if legally permissible, the issue can become a political challenge (see below).

For UN aerial reconnaissance, the host states' guarantees in the SOFA of unrestricted freedom of movement should normally apply.[10] But the United Nations would probably develop a kind of "modalities arrangement" for purposes of air traffic control.

The United Nations respects human rights law, which includes provisions to respect individual privacy. In carrying out monitoring activities, the United Nations must "avoid arbitrary interference with [the] privacy, family, home or correspondence" of individuals, in accordance with the Universal Declaration of Human Rights (United Nations 1948: Article 12). In its monitoring work, the United Nations would need to uphold privacy rights except in "non-arbitrary" cases where the actions of the targeted individuals or groups affect the mandate of the mission. The United Nations can take measures to ensure it respects privacy during its surveillance.[11] In general, legal instruments are not impediments to the United Nations' work but, rather, enablers of it. Nonetheless, lawyers within the United Nations have complicated the matter on occasion, placing a legal straitjacket on UN activities, much to the consternation of UN commanders.

Political: The conflicting parties

Since peacekeeping operations (PKOs) are designed primarily to achieve or contribute to a political outcome, notably a sustainable peace between conflicting parties, political considerations play a major role in the selection of monitoring methods and technologies (Diehl 2002).

Ideally, technical monitoring, like UN observation in general, should have a confidence-building effect on the conflicting parties. Accordingly, opposition should come only from individuals and groups who oppose the peace agreement or process. All committed parties should see that it is in their own interest for the United Nations to identify violations and provide early warning of threats.

In reality, parties usually sign peace agreements reluctantly because they are unable to achieve their desired outcome through armed conflict (for example, a one-sided victory). They often remain deeply suspicious and accuse each other of all manner of violations. The parties rely on the United Nations to provide objective verification of the compliance of the other side, but often prepare for the possibility of renewed violence, especially by hiding their weapons. They frequently push the limits of the peace agreement and test the limits of the United Nations' verification capability. Violations may range from marginal to substantial: from delays in implementing peace accords to political manipulation/intimidation; from arms smuggling/stockpiling to deliberate killings for political ends.

For these reasons, some parties may not wish the PKO to deploy a comprehensive monitoring system that could readily detect their own infractions of the peace accords. They might complain that the United Nations is interfering, infringing or "spying" on them, or accuse the United Nations of violating its standard of impartiality. Here, technology can both help and hinder UN deployment. Imagery or other technical evidence of illegal activities can provide objective proof beyond the verbal or written reports from UN officers. But if the parties know that the United Nations can accomplish this level of verification, they may be less interested in bringing the organization into the peace process or allowing it freedom of observation. In the end, the acceptance by the parties of objective but intrusive monitoring is one important test of their political commitment to put the peace accords into practice.

In environments of tenuous commitment where the United Nations has to investigate both major and minor wrongdoings, a "cat and mouse" game is often played in which the conflicting parties try to hide violations and accuse one another in a "blame game". In the end, it is the duty of the United Nations to establish the most rigorous verification system possible. The world organization cannot afford to be an impotent bystander in areas of violent conflict where innocent lives are at stake. If the United

Nations wants more than a purely symbolic presence, it must be ready and able to identify significant violators of peace accords and perpetrators of human rights abuses. When warranted, it must be willing to "name and shame" such individuals and groups. Even more proactively, it must help locate and help arrest war criminals and major violators of human rights.

The parties may also have legitimate concerns about UN monitoring. They might fear that the PKO could gain compromising information about them that could lead to a loss of security, especially if the information were to be obtained by the other side.[12]

The United Nations has dealt with the parties' fears by reassuring them that it will act impartially, with the required level of confidentiality and in accordance with its mandate. The United Nations can alleviate fears associated with new technologies by providing similar assurances and guarantees, as well as detailed explanations of the United Nations' methods.[13] Information technology improves the ease of information transfer, but it also provides the tools to prevent and catch such unwanted transfers.

Although the United Nations' methods are transparent, collected raw data are generally not openly available. The United Nations can explore the concept of cooperative monitoring in which interpreted data or even imagery are provided regularly to all parties as a confidence-building measure (Dorn 2004). Other options for sharing information from video cameras and sensors are as follows:
- *all* information is provided to *all* parties for *all* events:
  - on a real-time basis
  - periodically (daily/weekly/monthly)
- only violations, major or minor, are reported:
  - to *all* parties
  - to the offending party only (as a protest)
  - to *all* UN member states
- violations are reported:
  - with *all* supporting evidence (information essential to demonstrate non-compliance)
  - with only supporting evidence that will not affect the military security of the offending party
  - with no supporting evidence

In some cases, conflicting parties have even considered allowing the United Nations to place real-time video feed on the Internet for public access, that is, using web cameras to view a hotspot. For instance, in the negotiations of the 2006 Comprehensive Peace Accord in Nepal, the parties asked the United Nations to install cameras for 24/7 surveillance of weapons storage depots of both Maoist insurgents and government forces. This was to help ensure that these arms were not removed. In the end the video imagery was not made public but kept on UN computers at the weapons storage site. But this example showed how technology was applied and how it was envisioned. The system included continuous video recording of the fenced-off storage sites, a series of floodlights for illumination and a means for UN civilian observers to sound the alarm in the event of unauthorized withdrawal of the weapons (Government of Nepal 2006). This example demonstrates that technology is so widely recognized as a tool in modern life that parties have requested the United Nations to deploy it in support of peace accords.

Political: The contributing states

Nations contribute military and police personnel to UN PKOs for a variety of reasons. These include: to make a contribution to international peace and security, to foster a national role and reputation in the world ("show the flag"), to gain experience for their troops in multinational forces serving in conflict zones and to earn additional income.[14] Consequently, some contributors might not want a decrease in the number of peacekeepers in the field. They might fear that technology could bring such reductions, just as some people feared that office automation technology would lead to empty offices. Such fears are unwarranted.

In most cases, technology would not result in decreasing troop numbers but would rather lead to their more effective employment. Most UN missions are already overstretched, with too few soldiers and civilians to carry out all the tasks mandated and implied in Security Council resolutions. Robust multidimensional operations in particular are difficult to staff and support. Technology would, in most cases, take away some of the tedium of routine observation and allow PKOs to shift peacekeepers into more proactive roles, such as rapid reaction forces. By facilitating greater situational awareness, including better early warning, technology would enable reaction forces to intervene in a more targeted fashion in crisis or volatile situations. Far from creating a bunker mentality, technical means can make UN peacekeepers more proactive because the responders would benefit from increased knowledge of their local areas and could adopt preventative tactics when venturing into new ones.

Some troop contributors have little or no monitoring technology in their national inventories. Their doctrine, training and technical experience may have been limited to binoculars. Being unfamiliar with advanced technologies, these contributors might resent or envy the employment of technologies by more advanced contingents. Technology could conceivably introduce an imbalance between national contingents. One solution is to raise the capacity of these developing-nation forces by providing them with the devices and training needed to meet a standard technological level. The technology gap that exists between contributing states should not mean that the United Nations has to operate at the lowest common denominator. Rather, the United Nations should strive to operate at the most effective level for reasonable cost and effort. The soldiers of developing nations have in the past shown great eagerness to try out new tools. "Strategic partnerships" to bridge the technology gap can be adopted between nations to address the equipment and training needs of developing nations.

Some developed nations have re-engaged in peacekeeping (for example, certain European nations deployed in Lebanon) and have shown that they are willing to bring in the technologies and capabilities that they feel are necessary, irrespective of whether the United Nations will reimburse them. The United Nations' Memorandum of Understanding with troop contributors allows for such National Support Elements and equipment. Sharing a range of technology and expertise with developing nations would raise the standard of UN missions.

Political: UN member states

Some technologically advanced states have sought to prevent the proliferation of certain monitoring technologies, fearing that these might fall into non-friendly or enemy hands. One example is the stringent US export control regime on its night-vision equipment.[15] This has prevented UN headquarters from answering calls from field commanders for third-generation (Gen 3) night-vision equipment. Thus, the UN missions must, at present, be satisfied with the generation 2+ (Gen 2+) equipment in UN stockpiles, although more advanced devices are still being brought to the field as Contingent-Owned Equipment.

More generally, some states would not want the United Nations to have "information power" that might challenge their intelligence dominance in certain areas. This is particularly true in strategic conflict zones where economic interests are at stake and/or where covert operations are taking place. On the other hand, there are many examples where major powers have shared sensitive information with the United Nations in order to help bring a more durable peace to war-torn regions. This includes imagery from satellites and over-flights. When the success of a PKO is in the interest of all member states, as PKOs usually are, support is often provided.

Nations that host future PKOs on their territory may harbour exaggerated fears that technology could be used to pry into their affairs or that the United Nations might overstep the bounds of proper behaviour by interfering with national sovereignty and possibly engaging in dubious or covert intelligence-gathering. UN peacekeeping history has few incidents on record of such deviant behaviour. In practice, the United Nations has tended to be overly cautious and sensitive, avoiding anything controversial, even if the stakes have been high. Furthermore, the United Nations can institute internal checks and balances to prevent the potential misuse of monitoring. As noted, the United Nations has pledged to observe legal prohibitions and international norms.[16]

Institutional and cultural

Amid the conflicting interests and demands of UN member states, the UN Secretariat impressively manages a large number of PKOs in some of the most difficult conflict regions of the globe, using troops and civilians from over 100 disparate nations. The Department of Peacekeeping Operations (DPKO) in New York struggles to provide the field with the resources needed to do the job satisfactorily while also developing general policy, doctrine and training materials for PKOs, starting at the most basic level.

Field personnel, especially from developed nations, often complain that they are deployed in UN missions without sufficient tools, particularly the ones to which they have grown accustomed under national or allied arrangements. In the case of the UN mission in the DRC (MONUC), military commanders pleaded for modern surveillance technologies to carry out their ambitious monitoring mandates over vast territories. The UN system at headquarters, which must budget, fund and procure the technology, has often been slow or inadequate in its response. When not all UN actors sense the urgency and also face member state demands to decrease the overall cost of peacekeeping, it has been difficult to justify significant purchases of monitoring technology despite their potential or proven utility.

The military staff at UN headquarters are generally quite aware of the role that monitoring technology can play in PKOs and are sympathetic to the calls from the field. Soldiers are accustomed to seeking operational advantage from technology, whether in war-fighting or peacekeeping. Officers with NATO experience are aware that the alliance has over a dozen agencies devoted to technology and over 20 military advisory groups and committees (see the list in Table 7.4) to deal with science and technology issues. By contrast, military technologies are foreign to most civilians in the UN Secretariat. Staff who have never used or seen technologies in operation are only vaguely aware of the benefits/limitations and often exhibit a degree of "technophobia". They might even fear that technology is too military for peace. The solution is, of course, to raise awareness of technological options through education.

Some UN officials may also be concerned that member states would complain that the United Nations was overstepping its bounds in deploying sophisticated watching devices, despite the monitoring mandates. New information gained from technologies may also pressure and raise expectations for the United Nations to respond to early warning signals, removing the option of pleading ignorance about past or present threats. In the end, technical signals should help the United Nations become more proactive and responsive to the needs of inhabitants in conflict areas.

Humanitarians speak of the need for "humanitarian space" and worry about the possible over-militarization of operations. Some may not be aware that monitoring technologies can also be civilian run. In fact, humanitarian space relies extensively on communications technologies and many life-supporting devices such as water purification units. Using cameras instead of heavily armed soldiers can even reduce the level of military presence. When demilitarization is required, the step to civilian or appropriate joint civilian–military technology should not be difficult.

Financial

The cost of most monitoring devices is no longer a major obstacle. Prices have plummeted in recent years owing to advances in science and technology, as well as to the growing commercial marketplace. At the very low-cost end, motion detectors/illuminators can be obtained for as little as $20 and solar-powered versions are available at less than $50 per unit. This makes them cheap enough to use widely in refugee camps and even unattended places. Theft could be a problem, but at this low price there is little lost.

More expensive items such as video cameras (typically $500–2,000 each) for closed-circuit television (CCTV) systems and night-vision devices ($2,000 for Gen 2+ goggles) are well within normal discretionary budgets, as are hand-held metal detectors ($1,500) and acoustic/seismic systems ($1,500 for a set of a dozen sensors). Satellite imagery ($300–3,000 per image) becomes costly only when purchased in quantity or in near real time. (Some imagery, as in the older imagery on "Google Earth", is free.) Thermal (far-infrared) imaging devices are more expensive ($5,000 and above) and X-ray screening machines considerably more (over $25,000), as are various ground/aerial surveillance and artillery-locating radars (over $30,000).

The purchase of these devices, however, is only part of the overall cost, which must cover the entire lifecycle of the equipment. This includes procurement, transportation, installation, maintenance, repair, storage and disposal. Fortunately, the United Nations has become much better at equipment management over the past decade, especially through the development of better inventory methods and maintenance capabilities at the UN Logistics Base in Brindisi, Italy.

The most expensive types of surveillance are those involving aircraft (typically $1,000–2,500 per hour of flight for a wet lease[17]). When MONUC sought a commercial airborne surveillance service, DPKO budgeted $10–20 million per year, though the system was not deployed. If extensive use is to be made of aerial reconnaissance in several missions for several years, it might be cost-effective for the United Nations to procure one or more small aircraft and train its own civilian crews.

For unmanned aerial vehicles (UAVs), the United Nations might initially rely on certain troop-contributing countries that are rapidly gaining experience in deploying UAVs to operations. For instance, Belgium has deployed UAVs in Bosnia and the DRC under the UN-assisting European Union Force. As mini-UAV costs decrease and capabilities increase, the United Nations could consider purchasing some in the future.[18] A set of three mini-UAVs could be purchased for less than an annual dry lease for one manned aircraft.[19]

More challenging than equipment costs, however, can be the specialized training programmes for UN personnel to operate more advanced equipment. As mentioned, data analysis needs trained specialists. Several weeks of training and testing are required to operate even relatively simple systems, such as the ones used for X-ray screening.[20] This would be necessary for the equipment to become part of a standing "UN capability". Trainers from private corporations, including the equipment manufacturers, can be used to meet some of the training needs.

By using troop-contributing countries or wet-lease contractors, the training of military or contracted personnel can be done outside the United Nations, though such loans and leases may be more expensive than UN-owned and UN-operated equipment.[21] When the United Nations Interim Force in Lebanon was substantially expanded and upgraded after the 2006 war, the United Kingdom offered to provide UK-manned AWACS surveillance aircraft[22] – an offer that the United Nations had to turn down because of cost. Germany deployed frigates to patrol the coastline in the Mediterranean Sea and France sent a squadron of advanced UAVs. The full cost to lease such items would be millions of dollars a month, so the United Nations agreed to pay only a relatively small portion of the real cost.

Although monitoring is an essential, if not primary, function of all missions, monitoring equipment costs are currently not even 1 per cent of UN mission costs. The equipment costs are also minimal in comparison with the amounts the United Nations currently pays for aerial transport and personnel costs.[23] The United Nations spent over $8 billion on peace operations in 2009–2010. By contrast, a substantial increase in monitoring equipment in several missions could be gained with several million dollars. In short, the financial aspects of most monitoring technologies should not pose a significant obstacle, given the significant force-multiplier effect.

Other problems, pitfalls and hazards

Additional problems can be associated with technical monitoring:
- *Over-reliance.* If the United Nations were to become largely or completely dependent on technology, this would be a vulnerability. If devices malfunction or break down, experience a failure of electrical power or provide false information, the United Nations could find itself in difficult or embarrassing situations. Thus there is a need for constant testing, evaluation and cross-referencing with other sources, and for creating natural redundancies in the system. Direct human observation must continue to play a major part in the United Nations' information-gathering efforts.
- *Countermeasures.* Some technologies are susceptible to countermeasures that parties may take to evade detection. For instance, overhead nets can provide camouflage against day and night surveillance and GPS signals can be jammed. The United Nations should be aware of these possibilities, although most potential adversaries are not capable of sophisticated countermeasures.
- *Industrial lobbying.* DPKO already finds itself the target of lobbyists and commercial vendors who seek to promote their wares. Technologies cannot be justified for their own sake. They need to fulfil a definite purpose in peacekeeping (see Chapter 3). Commercial agents with past or present links to the organization may seek to exert undue influence on technology purchases. Given the strong defence lobby in some countries, particularly the host country for UN headquarters (the United States), it is likely that a more technologically receptive United Nations would find itself the object of greater lobbying. This, however, could have a side benefit of increasing awareness of technologies, although with some nuisance.
- *"Middleman" corporations.* Such companies are an integral part of the defence lobby in many nations, and the firms often charge substantially marked-up prices for coordinating delivery of products produced by others. This sometimes results in cost inefficiencies and a lack of direct accountability.

Though the challenges of employing technologies are great, the benefits are greater. The costs of not using technology are far higher in terms of UN effectiveness and of possible lives lost. Given the many obstacles identified above, what can be done to improve UN capacity? The penultimate chapter provides both general and technology-specific recommendations.

Notes

1. Night driving on roads with no street lighting (e.g. jungle roads) is possible with night-vision goggles but users should first gain experience in simpler environments. Users need to be aware that night-vision devices can alter depth perception and exhibit distortions such as curving at the edges and phenomena such as "blooming" (halo effects around bright lights), "scintillation" (temporary bright spots) and black spots (small but often permanent).
2. For instance, commercial water-resistant global positioning devices used for hiking and climbing expeditions can be purchased for under $200.
3. Terrain can impose other limitations on the choice of sensors. In the open desert, where there are many, if not an infinite number of, possible paths through the sand, point sensors are of limited value because they measure signals at one small location only. Seismic devices are rendered ineffectual in the desert because seismic waves are quickly absorbed by the sand. Similarly, in difficult mountainous terrain where vehicles are unlikely to pass, buried magnetic sensors are of limited value.
4. This notion is well captured by General Alfred M. Gray: "Intelligence without communications is irrelevant; communications without intelligence is noise" (quoted by Robert David Steele in "Intelligence & Information: The Debate Continues", available at <http://www.oss.net/dynamaster/file_archive/050305/fa8baa703790c82a5afbb1ada54e96db/Steele%20on%20Intelligence.doc>, accessed 7 February 2011). See also Steele (2010b).
5. In the same study (Schwabe et al. 2001: 102), a survey of US police officers revealed: "Relatively few local police (less than 10 percent) felt that training requirements were an important factor with respect to the use of video cameras either in patrol cars or in fixed or mobile surveillance. Only 10 percent of departments considered training to be key with respect to acquisition of night vision/electro-optic devices, smart guns, and for most vehicle stopping/tracking devices (tire deflation spikes, stolen vehicle tracking) and digital imaging devices (fingerprints, mug shots)."
6. Email from Dan Hefkey, Ontario Provincial Police Inspector, to Michael Dube, Toronto, Canada, January 2009. Inspector Hefkey had served as the detachment/station commander for the Hinche and Thiotte detachments in Haiti in 1995.
7. Also the 1994 Convention on the Safety of United Nations and Associated Personnel states that "their equipment and premises shall not be made the object of attack or of any action that prevents them from discharging their mandate" (United Nations 1994).
8. The right to import is provided in Article 15. This document also serves as the basis for Status of Mission Agreements in cases where UN civilians and unarmed military observers, but not UN forces, are deployed.
9. Personal interview with David Hutchinson, Senior Legal Officer, Office of Legal Affairs, United Nations, New York, 26 January 2007.
10. "The United Nations peacekeeping operation and its members shall enjoy, together with its vehicles, vessels, aircraft and equipment, freedom of movement throughout the

[host country/territory]. The freedom shall, with respect to large movements ... be coordinated with the Government" (United Nations 1990: Article 12).

11. The United Nations could use lower-resolution cameras so as not to identify individuals (unless required) and exercise "shutter control" over the cameras and devices to ensure that the peacekeeping operation does not unduly observe innocent commercial or private activities.

12. This happened in one Bosnian city. As soldiers of the United Nations Protection Force observed the landing areas of mortar fire, they communicated these locations to regional headquarters by radio in the clear (non-encrypted). They did not know that Serb artillerymen were listening to the communications and using the information to correct their fire in order to make it more deadly. In such cases, encrypted communications are a must for the United Nations.

13. The United Nations could, for instance, outline the types of information that would be sought and the general methods and devices that would be employed. Furthermore, it could provide the parties with regular reports on its monitoring activities in a way that would not threaten the parties' security. At meetings of joint commissions or other bodies that bring all parties and the United Nations together, a regular feature could be the presentation of the results of UN verification in general terms.

14. For some states, peacekeeping is revenue generating.

15. To export night-vision equipment from the United States to the field, the United Nations would need an export licence from the US State Department under the US Government International Traffic in Arms Regulations rules. The US government allows third-generation technology to be exported to all NATO countries, plus Japan, South Korea, Australia, Egypt and Israel. So far, the requests of the Supply Section in the United Nations' Logistics Support Division for licences have all been turned down, on the basis that nations other than those listed above might gain access to the technology once it is deployed to the field. The United Nations currently gets most of its night-vision equipment (generation 2+) from a Canadian company.

16. There are examples, however, where nation-states have used UN peacekeeping and other operations as a cover to introduce their own intelligence personnel into the mission area. The United Nations Special Commission in Iraq is a likely case of this (Ritter 1999).

17. A wet lease for an aircraft arrangement would include at least some of the costs for crew, maintenance and fuel, as well as the lease of the aircraft itself. See <http://www.globalplanesearch.com/view/aircraft/aircraft-leasing-def.htm>.

18. The UAV would need to be certified for airworthiness, possibly by the nation that produced it.

19. A dry lease for an aircraft does not provide aircraft insurance, crew or maintenance services.

20. MONUC procured X-ray machines at a cost of over $500,000 for baggage-handling at the MONUC-run airports in the DRC. Many months after they were installed at airport departure areas, they had not been brought into use because the local personnel had not been trained to operate them.

21. For instance, the United Nations pays over $8,000 per month for two ground surveillance radars used by the Quick Reaction Force in the United Nations Mission in Liberia.

22. Airborne Early Warning and Control System aircraft cost over $200 million each to procure and between $10,000 and $25,000 per hour to operate (Beattie and Greenaway 1986).

23. It is estimated that almost a quarter of MONUC's annual budget of $1.1 billion is spent on aircraft and fuel.

10

Recommendations

The present study has shown that monitoring technologies are not yet "tools of the trade" in UN peace operations but that they can and should be. To accomplish this, a conscious effort is needed by the UN Secretariat, supported by member states, to incorporate appropriate technologies into peacekeeping operations (PKOs) and to raise technical awareness and standards generally. The following seven general recommendations offer ways to create progress.

General recommendations

General recommendation 1

The United Nations should update, develop and improve UN policies, doctrine and training materials to incorporate appropriate monitoring technologies

The generic documents used to develop and implement PKOs need to be updated to include modern technologies. Important guidance documents from the Department of Peacekeeping Operations (DPKO) include the "Capstone" document (DPKO and DFS 2008), the *Handbook on United Nations Multidimensional Peacekeeping Operations* (DPKO 2003) and the model Standard Operating Procedures (UNFICYP 2008b). The "New Horizon" paper (DPKO and DFS 2009) made an important step in recognizing technological need. Updating basic documents would help create a

Keeping watch: Monitoring, technology and innovation in UN peace operations, Dorn, United Nations University Press, 2011, ISBN 978-92-808-1198-8

more advanced "common operating paradigm" for technology-enabled monitoring. Furthermore, a new training document could be produced to describe the range of possible technologies, including night-vision devices, radars, seismic and acoustic sensors, and aerospace reconnaissance.

To engage member states in a dialogue on the issue, as the Special Committee on Peacekeeping has encouraged, DPKO could organize seminars for both military and civilian personnel. For instance, the Military and Police Advisers Community at the United Nations in New York is one appropriate forum for DPKO and governments to discuss possible technological contributions to specific missions and to peacekeeping in general.

To help plan specific operations, a "menu document" containing a list of technologies could be developed to supplement the Table of Organization and Equipment. From such a list the appropriate technologies could be incorporated into the Concept of Operations and Force Requirements for specific missions.

General recommendation 2

To gain experience, the United Nations should test, deploy and evaluate sensor suites on a trial and operational basis

To evaluate which sensors are the most appropriate and effective in various circumstances, the UN departments involved in peacekeeping could select pilot PKOs or locations within PKOs to incorporate a variety of technologies from different vendors. Once the technologies are installed, the United Nations could evaluate the change in situational awareness. For instance, video surveillance equipment and unattended ground sensors could be deployed to monitor potential hotspots. A slightly more expensive approach would include thermal imaging cameras for increased monitoring of night activities.

To better prepare UN troops, military observers, police and civilians for deployments to new or rapidly changing areas, the United Nations should routinely provide peacekeepers with ground, aerial and satellite images. It should also provide them with access to geographic information system (GIS) databases filled with mission information to give them a greater sense of terrain, locations, events, and so on.

In the few cases where the United Nations has already deployed technologies in the field, such as the Interim Force in Lebanon, assessments should be made of the impact and effectiveness of these technologies. At present, there is no programme in place to systematically conduct such evaluations. The Contingent-Owned Equipment (COE) system provides for inspections to verify whether designated equipment is functional, not whether it is being effectively used. The Peacekeeping Best Practices Unit of DPKO could conduct a more operational survey of current practice along with lessons to be learned. Case studies, similar to the ones presented in Chapters 6 and 7, would help develop practical knowledge.

In missions where there is already a clearly expressed demand for technology, such as the requirement of the United Nations Organization Stabilization Mission in the Democratic Republic of the Congo (DRC) for aerial surveillance over the eastern DRC, the United Nations could implement a trial programme. If this is successful, the capacity could be continued and eventually even handed over to the host state. More generally, in the United Nations Mission in the DRC (MONUC), DPKO should revisit and implement the recommendations of the Joint Assessment Mission on surveillance assets.

General recommendation 3

DPKO should identify countries that are capable of providing monitoring equipment and expertise to UN missions. It should invite them to share some of their technological expertise and experiences generally. More importantly, these nations should be encouraged to provide equipment for specific missions, on a loan or lease basis, possibly with crews to serve the equipment

Some developed nations might prefer to offer specialized expertise rather than large numbers of troops to the United Nations for peace operations. A small number of national specialists equipped with advanced technologies can make a significant positive impact on a mission. Such countries could be approached and their capacities evaluated before formal requests are made. DPKO could conduct a survey of such technologically equipped nations.

The use of national capacities makes more sense for larger-ticket items such as sophisticated monitoring systems for which the purchasing costs are prohibitive. However, when such a country is not available, the United Nations could seek an outsource vendor, who would take complete responsibility for the equipment and for project management.

In general, the United Nations has yet to move from personal equipment (for example, night-vision goggles) to mission-operated and crew-served monitoring systems such as unattended sensors and radars that offer the benefits of round-the-clock surveillance. Some UN-owned equipment could be operated by civilians directly under UN employment.

General recommendation 4

The United Nations should revise and update the technical documents, particularly the COE Manual, so the requirements are clearer, more detailed and more specific

The important COE Manual provides the basis for the Memorandum of Understanding (MOU) between the United Nations and the contributing nations. The 2008 Manual (United Nations 2008) includes the most detailed treatment of monitoring technologies of any UN peacekeeping document, but there is still much to correct and improve.

In the self-sustainment category, the categories of observation and identification are poorly defined, leading to many uncertainties. Nations and even COE inspectors do not know what quantity or quality of equipment is required to meet the vague COE standards.[1]

In future updates of the Manual by the COE Working Group, these monitoring technology sections should be rewritten to provide greater detail and precision and to remove ambiguities. An annex should be added to these sections to list specific requirements. In the interim, UN field missions should specify and clarify their observation and identification requirements.

Other technical documents that need updating are the Tables of Organization and Equipment (DPKO (n.d.[b]), and the Standard Cost Manual (DPKO 2005a).

General recommendation 5

The United Nations should build on recent progress in developing geographic information systems

The Cartographic Section at UN headquarters and the GIS units in the field produce excellent paper maps using modern software and advanced satellite imagery (in some cases high-resolution). But the United Nations has yet to move from cartography to geomatics, in which users in the field can access and update maps and other information through shared electronic databases. If users could input data directly into networked databases, a new wealth of up-to-date geospatial information would become available. For example, UN military observers could submit their reports to a centralized database, allowing future observers and visitors to view all previous reports relating to specific villages or areas. This would facilitate the rapid transfer of information between neighbouring areas in the mission and up to (and back down from) mission HQ. For such types of application, commercial GIS database software, with user-friendly interfaces to input new information, is now widely available. Some parts of the database could be open for public input, allowing for "crowdsourced" information. The database could also draw from social media to help identify the latest developments.

The United Nations lacks a centralized database of the imagery that is ordered commercially and of the GIS paper products that are produced in the missions. It does not even have a catalogue using thumbnails. The DPKO intranet, established in 2006, could serve as a platform for the database, providing access mission-wide and at UN headquarters. Other DPKO databases are well established.[2]

General recommendation 6

UN reports should include imagery, both still and video links, and provide electronic access to primary source data from the field

Peacekeepers are only beginning to incorporate digital (still) imagery in their reports from patrols, visits or after-action reviews of operations. This practice is not yet used in the situation reports that are sent to UN headquarters. In the future, imagery could be included through links to GIS databases from which analysts and decision-makers in the field and at UN headquarters could get a clearer picture of conditions and activities in the field. Video clips could also be included, provided that wider-bandwidth communications channels are available. To gain maximum benefit, experts in image analysis should be deployed to the field, particularly within the Joint Operations Centre and Joint Mission Analysis Centre structures.

General recommendation 7

The United Nations should increase the capacity of UN headquarters to select, stockpile and maintain technologies and to apply truly innovative methods of technical monitoring

The United Nations need not become self-reliant in all technologies because troop-contributing countries and contractors can help fill the gaps. It should, however, have a basic stockpile of technologies upon which it can draw, as and when required. For instance, it should increase the number of night-vision goggles available (currently fewer than 500 goggles of an older generation) both for quick deployment and for contingents without adequate night-vision equipment (NVE). The stockpile should include thermal imagers and third-generation image intensifiers. To procure such devices, it may be necessary to obtain export licences from some leading manufacturing states. The member states should be able to grant special permits to the United Nations, given that the equipment is for peace-keeping.

A small team of specialists could be assembled at UN headquarters with familiarity of monitoring methods and technologies. They could be part of a new monitoring technology service or technology support office. This resident capacity would keep abreast of recent advances in technology and fill the need at UN headquarters in much the same way that the Communications and Information Technology Service (CITS) fulfils that function. The individuals could also become familiar with the specialized technological capacities of the national contingent so that they could advise on which nations to approach for technical contributions. For UN equipment purchases, they could develop specific selection criteria, including the principles of modularity and flexibility, so that equipment could be moved between missions as conditions warrant.

A UN team of technical experts at a technology support centre would create institutional memory on technical monitoring, so that lessons learned about equipment and techniques would be applied to future operations. The team could conduct capability/equipment performance reviews so that better sensors would be purchased. They could also assist with technical assessments during mission start-up.

These technical experts could also help UN officials and conflicting parties, when requested, to incorporate optimal technical monitoring solutions into the design and implementation of peace agreements. They could help explore "cooperative monitoring" by developing protocols for regular sharing of technical results with parties. Possible information-sharing arrangements have been listed in Chapter 9.

Specific recommendations

This mismatch between the scope of modern peacekeeping and its tools is creating serious strains for UN Peacekeeping at a time when it is being asked to do more.
DPKO and DFS (2009: 4)

Many specific technological tools can and should be introduced into the field. The following recommendations, naming over 30 technologies, are made in point form for brevity, grouping technologies into three cost categories (low, medium and high). Illustrative and typical purchase prices per device are provided in US dollars. The costs for signal transmission (wires or wireless), analysis and operators (including training) are not included. Similarly, the costs over the equipment lifecycle for supplies, maintenance, storage and disposal would be additional. In some cases, these other costs can be significant. However, as many of these technologies are increasingly commercialized, these lifecycle costs, like the prices of the devices themselves, will probably decrease in coming years.

Low-cost technologies ($50–$10,000 per device)

- Provide digital still and video **cameras** (camcorders) to peacekeepers tasked with monitoring; for example, one for each UN military observer or team in most missions.[3] These can capture images or clips from the field that can be added to UN reports or referenced in them to a database. Of course, rules for image-taking are needed, depending on the situation and local sensitivities. The typical cost of a still-image camera is $300. A quality video camcorder is about $500.

- Employ **remote video cameras** to monitor hotspots even when no peacekeepers are present. The United Nations Peacekeeping Force in Cyprus made pioneering use of surveillance cameras to monitor opposing forces along the Green Line in Nicosia (see the case study in Chapter 6). The United Nations should employ cameras in many other hotspots where it has a mandate to monitor conflicts and protect civilians. In some missions this would mean flash points, threatened towns, protected sites (for example, refugee camps) or across large conflict regions. Cameras can be installed to help prevent trespassing and the illegal trafficking of arms, natural resources and human beings. Each remote camera with connection could cost as little as $500. The data could be sent in real time or downloaded by passing patrols, depending on the urgency. Means to protect the cameras from theft and vandalism would need to be used in some cases.

- Deploy "**dummy cameras**" (camera housing without the expensive electronics inside) for short periods to deter violators and to test the vulnerability of cameras to vandalism, theft and destruction. Cost: $50.

- Equip selected peacekeepers with **helmet cameras**, which have become standard kit in many militaries (and are now even used by mountain bikers). They could be useful for UN operations. The view seen by a soldier can be recorded in a pocket device and even transmitted in real time to other soldiers and commanding officers, as well as to higher-ups in the headquarters. This could be a valuable information-gathering tool. Cost: $500 and upwards.

- Use **night-vision devices** of various kinds in areas where night violence is a concern. These include cameras with low-light sensing (image intensifiers) and cameras for infrared detection. In some locations, floodlights or infrared illuminators could be added. The recording capability for night vision could be useful for evidence gathering. Cost for low-light cameras (<10 lux): $1,000. Infrared cameras: $2,000 and upwards.

- Illuminators and cameras can be triggered by **motion detectors** to warn trespassers and alert the watchkeeper of any movements or changes. This would show potential trespassers that there is a UN monitoring "presence". In areas with no available power, solar-powered detector/illuminator systems can potentially be deployed. Illuminated signs could warn trespassers that they are entering an out-of-bounds, dangerous or monitored area. Solar-powered illuminators with motion detectors are available for under $100 each. Ruggedized versions will be more expensive.

- Install computer **software** to aid in the interpretation of signals, especially for motion detection, pattern recognition and filtering out false alarms. Such software is readily available, some with cameras. Typical cost: $500 per licence.

- Create a system to inspect and test the **night-vision equipment** of contributing countries. An example would be to verify a contingent's ability to detect the movement of a participating person at intervals of 100 metres. The COE Manual standard to detect/categorize persons at 1,000 metres is unlikely to be attained by most contingents in the field. So an assessment of the range for detection could help establish new levels. Units can be presented with the results of their tests. This would allow the United Nations to identify when the NVE is substandard and how much the COE technology needs to be improved. It would encourage units to bring better night-vision equipment. In cases where NVE is essential (for example, Special Forces operating in jungles) and the contingent is unable to provide it (especially contingents from developing countries), the United Nations should be capable of doing so.

- Use **microphones** attached to remote video cameras to record sounds in the most sensitive areas. Unusual sounds could also trigger alerts at the operations centre. Microphones are included with many cameras. Otherwise the cost to add can be small: $100.

- Use **laser range-finders** to detect trespassing across borders or into restricted zones. Cost: $100 and upwards. Maximum ranges: 1,000 to 20,000 metres. Some laser range-finders are combined with GPS units so the exact position of distant objects can be determined.

- Use powerful (eye-safe) visible laser pointers or **laser designators** to let potential combatants know that they are being watched and can be targeted if they resort to violence or otherwise violate the peace. Caution should be exercised in the application because some combatants may become nervous and aggressive if they assume they are being targeted. Cost: $100–$1,000.

- Upgrade the United Nations' capability from "cartography" (map-making) to true **geographic information systems** (GIS). Satellite imagery should be purchased to properly geo-reference the areas and sites where peacekeepers are deployed. A GIS system needs to be developed in which UN observers and liaison officers can enter data and reports directly into a spatial database and access it from anywhere in real time. Cost for a typical GIS software licence: $400. GIS server (computer): $10,000.

- Purchase **smartphones** for all field missions where data as well as voice transmission is possible through existing cell phone networks. This will allow the peacekeepers to have access to a world of data (for example, the Internet), as well as to transmit new information through web-based applications and email. Typical cost: $300 per device plus $70/month per subscription.

- Deploy **acoustic/seismic sensors** near sensitive areas to detect the movement of personnel or weapons. These sensors could trigger cameras and/or patrols. They can be both a security measure and a means of verification of peace agreements. Cost: $300.

- Equip selected peacekeepers and liaison officers with portable **DVD players** to show recordings to leaders or representatives of conflict parties and local communities, especially when entering into negotiations or scrutinizing incidents. Charges of wrong-doing are much more convincing when imagery evidence is shown. Cost: $100.

Medium-cost technologies ($10,000–$100,000)

- Deploy **suites of sensors** on ground vehicles (land cruisers) to key locations of immediate concern. Cost for surveillance suite (day camera, infrared, radar): $50,000.

- Place **ground surveillance radars** (GSRs) to help detect movements into and within sensitive areas. This will greatly improve night-time awareness. GSRs can be a valuable protection measure around UN camps, field units and refugee camps. GSR (radar range for person >5 km): $20,000 and upwards.

- Acquire **maritime radars** for use on patrol boats and on shore to spot boats moving along or across rivers. They can be programmed to emit an audible signal (for example, a series of beeps) when a boat approaches within a pre-programmed distance. Cost (entire system, radar range >30 nautical miles): $5,000 and upwards.

- Deploy tethered balloons holding day/night video cameras to provide a high and wide view of areas around UN locations. An **aerostat** marked with UN letters could also serve as a useful landmark or boundary demarcation point. However, the United Nations must be prepared to repair or replace the balloon and camera should it be shot down.

Compartmentalized and self-sealing aerostats can mitigate some of the costs of repair. Balloon cost: $10,000 and upwards.

- Provide a **live network link** to regional, mission and UN headquarters from UN cameras, whether they are on aircraft, ground vehicles or fixed, attended or unattended. Currently UN missions have little or no capacity to link live to command-and-control elements or higher units. With modern network technology, it should be relatively easy, provided the bandwidth is increased, to provide leaders in Force HQ and Sector HQ with the ability to see what is going on in their area of responsibility. This would help a Quick Reaction Force to be aware of incidents in areas to which they are about to deploy. Airborne imagery could also be transmitted in real time to soldiers on the ground with remote video terminals and to sector headquarters. In particularly dangerous/hostile areas, possible ambushes can be identified in this way. Cost: $50,000 and upwards.

High-cost technologies ($100,000 – millions)

- Deploy **armoured reconnaissance vehicles** with various sensor suites (for example, radars, infrared and electro-optical). This would greatly increase the mission's day/night surveillance capacity, especially in dangerous zones where people need to be protected. The vehicles could possess extendable masts equipped with a variety of sensors (day/night cameras and radars). The ability to transmit imagery from the sensors to both headquarters and units would be valuable. Reconnaissance units are ill equipped in most UN missions, except in the United Nations Interim Force in Lebanon. The Coyote reconnaissance vehicle deployed by Canada in the United Nations Mission in Ethiopia and Eritrea during 2000–2001 proved to be of immense value in monitoring the Temporary Security Zone. Cost for vehicle: $500,000 and up; sensor suite: $50,000 and up.

- Deploy **reconnaissance aircraft** equipped with gyro-stabilized camera pods for high-resolution videography. Make use of the night-vision (forward-looking infrared) cameras in daytime as well as at night. Cost for stabilized pod with day/night camera: $50,000; aircraft use: $1,500/ hour.

- Deploy **artillery-tracking radars** to detect and track projectiles (mortars, rockets, bombs, missiles) moving through the air. The trajectories can be traced back to their point of origin or forward to the point of impact. These radars can be used for self-defence or for verifying a cease-fire and determining who shot first. Their presence can serve as a deterrent to first use of artillery. Cost: $100,000 and upwards.

- Deploy unmanned aerial vehicles (**UAVs**) for surveillance. These can be of many sizes and capabilities, including mini-UAVs that are hand-launched and sub-tactical UAVs that are virtually invisible at higher altitudes, as well as tactical UAVs with long ranges. Cost for mini UAV: $50,000; for sub-tactical UAV: $500,000; for tactical UAV: $2 million.

For the United Nations, most of these high-cost technologies would be leased as major equipment through the COE programme. In MONUC, the Lama helicopters are leased from India by the United Nations for about $250,000 per year and the Mi-35s are leased at $950,000 per year.

Further recommendations

· To help incorporate the technologies listed above, a series of broader activities could be carried out, including the following:

- Develop the United Nations' internal capacity for **maintenance** of technologies (cameras, sensors, and so on). An existing organization, such as CITS, could be expanded or a new service could be created.

- Increase the internal **connectivity** of remote cameras and sensors to the United Nations' computer network. It is possible to transmit streaming video to wireless devices. For a future camera system, use standard formats, not software specific to the camera.

- Launch a second low–medium-cost **project** with a longer timeframe (more than one fiscal year).

- Launch a **pilot project** for remote surveillance of a hotspot using a variety of technology types. This could result in a longer-term commitment for appropriate and tested equipment.

- Develop a **monitoring technology policy**. As the United Nations Special Committee on Peacekeeping Operations has requested, a policy on monitoring and surveillance technology is being developed. It can serve a useful purpose as UN headquarters and the field operations struggle with the application of such devices.

- Include **imagery** in reports from the field and move away from text-limited messages. Imagery adds a sense of the environment that words alone cannot convey.

- Employ **image analysts** in the field. Basic analysis can be done by regular military/civilian personnel, but for results of higher resolution and deeper interpretation, especially when conflicting parties are trying to hide objects or activities, trained experts are needed.

- Adjust the basic **mission planning documents** (Force Requirements, Concept of Operations and Intelligence directives) to include monitoring and surveillance capabilities.

- As a confidence-building measure, consider sharing some video imagery with the opposing forces, either periodically or in real time. This might not be appropriate in "hot" conflicts in which the protagonists are resistant or might misuse information or misinterpret it. But, if the protagonists act responsibly, it can be a tremendous boost to the peace process. New technologies can provide many ways to share imagery and data from sensors and cameras. The United Nations could retain "shutter control" to cut off the signal feed if need be. Such "**cooperative monitoring**" arrangements could create transparency and instil confidence that the provisions of a peace agreement are being respected. It could also provide early warning when the provisions are being violated.

- For each technological application, consider the four types of **technology provider**: contributing countries; the United Nations Secretariat for purchased equipment; contracted services; and partnerships with other organizations (regional organizations or alliances or coalitions).

- Beyond hardware and software, develop "**peopleware**" by hosting seminars on the utility and challenges of various technologies. Further integrate staff, tools, processes and information flows so that monitoring and surveillance effectiveness are maximized.

- The United Nations should host a **conference** of high-ranking military officers who have served on UN missions that utilized technology. The purpose of the conference would be to develop a list of the highest-priority items of equipment that the United Nations would seek to purchase to augment the monitoring and surveillance capacity and general situational awareness of its missions.

Notes

1. The COE Manual does not give any sense of the required number or type of night-vision devices, and does not specify how this issue is to be resolved (for example, through mission-specific standards). The Manual, for instance, makes no distinction between image intensifiers and thermal imagers. Similarly, the recording devices listed in the identification

category are not defined. Indeed, the section title "Identification" is a misnomer; it should really be titled "Recording" because it is about capturing images for processing and dissemination. The section could, at least, list the capability for recording night-vision images. Being the result of outdated versions, the 2008 COE Manual does not recognize the new capacities of digital cameras and computers (for example, laptops) for storage, photo editing and databasing.

2. The COE unit has a well-developed COE Database that is accessible from the field, incorporating scanned copies of all the MOU with contributing states, for consultation by COE inspectors, and the verification reports from COE inspections.

3. It is also recommended that the COE Manual specify the number of such devices to be deployed per unit of troops or police (for example, per company or per 100 personnel).

11

Conclusions

The United Nations has gained more experience as a monitor of peace agreements than any other organization in history. But it is still far from maintaining an ever-watchful and attentive eye on the common interest that President Woodrow Wilson proposed in 1919 at the dawn of international organization. Though its mandates for monitoring and verification have expanded considerably, the United Nations is inadequately equipped for its evolving field operations.

Technological progress in the world has also been evolutionary, even "revolutionary" in the digital and information domains. Monitoring technologies, in particular, are advancing at a rapid rate. For instance, the new generation of unattended ground sensors incorporates video, seismic, magnetic and acoustic capabilities all in one small device. Each multi-sensor also includes a processor and transmitter to send analysed data by satellite. Many sensors can be dispersed by plane and their signals gathered in mobile laptop computers to determine the directions and characteristics of moving objects across large areas.

This process of technological convergence, where previously separate technologies are combined into single systems, is readily seen in the commercial cell phone market. A smartphone can contain a cell phone, a voice recorder, still and video cameras, GPS, TV viewer and Internet browser, as well as email and text messaging. Inbuilt video cameras are available in high definition and for low-light imaging. In other devices, ever-more-capable cameras are giving new forms of imagery: ultra-high definition, hyperspectral, panoramic (360 degrees – viewer controllable),

Keeping watch: Monitoring, technology and innovation in UN peace operations, Dorn, United Nations University Press, 2011, ISBN 978-92-808-1198-8

even three-dimensional. Cameras are becoming smaller (through industrially-driven miniaturization) and more integrated, with compatible digital signals and files sharable among many types of device. The outputs are increasingly shared through the Internet using social and professional media.

This revolution in commercial off-the-shelf technologies means that the United Nations can look forward to more tools with which to creatively gather information and conduct its monitoring. Modern technology offers the United Nations a wide array of monitoring systems that are continually improving in capacity while decreasing in cost. This study has examined these technologies and reviewed the relevant UN experience with monitoring and technology. It has explored the benefits and potential drawbacks of technical monitoring, including the operational, legal, political, institutional and financial challenges. From this work, four principal conclusions can be drawn.

Conclusion 1: There is no "technological fix" to the problem of human conflict. Technology can, however, be of immense value in monitoring, preventing and mitigating conflict, especially as a cease-fire or peace agreement is being implemented.

Although the human dimension of peacekeeping must always remain front and centre, technologies can be valuable tools in the hands of peacekeepers. They are key enablers.

Conclusion 2: Technical monitoring can increase the safety and security of peacekeepers, as well as the effectiveness of their mission.

Technology offers possibilities for wide-area, high-resolution and continuous surveillance, helping the United Nations to identify threats to personnel and the mission. It permits monitoring of dangerous areas where it would be unsafe or unwise to send human observers. Aerial surveillance offers vast opportunities for rapid and remote monitoring of otherwise inaccessible areas. Night surveillance, a traditional lacuna in UN peacekeeping, is made possible with modern devices. In addition, imagery can be disseminated rapidly for early warning, for in-depth analysis and as evidence in future legal or other proceedings. In complex multidimensional peace operations, modern technologies can help fill the "monitoring gap" between the demanding mandates given to field operations and the United Nations' limited capacities.

Conclusion 3: The United Nations currently lacks the equipment, resources and preparation/training needed for an effective and efficient use of modern monitoring technology, and instead relies mainly on primitive or obsolete methods and devices.

A review of UN experience in technology shows that the world organization has used *some* monitoring technologies in *some* missions but mostly in an ad hoc and *unsystematic* fashion. For example, ground surveillance radar is currently deployed by only a single mission.[1] The United Nations has begun to employ digital and video cameras in recent years, but this is not regular practice. The world organization has yet to deploy remote-controlled video cameras to its monitor hotspots, except in Nicosia, Cyprus. Significantly, the parties to the 2006 Nepal peace agreement asked for video monitoring of weapons cantonment sites. This was done to supplement the UN monitors already on site (see Chapter 8). The United Nations owns some 400 image-intensification systems for night viewing, but these are older second-generation devices not coupled with cameras for recording and are too few in number to meet the need. Thermal imagers are not in the UN stockpile. The United Nations has no direct experience with seismic or acoustic sensor systems. Furthermore, the organization does not routinely deploy motion sensors – a simple, cheap and readily available technology.

Deploying multiple sensors (for example, infrared and radar systems) on advanced mobile platforms such as light reconnaissance vehicles and unmanned aerial vehicles (UAVs) can offer great benefits. But the United Nations does not deploy these standard sensor systems in its operations. In fact, UAVs have yet to be deployed by the United Nations, although they were brought by a partner (the European Union Force) to temporarily support the UN operation in the Democratic Republic of the Congo (DRC) in 2006.

More alarmingly, there is an absence of policies, doctrine, Standard Operating Procedures (SOPs) and training materials regarding high-tech monitoring equipment. For example, the United Nations has no policies or procedures for any type of radar use – whether for aerial or ground surveillance, or for locating artillery and underground probing. The equipment guidelines in the draft SOPs, written for traditional peacekeeping, are out of date by at least a decade. The SOPs have not kept up with either technological advancement or the more proactive UN approach used in some field missions. Many recommendations have been made in this book to further development in this area.

Fortunately, a framework has been established in recent years to create, update and improve peacekeeping doctrine and the policy directives of the Department of Peacekeeping Operations. A policy on monitoring technologies was finally developed in 2010. This could be of immense value as new technologies are being considered, tested and deployed.

Because of the United Nations' "relative backwardness" in military equipment, many developed nations prefer to deploy their forces under other organizations and alliances (for example, the North Atlantic Treaty Organization and coalitions of the willing). In order to encourage these nations to re-engage in UN peacekeeping, the United Nations and its member states should encourage the deployment of at least some of the advanced tools that have long been standard "kit" for modern militaries.[2]

Conclusion 4: The United Nations has proved capable in the past of innovation in peacekeeping and it has incorporated some new and relatively advanced technologies into its operations.

The United Nations has impressively evolved its peace operations over many decades. Yet, while the functions have multiplied, the tools have not kept pace. Great political innovation has occurred with little technological innovation. However, there are some areas where the United Nations has demonstrated substantial technological progress.

It has developed a world-class communications and information technology (CIT) system. Given the difficult operational environments and the urgent demands for instantaneous communications in the field, the United Nations has achieved, if not set, a global standard for rapid CIT deployment to remote conflict areas.

There have also been a few success stories with monitoring technology. The Carlog system is deployed in most PKOs to track where UN vehicles have been and how they have been handled, thus improving fleet awareness, increasing accountability and efficiencies in time and fuel, and also reducing accidents. Real-time tracking is an option that could be pursued in the future for high-value or high-risk vehicles or convoys. Similarly, the United Nations' use of geographic information systems has increased dramatically in the past decade, though much more can be done. High-resolution commercial satellite imagery (including that supplied through the United Nations Operational Satellite Applications Programme) is now routinely used to create more accurate and up-to-date maps, although not to inform real-time operations. Aerial reconnaissance has been deployed in several missions to great effect. For instance, forward-looking infrared devices in helicopters in the eastern DRC and East Timor have helped to save the lives of peacekeepers and civilians. Also, useful radars were brought into the United Nations Interim Force in Lebanon in 2006 by troop-contributing countries, mostly through their National Support Element.

More generally, the United Nations has built up extensive experience with equipment handling and accounting in PKOs – whether the equipment is UN owned or contingent owned. For instance, the system of inspection for Contingent-Owned Equipment in the field is well established and should be capable, with some of the improvements suggested in this work, of handling more advanced technologies.

With a host of activities to monitor – from elections to disarmament to sanctions and a myriad of threats – the world organization needs to broaden its technology base and explore innovative monitoring strategies. Technical monitoring may be just one component of UN operations, but it is an essential one that gives the United Nations greater "information power". Monitoring technologies are legitimate tools – legal under international law – that host states and conflicting parties should welcome because these tools allow the United Nations to do a more effective job as an impartial observer of commitments. The United Nations can thereby help create a more sustainable peace in war-torn areas. These devices can also enhance the safety of UN civilian and military personnel. Finally, technology could help the United Nations take a more proactive approach – moving from a "culture of reaction" towards a "culture of prevention". For proactive peacekeeping, superior situational awareness is essential. Monitoring technologies are particularly important tools of this trade. They can help the United Nations to develop a much more watchful and attentive eye to serve its mission for peace.

Notes

1. The United Nations Interim Force in Lebanon currently deploys several types of advanced radar (as described in Chapter 8). In the past, the Quick Reaction Force in the United Nations Mission in Liberia used ground surveillance radars.
2. In Western military jargon, a major part of deployed capability is referred to as ISTAR ("Intelligence, Surveillance, Target Acquisition and Reconnaissance").

Appendices

Appendix 1

United Nations peacekeeping operations, 1948–2010, organized into four categories: Observer missions; Interposed forces; Multidimensional operations; Transitional administrations

Current operations are indicated by bold abbreviations, which can be found on the map in Figure 2.1 (page 9).

Keeping watch: Monitoring, technology and innovation in UN peace operations, Dorn, United Nations University Press, 2011, ISBN 978-92-808-1198-8

Table A1.1 Observer missions

Name	Abbreviation (current missions in bold)	Main location(s)	Mandate	Initial Security Council Resolution	Year(s)
UN Truce Supervision Organization	**UNTSO**	Palestine, later other areas[a]	Observe cease-fire and later the armistice between Israel and neighbouring Arab states	50 (1948)	1948–
UN Military Observer Group in India and Pakistan	**UNMOGIP**	State of Jammu and Kashmir	Observe cease-fire and cease-fire line;[b] investigate complaints of violations	47 (1948)	1949–
UN Observation Group in Lebanon	UNOGIL	Lebanon	Identify infiltration of personnel or arms; keep Security Council informed	128 (1958)	1958
UN Yemen Observation Mission	UNYOM	Yemen (especially Demilitarized Zone along section of Saudi border)	Observe Disengagement Agreement between Saudi Arabia, United Arab Republic and Yemen	179 (1963)	1963–1964
Mission of the Representative of the Secretary-General in the Dominican Republic	DOMREP	Dominican Republic	Observe situation and report on breaches of cease-fire	203 (1965)	1965–1966
UN India–Pakistan Observation Mission	UNIPOM	India–Pakistan border	Supervise cease-fire and observe withdrawal	211 (1965)	1965–1966
UN Iran–Iraq Military Observer Group	UNIIMOG	Iran and Iraq (border areas)	Monitor cease-fire and supervise withdrawal of forces at end of Iran–Iraq war	588 (1987)	1988–1991
UN Good Offices Mission in Afghanistan and Pakistan	UNGOMAP	Afghanistan and Pakistan	Observe Soviet troop withdrawals from Afghanistan; investigate and report violations of Geneva Accords and non-intervention agreement	622 (1988)	1988–1990

214

Mission	Acronym	Location	Task	Resolution	Period
UN Angola Verification Mission	UNAVEM I	Southern Angola	Verify departure of Cuban troops	626 (1988)	1988–1991
UN Observer Group in Central America	ONUCA	Costa Rica, El Salvador, Guatemala, Honduras and Nicaragua	Oversee regional peace plan, including demobilization of Contras	644 (1989)	1989–1992
UN Mission for the Referendum in Western Sahara	**MINURSO**	Western Sahara	Observe cease-fire and confinement of Moroccan troops and, later, Polisario forces; organize referendum	690 (1991)	1991–
UN Observer Mission in El Salvador	ONUSAL	El Salvador	Monitor agreements between Government of El Salvador and FMLN[c]	693 (1991)	1991–1995
UN Angola Verification Mission II	UNAVEM II	Angola	Verify various Angolan Peace Accords and supervise 1992 elections	697 (1991)	1991–1995
UN Advance Mission in Cambodia	UNAMIC	Cambodia	Supervise cease-fire prior to establishment of UNTAC; provide mine-awareness training to civilians	717 (1991)	1991–1992
UN Observer Mission Uganda–Rwanda	UNOMUR	Uganda–Rwanda border	Monitor border to verify no passage of military aid	846 (1993)	1993–1994
UN Observer Mission in Georgia	UNOMIG	Georgia (Abkhazia)	Observe cease-fire; monitor Abkhazian and Georgian forces as well as Russian military contingents	849 (1993)	1993–2009
UN Observer Mission in Liberia	UNOMIL	Liberia	Work with ECOMOG[d] for implementation of Cotonou Peace Agreement	866 (1993)	1993–1997
UN Aouzou Strip Observer Group	UNASOG	Republic of Chad	Verify withdrawal of Libyan administration and forces	915 (1994)	1994

Table A1.1 (cont.)

Name	Abbreviation (current missions in bold)	Main location(s)	Mandate	Initial Security Council Resolution	Year(s)
UN Mission of Observers in Tajikistan	UNMOT	Tajikistan	Monitor cease-fire on Tajik–Afghan border; investigate cease-fire violations and report them to UN	968 (1994)	1994–2000
UN Mission of Observers in Prevlaka	UNMOP	Prevlaka Peninsula, Croatia	Monitor demilitarization of Prevlaka Peninsula	1038 (1996)	1996–2002
UN Verification Mission in Guatemala	MINUGUA	Guatemala	Verify fulfilment of cease-fire provisions of 1996 Peace Accords; later verify disarmament, human rights and other tasks	1101 (1996)	1997–2003
UN Observer Mission in Angola	MONUA	Angola	Assist in consolidating peace and national reconciliation; enhance democratic development	1118 (1997)	1997–1999
UN Observer Mission in Sierra Leone	UNOMSIL	Sierra Leone	Monitor and advise on disarmament of combatants and restructuring of national security forces; report on human rights abuses	1181 (1998)	1998–1999

Notes:
[a] Later Suez Canal area, Golan Heights, Lebanon and the Sinai.
[b] The cease-fire line later became the "Line of Control".
[c] Frente Farabundo Martí para la Liberación Nacional: a rebel group in opposition to the El Salvador government. Later, ONUSAL was mandated with election supervision.
[d] Economic Community of West African States Military Observer Group: a separate peacekeeping force composed of 4,000 troops from Nigeria, Gambia, Ghana, Guinea, Algeria and Sierra Leone.

Table A1.2 Interposed forces

Name	Abbreviation (current missions in bold)	Main location(s)	Mandate	Initial Security Council Resolution	Year(s)
UN Emergency Force	UNEF I	Sinai Peninsula and Gaza Strip	Secure cease-fire and removal of foreign (France, Israel, UK) forces from Egypt; serve as buffer between Israeli and Egyptian forces	General Assembly (GA) Resolution 998 (ES-1)	1956–1967
UN Peacekeeping Force in Cyprus	**UNFICYP**	Nicosia	Maintain cease-fire zones and, after 1974, supervise "buffer zone"	186 (1964)	1964–
UN Emergency Force II	UNEF II	Sinai Peninsula and Suez Canal	Supervise cease-fire after Yom Kippur War and later 1974 and 1975 Egyptian/Israeli agreements; deploy troops to buffer zone	340 (1973)	1973–1979
UN Disengagement Observer Force	**UNDOF**	Syrian Golan Heights	Maintain cease-fire between Israel and Syria; supervise disengagement of forces and areas of limitation and separation	350 (1974)	1974–
UN Interim Force in Lebanon	**UNIFIL**	Southern Lebanon	Confirm withdrawal of Israeli forces from southern Lebanon; assist Lebanese government to return to authority; after 2006, monitor cease-fire, Lebanese forces and humanitarians	425 (1978)	1978–

Table A1.2 (cont.)

Name	Abbreviation (current missions in bold)	Main location(s)	Mandate	Initial Security Council Resolution	Year(s)
UN Iraq–Kuwait Observation Mission	UNIKOM	Iraq/Kuwait border	Monitor Khawr 'Abd Allah waterway and Demilitarized Zone along border; observe any hostile acts; deter border violations	687 (1991)	1991–2003
UN Preventive Deployment Force	UNPREDEP	Former Yugoslav Republic of Macedonia	Replaced UNPROFOR in Macedonia; monitor border area for events that could undermine stability and threaten Macedonia; act as "trip-wire"	983 (1995)	1995–1999
UN Mission in Ethiopia and Eritrea	UNMEE	Ethiopia, Eritrea	Monitor cessation of hostilities and temporary security zone; assist in ensuring observance of security commitments agreed by parties	1320 (2000)	2000–2008

Table A1.3 Multidimensional operations

Name	Abbreviation (current missions in bold)	Main location(s)	Mandate	Initial Security Council Resolution	Year(s)
UN Operation in the Congo	ONUC	Republic of the Congo	Ensure withdrawal of Belgian forces; assist government with law and order; later, prevent civil war and secure removal of all foreign mercenary personnel	143 (1960)	1960–1964
UN Transition Assistance Group	UNTAG	Namibia	Supervise transition of Namibia from South African rule to independence	435 (1978)	1989–1990
UN Protection Force – later UN Peace Forces, UN Confidence Restoration Operation	UNPROFOR – later UNPF, UNCRO	Bosnia and Herzegovina, Croatia, Fed. Rep. of Yugoslavia (Serbia and Montenegro), Macedonia	Create a secure environment for negotiation of overall settlement to Yugoslav crisis; ensure demilitarization of UN Protected Areas by conflicting parties; support humanitarian relief	743 (1992)	1992–1995
UN Transitional Authority in Cambodia	UNTAC	Cambodia	Ensure implementation of 1991 peace agreements;[a] supervise government, disarmament, refugee return; organize election	745 (1992)	1992–1993
UN Operation in Somalia I	UNOSOM I	Somalia	Monitor cease-fire; later, work with the USA's Unified Task Force for humanitarian assistance	751 (1992)	1992–1993
UN Operation in Mozambique	ONUMOZ	Mozambique	Help implement peace agreement; monitor cease-fire and withdrawal of foreign forces, also elections and humanitarian assistance	782 (1992)	1992–1994
UN Operation in Somalia II	UNOSOM II	Somalia	Establish a secure environment for humanitarian relief operations; disarmament, reconciliation, arrest of warlord	814 (1993)	1993–1995

219

Table A1.3 (cont.)

Name	Abbreviation (current missions in bold)	Main location(s)	Mandate	Initial Security Council Resolution	Year(s)
UN Mission in Haiti	UNMIH	Haiti	Help implement Governors Island Agreement; later, help security, professionalize Haitian armed forces and create police force; help with elections	867 (1993)	1993–1996
UN Assistance Mission for Rwanda	UNAMIR	Rwanda	Ensure the security of cease-fire zone; assist with mine clearance, election preparation and humanitarian concerns	872 (1993)	1993–1996
UN Angola Verification Mission III	UNAVEM III	Angola	Assist in establishing peace and national reconciliation between the government and rebel force	976 (1995)	1995–1997
UN Confidence Restoration Operation in Croatia	UNCRO	Croatia	Replaced UNPROFOR in Croatia: facilitate humanitarian assistance throughout Croatia; monitor demilitarization of Prevlaka Peninsula	981 (1995)	1995–1996
UN Mission in Bosnia and Herzegovina	UNMIBH; established IPTF[b] and UN civilian office	Bosnia and Herzegovina	Assist with law enforcement activities and police reform; coordinate UN and NATO activities for humanitarian relief and refugees, de-mining, human rights, elections, infrastructure and economic reconstruction	1035 (1995)	1995–2002
UN Support Mission in Haiti	UNSMIH	Haiti	Help maintain secure and stable environment; assist with establishment and training of national police force; support economic rehabilitation	1053 (1996)	1996–1997

220

Mission	Acronym	Location	Mandate	Resolution	Dates
UN Transition Mission in Haiti	UNTMIH	Haiti	Assist in professionalization of Haitian National Police; promote economic rehabilitation	1123 (1997)	1997
UN Civilian Police Mission in Haiti	MIPONUH	Haiti	Oversee technical assistance to Haitian National Police (funded by the UN Development Programme)	1141 (1997)	1997–2000
UN Civilian Police Support Group	UNPSG	Eastern Slavonia, Baranja and Western Sirmium (Croatia)	Monitor Croatian police in Danube region; ensure safe return of displaced people	1145 (1997)	1998
UN Mission in the Central African Republic	MINURCA	Central African Republic	Promote national reconciliation, security and safety; provide advice on development of police programme and for elections	1159 (1996)	1998–2000
UN Mission in Sierra Leone	UNAMSIL	Sierra Leone	Cooperate with government and other parties in implementing Lomé Peace Agreement; assist with disarmament, demobilization and reintegration of ex-combatants	1270 (1999)	1999–2005
UN Organization Mission in the Democratic Republic of the Congo	MONUC / **MONUSCO**[c]	DRC	Monitor cease-fire; facilitate disengagement; later, protect civilians, support DRC government in stabilization and peace consolidation	1291 (2000)	1999–
UN Assistance Mission in Afghanistan	**UNAMA**	Afghanistan	Promote national reconciliation; various peacebuilding tasks entrusted to UN in Bonn Agreement, including human rights, rule of law and gender issues; manage all UN humanitarian, relief, recovery and reconstruction activities	1401 (2002)	2002–
UN Mission of Support in East Timor	UNMISET	East Timor (Timor-Leste)	Provide assistance to East Timor as operational responsibilities are fully devolved to East Timor authorities	1410 (2002)	2002–2005

Table A1.3 (cont.)

Name	Abbreviation (current missions in bold)	Main location(s)	Mandate	Initial Security Council Resolution	Year(s)
UN Mission in Liberia	**UNMIL**	Liberia	Support implementation of Ceasefire Agreement and peace process; protect civilians; support humanitarian and human rights and security reform	1509 (2003)	2003–
UN Operation in Côte d'Ivoire	**UNOCI**	Côte d'Ivoire	Monitor cessation of hostilities, armed groups and arms embargo; support DDRRR,[d] law and order, elections, security sector reform; protect civilians; humanitarian assistance and human rights	1528 (2004)	2004–
UN Stabilization Mission in Haiti	**MINUSTAH**	Haiti	Foster secure and stable environment and security sector reform; protect civilians; support national dialogue and reconciliation, elections, human rights; assist in promoting good governance; support disaster recovery	1542 (2004)	2004–
UN Operation in Burundi	ONUB	Burundi	Help restore peace; ensure cease-fire; support national reconciliation and Arusha Agreement; contribute to disarmament, humanitarian assistance and elections; monitor arms flow and borders; facilitate return of refugees; protect civilians; support security sector and judicial reform; protect human rights	1545 (2004)	2004–2006

UNMIS	UN Mission in Sudan	Southern Sudan	Support Comprehensive Peace Agreement; monitor Ceasefire Agreement and armed groups; assist with disarmament, demobilization and reintegration; help establish security and restructure police service; promote rule of law, human rights, elections and referendums; facilitate return of refugees; protect civilians	1590 (2005)	2005–
UNMIT	UN Integrated Mission in Timor-Leste	Timor-Leste	Support democratic governance, political dialogue, elections, national police, security sector review; assist human rights	1704 (2006)	2006–
UNAMID	African Union/United Nations Hybrid Operation in Darfur	Darfur (Sudan)	Support Darfur Peace Agreement; protect civilians; prevent armed attacks; monitor withdrawal of weapons; facilitate humanitarian assistance; verify cease-fire agreements; contribute to security; promote human rights and rule of law; monitor borders	1769 (2007)	2007–
MINURCAT	UN Mission in the Central African Republic and Chad	Central African Republic and Chad	Help create security; protect civilians and assist return of refugees; promote reconstruction and economic and social development; promote human rights and the rule of law	1778 (2007)	2007–2010

[a] Agreements on the Comprehensive Political Settlement of the Cambodia conflict.
[b] The International Police Task Force was created to support law enforcement.
[c] MONUC was replaced by MONUSCO on 1 July 2010.
[d] Disarmament, demobilization, reintegration, repatriation and resettlement.

Table A1.4 Transitional administrations

Name	Abbreviation (current missions in bold)	Location	Functions	Security Council Resolution	Year(s)
UN Temporary Executive Authority	UNTEA	West New Guinea (West Papua), currently part of Indonesia	For 6 months, accept governance of territory from the Netherlands before turning it over to Indonesia; act with full authority to administer territory, to maintain law and order, to protect rights of inhabitants and to ensure uninterrupted, normal services	GA 1752 (XVII)	1962–1963
UN Security Force in West New Guinea (West Irian)	UNSF	West New Guinea (West Papua)	Security arm of UNTEA: maintain law and order; monitor cease-fire area	GA 1752 (XVII)	1962–1963
UN Transitional Administration for Eastern Slavonia, Baranja and Western Sirmium	UNTAES, followed by UN Police Support Group (UNPSG)	Eastern Slavonia, Baranja and Western Sirmium (Croatia)	Govern region for 12 months; maintain security; facilitate demilitarization; ensure safe return of refugees and implementation of Basic Agreement; organize elections	1037 (1996)	1996–1998
UN Interim Administration Mission in Kosovo	**UNMIK**	Kosovo	Administer (govern) territory of Kosovo; wide-ranging tasks, such as overseeing health and education, banking and finance, post and telecommunications, and law and order; organize elections	1244 (1999)	1999–
UN Transitional Administration in East Timor	UNTAET	East Timor	Administer the territory, exercise legislative and executive authority during transition period and support capacity-building for self-government	1272 (1999)	1999–2002

224

Appendix 2

Special Committee on Peacekeeping (C34) annual reports: Excerpts on monitoring and surveillance technology

The United Nations Special Committee on Peacekeeping is composed of 124 member states that are past or current contributors to peacekeeping operations. The Committee is mandated to conduct a "comprehensive review of all issues relating to peacekeeping". After each annual "substantive" session, it presents a consensus report to the UN General Assembly. The following are passages from those annual reports that deal with peacekeeping technology (especially monitoring and surveillance technology). **Bold font** and <u>underlining</u> have been added to certain keywords for ease of scanning.

_1989_ _(UN Doc. A/44/301)_

> "With regard to the use of **high technology** in peacekeeping operations, it was indicated that, in view of its complexity, the issue needed to be <u>**further explored**</u>."

Annex: Working Paper No. 2, "Proposals on Peacekeeping" (submitted by delegations). B.2. High technology:

> "19. A study should be undertaken on possible uses of high technology, such as surveillance satellites, automatic sensors, radar and night-vision-equipment."

_1990_ _(UN Doc. A/45/330)_

> "19. On the possible application of **high technology** to peace-keeping operations, the issues of **economic feasibility** as well as political advisability of using such technology in this field were raised. It was felt, therefore, that <u>**further**</u>

Keeping watch: Monitoring, technology and innovation in UN peace operations, Dorn,
United Nations University Press, 2011, ISBN 978-92-808-1198-8

discussion on the subject would be needed. In the course of the discussion, the Canadian delegation presented a study on '**overhead** remote sensing for United Nations peace-keeping,' which was highly appreciated by the working group."

1991 (UN Doc. A/46/254)

"14. Most delegations welcomed the progress made so far on the question of resources for United Nations peace-keeping operations. They felt that **further consideration** should be given to improvements in such matters as the use of civilians, training of peace-keepers, supply and stockpiling, and the **applications of high technology**."

1992 (UN Doc. A/47/253)

"96. However, while supporting reforms to enable the United Nations to assess quickly and accurately information on potential threats to international peace and security, some delegations were of the view that the United Nations **did not need** independent **high-tech means** for intelligence gathering. What was needed were better ties with national services that could provide detailed up-to-date information which would facilitate the United Nations analysis of options. In this respect, it was suggested that Member States should undertake to supply, at the request of the Secretary-General, the information which would permit an evaluation of the situation concerning international peace and security. If a Member State so requested, such information should be regarded as confidential."

2001 (UN Doc. A/55/1024)

"13. Many delegations endorsed the need expressed in the report of the Secretary-General for **additional resources**, as well as the better use of existing ones, in order to improve the functioning of the Department of Peacekeeping Operations. The same delegations underlined the **need** for an enhanced use of **information technology**."

2005 (UN Doc. A/59/19/Rev.1)

"67. The Special Committee agrees that as the United Nations enhances its capacity to gather field information and assess risks, all forms of **technical monitoring and surveillance** means, in particular **aerial** monitoring capabilities as part of United Nations missions, should be **explored** as a means to ensure the safety of peacekeepers, particularly in volatile and dangerous conditions and in situations too dangerous for visual monitoring from the ground. The Special Committee requests the Secretary-General to provide in his next report to the Committee a **comprehensive assessment** in that regard and on the basis of lessons learned."

2006 (UN Doc. A/60/19)

"56. The Special Committee stresses the **need for priority action** by the Department of Peacekeeping Operations to examine how all forms of technical monitoring and surveillance means, in particular aerial monitoring capabilities, can be used by the United Nations to ensure the safety and security of United Nations peacekeeping personnel, particularly those peacekeepers who are deployed in volatile and dangerous conditions, and in situations too dangerous for monitoring from the ground. The Special Committee recommends that the Department of Peacekeeping Operations engage troop-contributing countries in a **dialogue** on this issue. The Special Committee reiterates yet again its request to the Secretary-General to provide the Special Committee in his next report with a comprehensive assessment in this regard."

2007 (UN Doc. A/61/19)

"45. The Special Committee **welcomes the study** launched by the Secretariat on the use of advanced monitoring and surveillance technologies to tangibly improve operational capabilities, achieve results in the field and promote the safety and security of peacekeeping personnel. Recognizing the urgent need for Peacekeeping Operations to **standardize** the use of advanced technology, particularly in missions operating in dangerous environments or mandated with challenging tasks, the Special Committee requests the Secretariat to **develop appropriate modalities** for the use of advanced monitoring and surveillance technologies with due attention to legal, operational, technical and financial considerations as well as the consent of the countries concerned with regards to their application in the field.

46. The Special Committee calls on the Secretariat to *engage* in the utilization of advanced monitoring and surveillance technologies where appropriate, particularly in more dangerous missions, and **present a report** to the C-34 in its next session on the steps taken by the Secretariat towards achieving these ends and any further suggestions for consideration by the Special Committee. The Special Committee *encourages dialogue* among member states and between member states and the Secretariat to meet the objectives stated above."

2008 (UN Doc. A/62/19)

"50. The Special Committee requests the Department of Peacekeeping Operations to present a **progress report** to it before its 2009 substantive session on the use of advanced monitoring and surveillance technologies in United Nations peacekeeping operations. The Special Committee continues to request the Secretariat to **develop appropriate modalities** for the use of advanced monitoring and surveillance technologies with due attention to legal, operational, technical and financial considerations as well as the consent of the countries concerned with regard to their application in the field."

2009 (UN Doc. A/63/19)

"42. The Special Committee notes the **progress** made towards a wider and systemic use of technology in peacekeeping operations. However, the Special Committee believes **further progress** is required. In this regard, the Special Committee requests the development of a United Nations **policy** on monitoring and surveillance technology, and looks forward to a **report** on this subject within six months of the issuance of this Committee's findings. The Special Committee believes that due attention should be given to legal, operational, technical and financial considerations and especially the consent of the countries concerned with regard to their application in the field."

2010 (UN Doc. A/64/19)

"43. The Special Committee notes the **progress** made towards a **wider and systemic use of technology** in peacekeeping operations. However, the Special Committee believes **further effort** in this direction is required. In this regard, the Special Committee requests the Secretariat to continue its work towards the finalization of the **draft policy** for the use of monitoring and surveillance technology in the field missions, and looks forward to a **report** on this subject within six months of the issuance of this Committee's 2010 report. The Special Committee looks forward to considering the legal, operational, technical and financial considerations contained in the report and especially the element of the consent of the countries concerned with regard to the application of such means in the field."

Appendix 3

Possible sensing technologies for peacekeeping, categorized by type of signal detected

Table A3.1 Possible sensing technologies for peacekeeping by type of signal measured

Technology	Quantity measured	Examples of use
Electromagnetic sensing (passive)	Electromagnetic radiation, emitted or reflected, of wavelength …	
Visible light imaging (using film or charge-coupled device)	0.4–0.7 µm	Photograph or video troops, tanks, vehicles in a demilitarized/conflict zone
Infrared (IR) imaging (i.e. heat sensing)		Locate operating vehicles, warm bodies moving across cease-fire lines or prohibited areas at night, aid to patrols
Near infrared	0.7–1.4 µm	
Short wave (SWIR)	1.4–3.0 µm	
Mid wave (MWIR)	3.0–9.0 µm	
Long wave (LWIR)	9.0–12.0 µm	
Far-IR	12.0–300.0 µm	
Radio-wave monitoring	>30 cm (HF: 3–30 MHz; VHF: 30–300 MHz; UHF: 300 MHz – 3 GHz)	Receive and monitor radio and cellular communications
Electromagnetic sensing (active)	Electromagnetic radiation, originating from the sensor system and reflected by object, in the wavelength range …	
LIDAR (Light Detection and Ranging)	0.4–1.1 µm	Determine vehicle speed, location of combatants' positions
RADAR (Radio Detecting and Ranging)		
Ground surveillance radar	3–30 cm (X-band: 8–12 GHz; K-band: 18–26 GHz; K_a band: 26–40 GHz)	Detect person entering monitored zone
Ground-penetrating radar	0.3–10 m (30–900 MHz, typically)	Find buried weapons or mass graves
Wall-penetrating radar	3–30 cm (1–10 GHz)	Detect people inside rooms (e.g. hostage situations)
Doppler radar	0.1–100 cm	Determine vehicle speed
Synthetic aperture radar	3–50 cm	Spot weapons and deployments, day and night and in all weather conditions

Method	Description	Application
Aerial surveillance radar	3–50 cm	Detect planes violating no-fly zones
X-ray detection and imaging	0.03–3 nanometres	Identify weapons inside metal/wooden cases or beneath personal clothing
Magnetic (and quasi-static electric field) detection	Magnetic field perturbations due to large ferromagnetic objects	Detect mines in fields, vehicles passing on roads
Acoustic wave sensing		
Seismic sensing (long-range) using a seismometer	Elastic waves travelling through the Earth's interior and along its surface	Detect underground explosions (e.g. in explosives testing and in mining)
Seismic detection (short-range) using a geophone	Elastic waves travelling along the Earth's surface	Detect vehicle or combatant intrusion into restricted areas
Sonar (Sound Navigation and Ranging) detection	Acoustic waves, in water, of wavelength 10 cm – 1 km (passive), 0.1–30 cm (active)	Observe ship passage into restricted areas or presence of sea-mines
Ultrasound probing	Sound wave frequency >20 kHz	Probe artillery shells for chemical weapon agents
Microphone	Sound waves in air of frequency 20 Hz – 20 kHz (wavelength 1 cm – 20 m)	Determine which side/party fired first; provide alert if tanks are travelling along roads or removed from storage
Pressure and strain sensing	Pressure (or strain) applied on contact with…	
Strain sensitive cable	A cable (fibre-optic or piezoelectric) or pneumatic tube	Detect vehicles moving on monitored roads, e.g. before or near checkpoint
Weight scale	Pressure-sensitive plate	Weigh truck passing atop scale for sanctions monitoring

Appendix 4

Summary of the benefits of various monitoring technologies

Keeping watch: Monitoring, technology and innovation in UN peace operations, Dorn, United Nations University Press, 2011, ISBN 978-92-808-1198-8

Table A4.1 Summary of the benefits of various monitoring technologies

Monitoring technology	Benefits
Video monitors • video cameras • web cameras • closed-circuit television • digital video networks • aerial and space-based	• supplement observation by the human eye • zoom capability for higher-resolution imagery • monitor current conflict zones nearby, from the air or from a remote location • spot approaching threats in daytime and in illuminated areas at night (e.g. in UN compounds) • verify commitments made in peace agreements, spot violations of human rights • detect illegal activities, including malicious acts, smuggling or sanctions evasion • share imagery in real time and in reports • record events for future analysis or for use as evidence in commissions or tribunals
Night vision • image intensifiers • thermal imagers	• as above, but at night • allow for night patrols and monitoring of illegal movements of arms and personnel at night (including sanctions evasion and preparations for attack) • thermal imagers can operate in complete darkness whereas image intensifiers require some ambient light (e.g. moonlight or artificial illumination)
Motion detectors	• detect approaching humans or vehicles, especially at night • activate cameras, illuminators and/or alarms
Radars • air surveillance (ASR) • artillery locating • ground surveillance • ground penetrating (GPR) • synthetic aperture • marine • weather	• operate day and night • operate in all weather conditions • detect and/or image aircraft (ASR), ground vehicles or boats and individuals • locate the origins of artillery fire • discover buried weapons or mass graves (GPR) • warn of oncoming storms or turbulence

Table A4.1 (cont.)

Monitoring technology	Benefits
X-ray machines	• examine baggage for dangerous/ prohibited items such as weapons
Acoustic sensors	• detect and locate small arms fire • detect movement of persons or vehicles
Seismic sensors • geophones • seismic arrays	• detect personnel/vehicles (geophones) • detect explosions (seismic arrays)
Chemical sensors	• detect explosives, poisons and possible chemical weapons
Metal detectors • hand-held wand • mine detector	• check for metal-containing weapons (hand-held wand) • detect mines
Pressure transducers • intrusion alarms • road monitor	• detect persons entering camps • detect vehicles trying to circumvent checkpoints
Radio-wave monitoring • signal-locating equipment • radio scanners / signal monitoring	• find source of radio transmission • intercept calls of hostage-takers
Positioning and tracking systems • Global Positioning System (GPS) • transponders and tags • radio frequency identification (RFID)	• determine location of observer or of distant objects (using GPS and laser range-finders) • relay position to remote monitors (transponders and tags) • identify equipment (including stored weapons, using RFID)

Note: Technologies less likely to be used in peacekeeping include: sonar, ultrasound, LIDAR, taut-wire fences, IR break-beam detectors, seals and tags. Nuclear detectors (Geiger counters) are needed only when nuclear materials present a danger.

Appendix 5

Summary of current and potential monitoring technologies in UN peacekeeping

Keeping watch: Monitoring, technology and innovation in UN peace operations, Dorn,
United Nations University Press, 2011, ISBN 978-92-808-1198-8

Table A5.1 Summary of current and potential monitoring technologies in UN peacekeeping

Types	Current UN uses	Potential UN activities
Video • video cameras	• used only in an ad hoc fashion in some missions • personal equipment often employed • no systematic plans, policies or guidelines for use	• use in all missions for patrols and in observation posts • use in an unattended fashion • specialized cameras in aircraft • record peace agreement violations or human rights abuses • maintain database of important clips
• closed-circuit television (CCTV)	• used to protect UN premises • one case of "hotspot" monitoring: Green Line in Nicosia	• remote viewing of hotspots and potential flashpoints
Night vision • image intensifiers	• too few possessed, or deployed in insufficient numbers • inadequate COE standards	• facilitate night patrols and night operations
• thermal imaging	• not used, except in a few advanced aircraft	• night foot/vehicular patrols • border control • forward-looking infrared in aircraft
Motion detectors • intrusion alarms	• underexploited technology	• protect refugee/UN camps • coupled with automatic illuminators
Radars • aerial surveillance radar	• used only in UNIFIL	• track aircraft violating no-fly zones or sanctions or transporting illegal materials • synthetic aperture radar for imaging from satellite and/or aircraft
• artillery-locating radar	• used only in UNIFIL	• determine the source of artillery fire • remove UN personnel from fire

Technology	Use in UN peacekeeping	Purpose
ground-penetrating radar	• not used	• discover underground weapons caches and mass graves • detect landmines and unexploded ordinance
ground surveillance radar	• used only in UNIFIL	• detect trespassers along line of control or demilitarized zone • catch illegal smuggling or aggression
X-ray machines • Baggage and shipments	• used in entrances to some buildings and UN-run airports	• examine cargo • detect human and or other forms of smuggling
Acoustic sensors • small arms fire location • movement of persons or vehicles	• not used (except makeshift)	• identify source of rifle fire for early warning and response • detect weapons being removed from cantonment
Seismic sensors • geophones/seismometers	• not used	• detect persons or vehicles passing through a certain area
Chemical sensors • explosives detector	• not used (except perhaps in Middle East PKOs)	• detect weapons and ammunition
Metal detectors • hand-held wand • mine detector	• used to detect metal on persons entering some premises • widely used for mine detection	• detect weapons and mines • improved sensors with better detection
Electronic monitors • signal-locating equipment • radio scanners / signal monitoring	• not used • not used systematically (except in Congo 1960–1964 and 2006–2007)	• for electronic countermeasures, e.g. detection of bugs in UN offices or of militia signals in jungles • for tactical operations, e.g. against hostage-takers

Table A5.1 (cont.)

Types	Current UN uses	Potential UN activities
Positioning and tracking systems • Global Positioning System (GPS) • Transponders and tags	• GPS used extensively; devices are individually owned, contingent owned and UN owned • Carlog used in most missions for UN vehicles	• real-time tracking of vehicles • radio-frequency identification used to track weapons and UN supplies
Information analysis • geographic information systems (GIS) • databases	• GIS capabilities increasing • used for mapping • Joint Operations Centre and Joint Mission Analysis Centre structures developing Standard Operating Procedures	• systems allowing user interaction and input for real-time picture

Appendix 6

Unattended ground sensors: Summary of a survey

A pioneering opinion survey on the potential use of unattended ground sensors (UGS) in UN peacekeeping was conducted in 1995 by European researchers (Altmann et al. 1998) and published by the United Nations Institute for Disarmament Research. Such UGS can be left in the field to send signals to peacekeepers. A questionnaire was sent out to peacekeepers and to officials at defence headquarters in various countries, gaining 114 responses out of 185 questionnaires sent. A full 90 per cent considered ground sensors useful in principle, across the range of possible activities considered (cease-fire lines, buffer/demilitarized zones, enclosed areas, safe havens and using portable sensors). Only 27 per cent had actual experience with ground sensors, mostly from other military activities, as would be expected because of the very limited application in current UN operations.

A majority (68 per cent) believed that the efficiency of a peacekeeping operation could be increased by using ground sensors, while 29 per cent disagreed. Some 40 per cent wanted to deploy sensors in a covert fashion, 36 per cent in a purely overt fashion, and 16 per cent wanted the capability for both modes of operation. Encrypted signals were preferred by 54 per cent, while open communication was chosen by 34 per cent, with only 7 per cent desiring both. The respondents expected that the unattended sensors should operate for weeks (46 per cent), as opposed to days (31 per cent) or months (22 per cent), before human intervention was required. The optimal detection range was 100–1,000 metres for most respondents (49 per cent), although some (25 per cent) wanted a longer

Keeping watch: Monitoring, technology and innovation in UN peace operations, Dorn,
United Nations University Press, 2011, ISBN 978-92-808-1198-8

distance and the rest (9 per cent) could settle for less. The main objects of detection were considered to be: people (84 per cent), trucks (75 per cent), tanks (45 per cent), helicopters (28 per cent) and aircraft (28 per cent). Most respondents desired detection within a few seconds (not minutes or hours) and were willing to accept a false-alarm rate of one per day, but not five per day. A slim majority considered that an acceptable training time would be one week (51 per cent), while some wanted only one day (35 per cent) and others a full month (7 per cent).

A few of the many desirable features cited for UGS were: theft-proof installation; remote on/off switching (for example, to activate sensors at the beginning of a curfew); the capability to differentiate between animals and humans, as well as between armed and unarmed persons; and compatibility with existing computer and communications systems. In addition to those inferred from the above, the listed concerns were: the possibility of increased complexity in the operation; the potential need for more troops to guard or periodically check the sensors and respond to the alerts; the need for technical expertise for operation and maintenance; the degradation of sensor capabilities owing to weather, terrain and other factors; increased UN involvement necessitated as a result of increased information.

Practical suggestions included: including the use of unattended sensors in the mission's mandate (or the Status-of-Forces Agreement) to lessen any fears the parties might have of unwarranted observation, and including backup systems and methods in case the sensors fail. In considering how peacekeeping expertise with sensors should in the future be increased, most felt that cooperation among nations is the best means to develop the technologies (41 per cent). Others preferred UN ownership (30 per cent), while the remainder preferred other means (29 per cent).

The respondents were almost exclusively from the military component of peacekeeping missions; the civilian members of the peacekeeping community were under-represented (only 5 per cent of the respondents). The survey covered a much more limited set of tools than the present work.

Appendix 7

Bibliography on monitoring technology for UN operations

Altmann, Jürgen, Horst Fischer and Henny van der Graaf (eds), *Sensors for Peace*, Geneva: United Nations Institute for Disarmament Research (UNIDIR), 1998.

Canada, Government of, *Overhead Remote Sensing for United Nations Peacekeeping*, Ottawa: Government of Canada (Department of External Affairs and International Trade), April 1990.

Diehl, Paul F., "The Political Implications of Using New Technologies in Peace Operations", *International Peacekeeping*, vol. 9, no. 3, 2002, pp. 1–24.

Dorn, Walter, *Peace-keeping Satellites: The Case for International Surveillance and Verification*, *Peace Research Reviews*, vol. 10, nos 5&6, 1987.

Dorn, A. Walter, *The Case for a United Nations Verification Agency: Disarmament under Effective International Control*, Ottawa: Canadian Institute for International Peace and Security, 1990.

Dorn, A. Walter, *Blue Sensors: Technology and Cooperative Monitoring in UN Peacekeeping*, Cooperative Monitoring Center Occasional Paper 36, SAND 2004-1380, Albuquerque, NM: Cooperative Monitoring Center, Sandia National Laboratories, April 2004. Available at <http://www.cmc.sandia.gov/cmc-papers/sand2004-1380.pdf> (accessed 10 December 2010).

Dorn, A. Walter, *Tools of the Trade? Monitoring and Surveillance Technologies in UN Peacekeeping* (commissioned report), New York: Peacekeeping Best Practices Unit, Department of Peacekeeping Operations, United Nations, 2007.

Dorn, A. Walter, "United Nations Peacekeeping Intelligence", in Loch Johnson (ed.), *The Oxford Handbook of National Security Intelligence*, New York: Oxford University Press, 2010, pp. 275–295.

Dunay, Pál et al., *Open Skies: A Cooperative Approach to Military Transparency and Confidence Building*, Geneva: UNIDIR, UN Publication GV.E.04.18, 2004.

Keeping watch: Monitoring, technology and innovation in UN peace operations, Dorn, United Nations University Press, 2011, ISBN 978-92-808-1198-8

Hanning, Hugh (ed.), *Peacekeeping and Technology: Concepts for the Future* (No. 17), New York: International Peace Academy, 1983.

International Peace Academy (IPA), *Weapons of Peace: How New Technologies Can Revitalize Peace-keeping: A Report of the IPA Task Force on Technology*, New York: IPA, 1980.

Jones, Peter, "Technology and Peacekeeping", *Peacekeeping and International Relations*, vol. 21, no. 6, November/December 1992.

Jong, Ben, Wies Platje and Robert David Steele (eds), *Peacekeeping Intelligence: Emerging Concepts for the Future*, Virginia: OSS International Press, 2003.

Keeley, James F. and Robert N. Huebert, *Commercial Satellite Imagery, and United Nations Peacekeeping: A View from Above*, Aldershot, UK: Ashgate, 2004.

Office of Technology Assessment, *Improving the Prospects for Future International Peace Operations*, U.S. Congress, OTA-BP-ISS-167, Washington, DC: US GPO, 1995.

Sullivan, Jeremiah (ed.), *Technology for Peace: Improving the Effectiveness of Multilateral Interventions*, Program in Arms Control, Disarmament, and International Security (ACDIS), University of Illinois at Urbana-Champagne, Urbana, 2000.

UN Department of Peacekeeping Operations, "The Use of Digital Satellite Images in United Nations Peacekeeping Operations: Discussion Paper", Peacekeeping Best Practices Unit, New York, 2003. Available at <http://pbpu.unlb.org/PBPS/Library/Satellite%20Image%20Discussion.pdf> (accessed 18 January 2011).

UN Department of Peacekeeping Operations, "Report of the Joint Assessment Mission (JAM) on Intelligence Assets Requirements of MONUC", April 2005.

UN Secretary-General, "Study on the Implications of Establishing an International Satellite Monitoring Agency", UN Doc. A/AC.206/14 of 6 August 1981.

UN Secretary-General, "Study on the Role of the United Nations in the Field of Verification", UN Doc. A/45/372 of 28 August 1990.

UN Secretary-General, "Verification in All Its Aspects, Including the Role of the United Nations in the Field of Verification: Report of the Secretary-General", UN Doc. A/50/377 of 22 September 1995.

Vannoni, Michael, *Sensors in the Sinai: A Precedent for Regional Cooperative Monitoring*, Sand Report SAND96-2574, Albuquerque, NM: Cooperative Monitoring Center, Sandia National Laboratories, 1996. Available at <http://www.cmc.sandia.gov/cmc-papers/sand96-2574.pdf> (accessed 18 January 2011).

References

Altmann, Jürgen, Horst Fischer and Henny van der Graaf, eds (1998), *Sensors for Peace*, Geneva: United Nations Institute for Disarmament Research (UNIDIR).

Bash, Brooks L. (1995), "Airpower and Peacekeeping", *Airpower Journal*, 9(1), <http://www.airpower.maxwell.af.mil/airchronicles/apj/apj95/spr95_files/bash.htm> (accessed 18 January 2011).

BBC News (2008), "Sudan 'Kills Refugees in Darfur'", *BBC News*, 26 August, <http://news.bbc.co.uk/2/hi/africa/7580778.stm> (accessed 7 January 2011).

Beattie, C. E. and K. R. Greenaway (1986), "Offering Up Canada's North", *Canadian Arctic Resources Committee* 14(4), <http://www.carc.org/pubs/v14no4/4.htm> (accessed 7 January 2011).

Blyth, Mike (2009), "Missions Look to SMS in Nigeria", *Kiwanja.net*, 4 June, <http://www.kiwanja.net/blog/2009/06/missions-look-to-sms-in-nigeria> (accessed 14 January 2011)

Burns, E. L. M. (1962), *Between Arab and Israeli*, Toronto: Clarke, Irwin & Co.

Camero Inc. (n.d.), "Xaver™ 400: Compact, Tactical Through-Wall Vision System", <http://www.camero-tech.com/xaver400.shtml> (accessed 7 January 2011).

Cammaert, Patrick (2005a), "Eastern Division Commander's Guidelines", 9 May, MONUC files.

Cammaert, Patrick (2005b), "Headquarters Eastern Division Requirement", message from Eastern Division Commander Maj. Gen. Cammaert to MONUC Force Commander, 24 June, MONUC files.

Cebrowski, Arthur K. and John J. Garstka, (1998), "Network-Centric Warfare: Its Origin and Future", *Proceedings of the U.S. Naval Institute*, January, <http://www.kinection.com/ncoic/ncw_origin_future.pdf> (accessed 7 January 2011).

Center for Army Lessons Learned (1995), "Haiti: The US Army and UN Peacekeeping, Initial Impressions", vol. III, Fort Leavenworth, KS: US Army Training and Doctrine Command.

Crossette, Barbara (1996), "UN Report Suggests Israeli Attack Was Not a Mistake", *New York Times*, 8 May.

Diehl, Paul (2002), "The Political Implications of Using New Technologies in Peace Operations", *International Peacekeeping*, 9(3), pp. 1–24.

Donoghue, Andrew (2009a), "Solar Powered iPhone Launched Amid Overheating Reports", *eWeek Europe*, 4 September, <http://www.eweekeurope.co.uk/news/news-mobile-wireless/solar-powered-iphone-case-launched-amid-overheating-reports-1756> (accessed 18 January 2011).

Donoghue, Andrew (2009b), "UK Troops in Afghanistan Want Solar Gadgets", *eWeek Europe*, 15 October, <http://www.eweekeurope.co.uk/news/news-mobile-wireless/uk-troops-in-afghanistan-want-solar-gadgets-2093> (accessed 18 January 2011).

Dorn, A. Walter (1987), *Peacekeeping Satellites: The Case for International Surveillance and Verification*, Peace Research Reviews, 10(5–6), <http://www.walterdorn.org/pub/19> (accessed 18 January 2011).

Dorn, A. Walter (1999), "The Cloak and the Blue Beret: Limitations on Intelligence in UN Peacekeeping", *International Journal of Intelligence and Counter Intelligence*, 12(4), pp. 414–447, <http://www.walterdorn.org/pub/16> (accessed 31 January 2011).

Dorn, A. Walter (2004), *Blue Sensors: Technology and Cooperative Monitoring in UN Peace Operations*, Cooperative Monitoring Center Occasional Paper 36 (SAND 2004-1380), Albuquerque, NM: Cooperative Monitoring Center, Sandia National Laboratories, April, <http://www.cmc.sandia.gov/cmc-papers/sand2004-1380.pdf> (accessed 18 January 2011).

Dorn, A. Walter (2005), "Intelligence at UN Headquarters? The Information and Research Unit and the Intervention in Eastern Zaire", *Intelligence and National Security*, 20(3), pp. 440–465, <http://www.walterdorn.org/pub/31> (accessed 31 January 2011).

Dorn, A. Walter (2009), "Intelligence-led Peacekeeping: The United Nations Stabilization Mission in Haiti (MINUSTAH), 2006–07", *Intelligence and National Security*, 24(6), pp. 805–835.

Dorn, A. Walter (2010), "United Nations Peacekeeping Intelligence", in Loch Johnson (ed.), *Oxford Handbook of National Security Intelligence*, New York: Oxford University Press, pp. 275–295, <http://www.walterdorn.org/pub/79> (accessed 31 January 2011).

Dorn, A. Walter and David J. H. Bell (1995), "Intelligence and Peacekeeping: The United Nations Operation in the Congo 1960–64", *International Peacekeeping*, 2(1), pp. 11–33, <http://www.walterdorn.org/pub/40> (accessed 31 January 2011).

Dorn, A. Walter and J. Matloff (2000), "Preventing the Bloodbath: Could the UN have Predicted and Prevented Genocide in Rwanda?", *Journal of Conflict Studies*, 20(1), pp. 9–52, <http://www.walterdorn.org/pub/35> (accessed 31 January 2011).

Dorn, A. Walter and Robert Pauk (2011), "Eyes on the Green Line: Human and Technological Surveillance by the United Nations Peacekeeping Force in Cyprus", *Journal of Conflict Studies* (forthcoming).

DPKO [Department of Peacekeeping Operations] (n.d.[a]), *United Nations Peacekeeping Training Manual: Training Guidelines and Exercises*, New York: Training and Evaluation Service, United Nations (undated, but developed in 1995 from Scandinavian training materials), <http://www.usaraf.army.mil/documents_pdf/READING_ROOM/UNpeacekeepingTngMan.pdf> (accessed 14 January 2011).

DPKO (n.d.[b]), "Tables of Organization and Equipment", <http://www.un.org/depts/dpko/training/tes_publications/books/logistics/TOE/TOE.pdf> (accessed 2008).

DPKO (1999), *Medical Support Manual for United Nations Peacekeeping Operations*, 2nd edn, New York: United Nations Department of Peacekeeping Operations.

DPKO (2002), *Selection Standards and Training Guidelines for United Nations Military Observers*, New York: United Nations.

DPKO (2003), *Handbook on United Nations Multidimensional Peacekeeping Operations*, New York: DPKO Peacekeeping Best Practices Unit, December.

DPKO (2005a), "Standard Cost Manual for Peacekeeping Operations", Revision 2005, UN Department of Peacekeeping Operations, New York.

DPKO (2005b), "Report of the Joint Assessment Mission on Intelligence Assets Requirements of MONUC (11 to 19 April 2005)" (JAM Report), DPKO internal document.

DPKO (2006a), "DPKO Policy Directive: Joint Operations Centres and Joint Mission Analysis Centres", Ref. POL/2006/3000/4, UN Department of Peacekeeping Operations, New York.

DPKO (2006b), "Policy on Cooperation and Coordination between the Department of Safety and Security (DSS) and the Department of Peacekeeping Operations (DPKO)", UN Department of Peacekeeping Operations, New York.

DPKO (2006c), "Standby Arrangements in the Service of Peace: Tables of Organization and Equipment" (draft).

DPKO (2007), "UNAMID Deployment, Background Fact Sheet", UN Department of Peacekeeping Operations, New York.

DPKO (2010a), "Monitoring and Surveillance Technology in Field Missions", draft policy of 29 April.

DPKO (2010b), "Background Note: 30 April 2010, United Nations Peacekeeping Operations", <http://www.un.org/en/peacekeeping/archive/2010/bnote0410.pdf> (accessed 18 January 2011).

DPKO and DFS (2008), *United Nations Peacekeeping Operations: Principles and Guidelines*, New York: Department of Peacekeeping Operations and Department of Field Support, <http://pbpu.unlb.org/pbps/Library/Capstone_Doctrine_ENG.pdf> (accessed 5 January 2011).

DPKO and DFS (2009), *A New Partnership Agenda: Charting a New Horizon for UN Peacekeeping*, New York: Department of Peacekeeping Operations and Department of Field Support, July, <http://www.un.org/en/peacekeeping/documents/newhorizon.pdf> (accessed 13 January 2011).

DSS [Department of Safety and Security] (2004), "Minimum Operating Security Standards: Instructions for Implementation", dated 1 July (endorsed by the Inter-Agency Security Management Network in May 2004).

Duncan, A. P. (2008a), Letter from UNFICYP Sector 2 Commander Lt. Col. A. P. Duncan to Turkish Forces Commander Col. V. Tarakci, 1 Wolf Regiment, 11 March.

Duncan, A. P. (2008b), Letter from Lt. Col. A. P. Duncan, Commanding Officer of HQ Sector 2, UNFICYP, to Col. Panayiotou, Commanding Officer, 9th Regiment, National Guard, 23 February.

Dziedzic, Michael and Robert M. Perito (2008), "Haiti: Confronting the Gangs of Port-au-Prince", Special Report 208, United States Institute of Peace, Washington DC, September, <http://www.usip.org/files/resources/sr208.pdf> (accessed 18 January 2011).

Economist (2009), "The Boom in Smart-phones: Cleverly Simple", *The Economist*, 1 October, <http://www.economist.com/businessfinance/displaystory.cfm?story_id=14563636> (accessed 7 January 2011).

Egypt–Israel (1979), "Treaty of Peace between the Arab Republic of Egypt and the State of Israel", United Nations, *Treaty Series*, vol. 1136, Registration No. I-17813, <http://treaties.un.org/pages/showDetails.aspx?objid=08000002800f1f88> (accessed 17 January 2011).

Ekpe, Bassey (2007), "The Intelligence Assets of the United Nations: Sources, Methods, and Implications", *International Journal of Intelligence and Counter Intelligence*, 20(3), pp. 377–400.

Erdik, Mustafa (2006), "Urban Earthquake Rapid Response and Early Warning Systems", in *First European Conference on Earthquake Engineering and Seismology*, Geneva, Switzerland, 3–8 September, <http://www.ecees.org/Paper/paper4004.pdf> (accessed October 2010).

EUSC [European Union Satellite Centre] (2010), homepage at <http://www.eusc.org> (accessed 18 January 2011).

Figoli, Maj. Gen. Herbert (2004), "UNFICYP 860 Concept of Operations", UNFICYP Force Commander, UNFICYP Memorandum, October.

Gabriel, Peter, Gillian Caldwell, Sara Federlein, Sam Gregory and Jenni Wolfson (2008), "Moving Images: WITNESS and Human Rights Advocacy", *Innovations: Technology, Governance, Globalization*, 3(2), pp. 35–60, <http://www.ndi.org/files/2329_sms_engpdf_06242008.pdf> (accessed 18 January 2011).

Gaouette, Michael and Michael MacKinnon (2007), "The UN Security Council and the Darfur Crisis: A Case Study of Weak and Ineffective Decision-Making", paper presented at the annual meeting of the International Studies Association 48th Annual Convention, Chicago, 28 February.

George, Alexander (1980), *Presidential Decisionmaking in Foreign Policy: The Effective Use of Information and Advice*, Boulder, CO: Westview Press.

Government of Nepal (2006), "Comprehensive Peace Agreement Held between Government of Nepal and Communist Party of Nepal", <http://www.reliefweb.int/rw/RWB.NSF/db900SID/VBOL-6VSHK8?OpenDocument> (accessed 10 December 2010).

Gryzb, Amanda, ed. (2009), *The World and Darfur*, Montreal: McGill-Queens University Press.

Guéhenno, Jean-Marie (2008), "Introduction of Low and Medium-cost Surveillance and Communications Technologies in UN Peacekeeping Missions" [Low–Medium-Cost Project], Code Cable to UN missions, 27 February.

Holmes, John [Under-Secretary-General for Humanitarian Affairs and Emergency Relief Coordinator] (2009), "Press Conference on Expulsion of Non-Governmental Organizations from Darfur", 16 March, <http://www.un. org/News/briefings/docs/2009/090316_Holmes.doc.htm> (accessed 18 January 2011).

ICISS [International Commission on Intervention and State Sovereignty] (2001), *The Responsibility to Protect: Report of the International Commission on Intervention and State Sovereignty*, Ottawa, Canada: International Development Research Centre, <http://www.iciss.ca> (accessed 6 January 2011).

Integrated Training Service (2008), "Report on the Strategic Peacekeeping Training Needs Assessment", <http://peacekeepingresourcehub.unlb.org/PBPS/Library/Strategic_Training_Needs_Assessment_-_Report%5B1%5D.pdf> (accessed 18 January 2011).

Internal Audit Division (2009), "Audit of Patrolling by United Nations Military Observers in UNMIL: Logistical Support for UNMIL Military Observers Needs Improvement", Audit Report, Office of Internal Oversight Services, United Nations, 13 April, <http://usun.state.gov/documents/organization/140721. pdf> (accessed 15 February 2011).

International Charter (2010), "International Charter: Space and Major Disasters", <http://www.disasterscharter.org/home> (accessed 6 January 2011).

Isberg, Jan-Gunnar (2004), "Urgent Operational Equipment Upgrades – Amendment", Facsimile transmission from Brigadier General Isberg (Acting Force Commander of MONUC) to Military Adviser P. C. Cammaert, 7 December.

Jones, Bruce, Richard Gowan and Jake Sherman (2009), *Building on Brahimi: Peacekeeping in an Era of Strategic Uncertainty*, NYU Center on International Cooperation, <http://www.cic.nyu.edu/Lead%20Page%20PDF/CIC%20New%20Horizons%20Report.pdf> (accessed 12 January 2011).

Jordans, Frank (2009), "World's Poor Drive Growth in Global Cell Phone Use", *USA Today*, 2 March.

Ker-Lindsay, James (2005), *EU Accession and UN Peacemaking in Cyprus*, Basingstoke: Palgrave Macmillan.

Ker-Lindsay, James (2006), "The UN Force in Cyprus after the 2004 Reunification Referendum", *International Peacekeeping*, 13(3), pp. 410–421.

Koch, George (1995), "Bosnia: How Our Troops View Their Equipment", *Vanguard* magazine (Toronto), January.

Kontos, C. William (1980), "Lessons from the U.S. Sinai Field Mission", in *Weapons of Peace*, New York: International Peace Academy.

Langille, H. Peter (2002a), *Bridging the Commitment–Capacity Gap: Existing Arrangements and Options for Enhancing UN Rapid Deployment*, Wayne, NJ: Center for United Nations' Reform Education, <http://www.globalpolicy.org/images/pdfs/1102langille.pdf> (accessed 18 January 2011).

Langille, H. Peter (2002b), "Bridging the Commitment–Capacity Gap: A Review of Existing Arrangements and Options for Enhancing UN Rapid Deployment", Center for UN Reform Education, New Jersey, <http://www.centerforunreform. org/node/67> (accessed 18 January 2011).

Langille, H. Peter and A. Walter Dorn (2011), "Technology to Enable the United Nations in Darfur," unpublished manuscript.

Lindley, Dan (2007), *Promoting Peace with Information: Transparency as a Tool of Security Regimes*, Princeton, NJ: Princeton University Press.

Lito, Doug (2010), "How Network Centric Operations Could Improve United Nations Peacekeeping Operations", Master of Defence Studies Research Project, Canadian Forces College, Toronto, Canada, <http://www.cfc.forces.gc.ca/papers/csc/csc36/mds/Lito.pdf> (accessed 7 January 2011).

Loudon, Melissa (2010), "Mapping SMS Incident Reports: A Review of Ushahidi and Managing News", MobileActive.org, <http://mobileactive.org/howtos/mapping-sms-incident-reports-review-ushahidi-and-managing-news> (accessed 7 January 2011).

Lovelock, Ben (2005), "Securing a Viable Peace: Defeating Militant Extremists – Fourth Generation Peace Implementation", in Jock Covey, Michael J. Dziedzic and Leonard R. Hawley (eds), *The Quest for Viable Peace: International Intervention and Strategies for Conflict Transformation*, Washington, DC: US Institute of Peace Press, pp. 139–140.

Lynd, Robert S. (1939), *Knowledge for What? The Place of Social Science in American Culture*, Princeton, NJ: Princeton University Press.

McGeer, Tad (1999), "*Laima*: The First Atlantic Crossing by Unmanned Aircraft", The Insitu Group, Washington DC, <http://www.aerovelco.com/papers/LaimaStory.pdf> (accessed 11 January 2011).

Martin, Nicholas C., Anand Varghese and Walter Dorn (2011), "Smartphones for Smart Peacebuilding", unpublished.

MINUSTAH [United Nations Stabilization Mission in Haiti] (2005), "Aftermath of the Cite of Soleil Operation Iron Fist Conducted 6 July 2005: Implications for MINUSTAH, Military Staff Assessment Paper", unpublished.

MINUSTAH (2007a), "After Action Review, Op Nazca", unpublished and undated document obtained from MINUSTAH, Port-au-Prince.

MINUSTAH (2007b), "After Action Report on Operation 'Jauru Sudamericano'".

Mitchell, Paul T. (2009), *Network Centric Warfare and Coalition Operations: The New Military Operating System*, London: Routledge.

MONUC [United Nations Organization Mission in the Democratic Republic of the Congo] (2005), Board of Inquiry, 3 August 2005, on the incident in Lugo, 2 June 2005, MONUC document.

MONUC (2006a), "After Mission Report", UNO-888, 26 November (0612h–0748h).

MONUC (2006b), "After Mission Report", UN-887, 26 November (0910h–1041h).

MONUC (2006c), "After Mission Report", UNO-886, 26 November (0945h–1116h).

MONUC (2006d), "After Mission Report", UNO-888, 26 November (1410h–1530h).

MONUC (2006e), "After Mission Report", UN-886, 26 November (1256h–1438h).

MONUC (2006f), "After Mission Report", UNO-887, 26 November (1705h–1831h).

MONUC (2007), "2006–7 Acquisition Plan – UN Mission in the Democratic Republic of Congo (MONUC)", <http://www.un.org/Depts/ptd/2007_monuc.htm> (accessed 18 January 2011).

MONUC (2008a), "SOP – Monitoring and Verification", Part 5, MONUC SOP 550, unpublished mission document.

MONUC (2008b), "After Mission Report", UN-888, 27 October 2008 (1645h–1810 h).

MONUC (2008c), "After Mission Report", UN-889, 28 October 2008.

MONUC (2008d), "After Mission Report", UN-888, 29 October 2008 (0855h–1027h).

MONUC (2008e), "After Mission Report", UNO-887, 29 October 2008 (1300h–1450h).

Multinational Force and Observers (1997), "Multinational Force and Observers: Servants of Peace", Office of Personnel and Publications, Multinational Force and Observers, Rome, Italy.

National Biometric Security Project (2005), *Biometric Technology Application Manual, Volume 1: Biometrics Basics*, <http://www.nationalbiometric.org/publications/BTAM_%20Book_%20Vol%20_1_%20final%2001-10-06.pdf> (accessed 18 January 2011).

NATO [North Atlantic Treaty Organization] (2005), *NATO Handbook*, Brussels: NATO.

NATO (2010a), "NATO Airborne Early Warning & Control Force, E-3A Component", <http://www.e3a.nato.int> (accessed 18 January 2011).

NATO (2010b), "NATO Glossary of Terms and Definitions", <http://www.nato.int/docu/stanag/aap006/aap6.htm> (accessed 18 January 2011).

Oberwarth, Cayle (2001), "Temporary Assignment in Africa Pushes the Peace Process Forward," unpublished Public Affairs document, available on the "Operation Eclipse" CD, Public Affairs, Department of National Defence, Ottawa.

Obiakor, Chikadibia Isaac (2008), "Status of Implementation of Low and Medium-cost Technology Projects in Missions", Code Cable from Lt. Gen. Obiakor to Susana Malcorra, Under-Secretary-General, Department of Field Support, 24 November.

O'Brien, Kevin A. (1998), "Military-Advisory Groups and African Security: Privatised Peacekeeping?", *International Peacekeeping*, 5(3), pp. 78–105.

Ostrowski, Andrzej (2008), "Chief of Staff Words", *Golan: the UNDOF Journal*, No. 114, January–March, <http://www.un.org/en/peacekeeping/missions/undof/documents/golan/Golan%20Journal%20114.pdf> (accessed 18 January 2011).

Parsch, Andreas (2005), "Tethered Aerostats", in *Directory of U.S. Military Rockets and Missiles*, Appendix 4: Undesignated Vehicles, <http://www.designation-systems.net/dusrm/app4/aerostats.html> (accessed 18 January 2011).

Paulsen, Ystein (1999), "Dutch Recce Platoon", *SFOR Informer*, No. 71, 29 September, <http://www.nato.int/SFOR/sfor-at-work/dutch-recce/t991001c.htm> (accessed 13 January 2011).

Polgreen, Lydia (2008), "A Massacre in Congo, Despite Nearby Support", *New York Times*, 11 December, <http://www.nytimes.com/2008/12/11/world/africa/11congo.html> (accessed 18 January 2011).

Poropudas, Timo (2009), "African Mobile Subs Grew 550 Percent in 5 years", *Mobile Monday*, 30 October, <http://www.mobilemonday.net/news/african-mobile-subs-grew-550-percent-in-5-years> (accessed 1 July 2010).

Port Orchard Independent (2008), "WSP Plan Irks Terrorists and Their Enablers", 30 July, <http://www.pnwlocalnews.com/kitsap/poi/opinion/26023824.html> (accessed 7 January 2011).

Reeves, Eric (2008), "Attack on UNAMID Forces in Darfur: The Khartoum Regime Is Responsible", *The Sudan Tribune*, 12 July, <http://www.sudantribune.com/spip.php?article27838> (accessed 18 January 2011).

Reeves, Eric (2009), "Death in Darfur: Total Mortality from Violence, Malnutrition and Disease: April/May", in Amanda F. Gryzb, *Darfur and the World*, Montreal: McGill-Queen's University Press, pp. 152–182.

Ritter, Scott (1999), *Endgame: Solving the Iraq Crisis – Once and for All*, New York: Simon & Schuster.

Roberts, Ashley (2008), "Reports Indicate Attack by Government Forces on Kalma Camp", *Save Darfur*, 25 August, <http://blogfordarfur.org/archives/80> (accessed 18 January 2011).

Schmitt, Eric (1995), "In U.S. Peacekeeper Arsenal, Weapons Honed for Bosnia", *New York Times*, 5 December.

Schuler, Ian (2008), "National Democratic Institute: SMS as a Tool in Election Observation", *Innovations*, 3(2), pp. 143–157, <http://www.ndi.org/files/2329_sms_engpdf_06242008.pdf> (accessed 18 January 2011).

Schwabe, William, Lois M. Davis and Brian Anthony Jackson (2001), "Challenges and Choices for Crime-fighting Technology: Federal Support of State and Local Law Enforcement", Science and Technology Policy Institute (Rand Corporation), MR 1349, Rand Corporation.

Shane, Scott and Christopher Drew (2009), "Officials Say Iraq Fighters Intercepted Drone Video", *New York Times*, 17 December, <http://www.nytimes.com/2009/12/18/world/middleeast/18drones.html> (accessed 18 January 2011).

Shetler-Jones, Philip (2008), "Intelligence in Integrated UN Peacekeeping Missions: The Joint Mission Analysis Centre", *International Peacekeeping*, 15(4), pp. 517–527.

Smith, Hugh (1994), "Intelligence and UN Peacekeeping", *Survival*, 36(3), pp. 174–192.

Steele, Robert David (2010a), "Intelligence for Earth: Clarity, Diversity, Integrity, & Sustainability", Earth Intelligence Network, Oakton, Virginia.

Steele, Robert David (2010b), *Human Intelligence: All Humans, All Minds, All the Time*, Carlisle, PA: Strategic Studies Institute, United States Army War College, <http://www.strategicstudiesinstitute.army.mil/pubs/display.cfm?pubID=991> (accessed 18 January 2011).

Stockton, Dale (2009), "Stolen Car King – LPR Technology Helps One Arizona Officer Identify More Than 400 Occupied Stolen Vehicles", *Law Officer*, 5(3), <http://www.lawofficer.com/article/investigation/stolen-car-king (accessed 18 January 2011).

Thomas, David (2001), "French and Canadians – Working Together to Learn", *SFOR Informer*, No. 104, 10 January, <http://www.nato.int/sfor/indexinf/104/s104p08a/t0101108a.htm> (accessed 18 January 2011).

Thucydides (1972), *History of the Peloponnesian War* (translation by Rex Warner), New York: Penguin Classics (revised edition).

UN Cartography Unit (2006), "Geographic Information System: Resource Planning and Budget Guidelines for Peacekeeping Missions", Specialist Support Services, Logistics Support Division, June.

UN Department of Public Information (1960), "Presentation 2235, 1E", Audio-visual Unit, United Nations, New York.

UN News Centre (2003), "Humanitarian and Security Situations in Western Sudan Reach New Lows, UN Agency Says", 5 December, <http://www.un.org/apps/news/storyAr.asp?NewsID=9094&Cr=sudan&Cr1=> (accessed 7 January 2011).

UN News Centre (2005), "UN Aviation Agency's Format for Biometric Passports Enters into Force", 12 July, <http://www.un.org/apps/news/story.asp?NewsID=14981&Cr=aviation&Cr1> (accessed 7 January 2011).

UN Secretary-General (1956), "Report of the Secretary-General on Basic Points for the Presence and Functioning in Egypt of the United Nations Emergency Force", UN Doc. A/3289, 4 November.

UN Secretary-General (1961), "Progress Report", UN Doc. A/4857, 30 August.

UN Secretary-General (1964), "Report by the Secretary-General to the Security Council on the United Nations Operation in Cyprus, for the Period 26 April to 8 June 1964", UN Doc. S/5764, 15 June.

UN Secretary-General (1974), "Report of the Secretary-General on the United Nations Operation in Cyprus", UN Doc. S/11294, 22 May.

UN Secretary-General (1975), "Report of the Secretary-General on the United Nations Operation in Cyprus", UN Doc. S/11717, 9 June.

UN Secretary-General (1984), "Letter Dated 14 June 1984 from the Secretary-General Addressed to the President of the Security Council", UN Doc. S/16627, 15 June.

UN Secretary-General (1987), "Letter Dated 87/09/18 from the Deputy Head of the Delegation of the Union of Soviet Socialist Republics to the 42nd Session Addressed to the Secretary-General", UN Doc. S/19143, 18 September.

UN Secretary-General (1992), "Report of the Secretary-General on the United Nations Operation in Cyprus", UN Doc. S/24917, 1 December.

UN Secretary-General (1993a), "Report of the Secretary-General on the United Nations Operation in Cyprus", UN Doc. S/25492, 30 March.

UN Secretary-General (1993b), "Report of the Secretary-General on the United Nations Operation in Cyprus", UN Doc. S/25912, 9 June.

UN Secretary-General (1993c), "Report of the Secretary-General on the United Nations Iraq-Kuwait Observation Mission, for the Period 1 October 1992–31 March 1993", UN Doc. S/25514, 2 April.

UN Secretary-General (1993d), "Report of the Secretary-General on the United Nations Operation in Cyprus", UN Doc. S/26777, 22 November.

UN Secretary-General (1995), "Verification in All Its Aspects, Including the Role of the United Nations in the Field of Verification", UN Doc. A/50/377, 22 September.

UN Secretary-General (1999), "Report of the Secretary-General on Prevention of Armed Conflict", UN Doc. S/1999/957, 8 September.

UN Secretary-General (2004), "Report of the Secretary-General on the United Nations Operation in Cyprus", UN Doc. S/2004/756, 24 September.

UN Secretary-General (2005), "Report of the Secretary-General on the United Nations Operation in Cyprus", UN Doc. S/2005/353, 27 May.

UN Secretary-General (2006), "Letter Dated 2006/09/28 from the Secretary-General Addressed to the President of the Security Council", UN Doc. S/2006/779, 29 September.

UN Secretary-General (2007), "Information Sensitivity, Classification and Handling", Secretary-General's Bulletin, UN Doc. ST/SGB/2007/6, 12 February.

UN Secretary-General (2008a), "Report of the Secretary on United Nations Operation in Cyprus", UN Doc. S/2008/744, 24 November.

UN Secretary-General (2008b), "Report of the Secretary-General on the Deployment of the African Union–United Nations Hybrid Operation in Darfur", UN Doc. S/2008/304, 9 May.

UN Secretary-General (2008c), "Report of the Secretary-General on the Deployment of the African Union–United Nations Hybrid Operation in Darfur", UN Doc. S/2008/558, 18 August.

UN Secretary-General (2009a), "Report of the Secretary-General on the Deployment of the African Union–United Nations Hybrid Operation in Darfur", UN Doc. S/2009/352, 13 July.

UN Secretary-General (2009b), "Report of the Secretary-General on the African Union–United Nations Hybrid Operation in Darfur", UN Doc. S/2009/592, 16 November.

UN Security Council (2000), *Report of the Panel on United Nations Peace Operations* (widely referred to as the "Brahimi Report", after its chairman, Lakhdar Brahimi), UN Doc. A/55/305–S/2000/809, 21 August.

UN Security Council (2004), "Report of the Group of Experts", formally titled "Letter dated 15 July 2004 from the Chairman of the Security Council Committee established pursuant to resolution 1533 (2004) concerning the Democratic Republic of the Congo addressed to the President of the Security Council", UN Doc. S/2004/551, 15 July, <http://www.un-casa.org/CASAUpload/ELibrary/S-2004-551.pdf> (accessed 6 January 2011).

UN Security Council (2008), "The Situation Concerning Haiti", UN Doc. S/RES/1840 (2008), 14 October.

UN Special Committee on Peacekeeping (2008), "Report of the Special Committee on Peacekeeping Operations and Its Working Group: 2008 Substantive Session (10 March–4 April and 3 July 2008)", *General Assembly Official Records*, Sixty-second Session, Supplement No. 19, UN Doc. A/62/19.

UN Special Committee on Peacekeeping (2009), "Report of the Special Committee on Peacekeeping Operations and Its Working Group: 2009 Substantive Session (23 February–20 March 2009)", *General Assembly Official Records*, Sixty-third Session, Supplement No. 19, UN Doc. A/63/19.

UN Special Committee on Peacekeeping (2010), "Report of the Special Committee on Peacekeeping Operations: 2010 Substantive Session (22 February–19 March 2010)", *General Assembly Official Records*, Sixty-fourth Session, Supplement No. 19, UN Doc. A/64/19.

UNAMID [African Union–United Nations Hybrid Operation in Darfur] (2008), "Introduction of Low and Medium-Cost Surveillance and Communications Technologies in UN Peacekeeping Missions", Code Cable to UN DPKO, 15 March.

UNAMID (2009), "Insecurity Incidents Report", 16 April.

UNFICYP [United Nations Peacekeeping Force in Cyprus] (2004a), *The Comprehensive Settlement of the Cyprus Problem*, 31 March, <http://www.unficyp.org/nqcontent.cfm?a_id=1637> (accessed 14 January 2011).

UNFICYP (2004b), "Close Circuit Television Monitoring Systems: Statement of Requirement", internal memorandum, January.

UNFICYP (2005), "Technical Statement of Work and Specifications for Amendment to CCTV Contract CON/CYP/04-089, Quantity 17 Additional Cameras", 26 July; obtained from UNFICYP while on official visit in January 2009.

UNFICYP (2007), "2006–7 Acquisition Plan – United Nations Peacekeeping Force in Cyprus (UNFICYP)", <http://www.un.org/Depts/ptd/2007_unificyp.htm> (accessed 7 January 2011).

UNFICYP (2008a), UN database entry, "Frezenburg [*sic*] House: Special Case File, Local Agreement"; obtained from UNFICYP files while on official visit in January 2009.

UNFICYP (2008b), "Standard Operating Procedures", November.

United Nations (1946), "Convention on the Privileges and Immunities of the United Nations", Adopted by the General Assembly of the United Nations on 13 February, United Nations, *Treaty Series*, vol. 1, <http://treaties.un.org/doc/Treaties/1946/12/19461214%2010-17%20PM/Ch_III_1p.pdf> (accessed 17 January 2011).

United Nations (1948), "Universal Declaration of Human Rights", Adopted by the General Assembly of the United Nations on 10 December, UN Doc A/810, <http://www.un.org/en/documents/udhr/index.shtml> (accessed 17 January 2011).

United Nations (1990), "Draft Model Status-of-Forces Agreement for Peacekeeping Operations Between the United Nations and Host Countries", UN Doc. A/45/594, 8 October.

United Nations (1994), "Convention on the Safety of United Nations and Associated Personnel", New York, 9 December, <http://www.un.org/law/cod/safety.htm> (accessed 17 January 2011).

United Nations (1996), *The Blue Helmets: A Review of United Nations Peacekeeping*, 3rd edn, New York: United Nations.

United Nations (1998–), "Security in the Field: Information for Staff Members of the United Nations System", updated online at <http://www.unops.org/security/> (password needed).

United Nations (2001), "Report of the Fact-Finding Investigation Relating to the Abduction of Three Israeli Soldiers on 7 October 2000 and Subsequent Relevant Events", New York, 2 August, <http://www.un.org/News/dh/latest/videorpt.htm> (accessed 18 January 2011).

United Nations (2005), *2005 World Summit Outcome*, UN Doc. A/RES/60/1, 24 October, <http://www.un.org/summit2005/documents.html> (accessed 6 January 2011).

United Nations (2008), *Manual on Policies and Procedures Concerning the Reimbursement and Control of Contingent-Owned Equipment of Troop/Police Contributors Participating in Peacekeeping Missions* [COE Manual], UN Doc. A/C.5/63/18, 29 January.

United Nations (2010), "Background Notes: 30 April 2010", United Nations Peacekeeping Operations, <http://www.un.org/en/peacekeeping/bnote.htm> (accessed 13 January 2011).

USHMM [United States Holocaust Memorial Museum] (2009), "United States Holocaust Memorial Museum Adds New Data to Google Earth Showing Twice as Many Destroyed Villages in Darfur", Press Release, 30 July.

Vannoni, Michael G. (1998), "Sensors in the Sinai: A Precedent for Regional Cooperative Monitoring", Sand Report SAND96-2574, Albuquerque, NM: Cooperative Monitoring Center, Sandia National Laboratories, <http://www.cmc.sandia.gov/cmc-papers/sand96-2574.pdf> (accessed 7 January 2011).

Veterans Affairs Canada (2006), "The Canadian Forces in Ethiopia and Eritrea", <http://www.vac-acc.gc.ca/content/history/CanadianForces/docs/ethiopia_e.pdf> (accessed 18 January 2011).

Vumii Inc. (2010), "Discoverii", <http://www.vumii.com/discoverii.htm> (accessed 7 January 2011).

Wainhouse, David W. (1966), *International Peace Observation: A History and Forecast*, Baltimore, MD: Johns Hopkins University Press.

Wentz, Larry K., ed. (1997), *Lessons From Bosnia: The IFOR Experience*, Washington, DC: National Defense University, available at <http://www.dodccrp.org/files/Wentz_Bosnia.pdf> (accessed 18 January 2011).

Wilson, Woodrow ([1919] 1986), "Protocol of a Plenary Session of the Inter-Allied Conference for the Preliminaries of Peace, January 25, 1919", in Arthur S. Link (ed.), *The Papers of Woodrow Wilson*, vol. 54, Princeton NJ: Princeton University Press.

Index

- Monitoring
- Protect, Pursue - face pursue...
  - Vigilance ADR
- Detain illegal traffic,
  - and support to follow gov
  Thirty Thugs ...

usual
Basic Infantryman
Teethwoman